The Savage Frontier

The Savage Frontier

The Pyrenees in
History and the Imagination

Matthew Carr

THE
NEW
PRESS

NEW YORK
LONDON

Requests for permission to reproduce selections from this book should be mailed to:
Permissions Department, The New Press, 120 Wall Street, 31st floor,
New York, NY 10005.

Published in the United States by The New Press, New York, 2018
Distributed by Two Rivers Distribution

ISBN 978-1-62097-427-8 (hc)
ISBN 978-1-62097-428-5 (ebook)
CIP data is available.

The New Press publishes books that promote and enrich public discussion and
understanding of the issues vital to our democracy and to a more equitable world.
These books are made possible by the enthusiasm of our readers; the support of a
committed group of donors, large and small; the collaboration of our many partners
in the independent media and the not-for-profit sector; booksellers, who often
hand-sell New Press books; librarians; and above all by our authors.

www.thenewpress.com

Map on page xi courtesy of Wikimedia Commons
Map on pages xii and xiii by Nick Trotter
Composition by Westchester Publishing Services
This book was set in Adobe Caslon Pro

Printed in the United States of America

2   4   6   8   10   9   7   5   3   1

Contents

Acknowledgments

Few books are written without the help of others. I want to thank Marta Marín Bráviz, the indefatigable local historian of Hecho, Aragon, for providing me with copies of her excellent magazine *Subordán,* and for many other useful tips and suggestions. The late Scott Goodall (1935–2016) went beyond the call of duty to facilitate my participation in the Chemin de la Liberté. Michael Richardson from the Art Space Gallery was extremely helpful in introducing me to Ray Atkins's work. Thanks also to Steve Waters, Andreu Jené, and so many others who shared these mountain trails with me and contributed to this book in ways that they may not even be aware of.

As always, much love to my wife Jane and my daughter Lara, who accompanied me on various Pyrenean jaunts. The anonymous narrator of Chris Marker's film *Sans Soleil* once described three Icelandic children playing on a volcanic beach as "the image of happiness." For me, the sight of the Bious pasturelands in 2016—when I walked with Jane and Lara through a Pyrenean wonderland of mountains, forest, water, and animals—will remain indelibly imprinted on my mind as an image of happiness and perfection on earth, and there are no two people I would rather have shared it with.

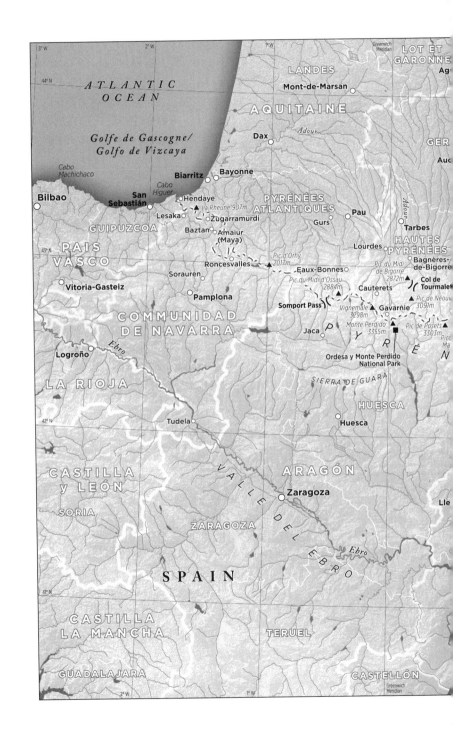

The Pyrénées

The Savage Frontier

From the Sacred Mountain

> We are not among those who have ideas only between books,
> stimulated by books—our habit is to think outdoors, walking,
> jumping, climbing, dancing, preferably on lonely mountains
> or right by the sea where even the paths become thoughtful.
>
> —Friedrich Nietzsche, *The Gay Science*[1]

At 2,969 feet (905 meters), the Pyrenean mountain known as La Rhune in French and Larrun in Basque is not, in theory, a particularly formidable physical challenge compared with the 10,000-foot (3,000-meter) peaks that proliferate in the Central Pyrenees. Its shaven, cone-like peak straddles the French-Spanish border at the point where the Atlantic Pyrenees begin to rise from the flat coastal strip, giving onto Navarre to the south and the French Basque province of Labourd to the north. For hikers undertaking the trans-Pyrenean trail from the Atlantic to the Mediterranean, La Rhune is a mere stepping-stone to the higher mountains farther west. It can easily be walked up and down in half a day, and French and Spanish families regularly do this most weekends.

Thousands of day-trippers also take the funicular railway, the Petit Train de La Rhune, which leads up to the summit from the Col de Saint-Ignace on the French side. Some go for a meal in the café-restaurant on the summit, to take some exercise, and to enjoy a mountain view. Others are attracted by La Rhune's esoteric history as a sacred mountain. Its slopes are littered with Neolithic dolmens, and the summit was once associated with magic, sorcery, and *akelarres*—the Basque term for witches' sabbaths—in the sixteenth and seventeenth centuries. As late as the eighteenth century, a monk lived permanently on the summit to keep the forces of darkness at bay.

Nowadays the constant stream of visitors makes such a vigil redundant. I hiked up the sacred mountain with my wife and daughter in August 2015, on the hottest day of what was then the hottest summer on record. Despite La Rhune's relatively modest height, the steep gradient and the scorching heat made the climb much harder than I had expected. We were soon wilting as we trudged slowly up the stony path beneath a flawless blue sky, past beige Pyrenean cattle and little groups of short-legged wild Pottok ponies. La Rhune was once covered in forest, but most of its trees have long since been stripped to clear the way for pastureland or provide wood for the French and Spanish navies. A few isolated vestiges still remain, and about halfway up the mountain we stopped to have lunch in a copse of tall pines. A handful of Pottoks were also taking shelter there, standing stock-still with that stolid patience and innocence that Walt Whitman once observed in animals.

On seeing us eat, some of them ambled slowly toward us and nuzzled hopefully at our rucksacks. It has not been long since these beautiful animals were hunted to near extinction in order to make salami, and their luminous brown eyes were difficult to refuse. As we shared some of our picnic with them, I looked back down toward the sea and the blue sky and I felt one of those moments of euphoria that I have often felt in the Pyrenees—a sense of having momentarily stepped out of the turbulent waters of twenty-first-century history and reconnected with a mountain world that was timelessly serene and benignly reassuring. The sensation was so pleasant that I was reluctant to step back out into the heat to continue our plodding progress toward the summit.

Soon the path grew significantly steeper, and we were surrounded by dozens of hikers walking up the curved track or clambering more directly over the slabs of rock that lay half-buried in the earth like giant stepping-stones. By the time we reached the summit, my daughter and I were red-faced and dehydrated, and we gorged on sugary soft drinks in the overcrowded visitors' complex while we waited for my wife to join us. Whatever La Rhune had been in the past, there was nothing sacred about the complex of restaurants, cafés, and souvenir shops that covered the summit. Below the picnicking families and walkers we could see the funicular, crawling caterpillar-like up and around the sharp stony ridge above La Petite Rhune—the Lesser Rhune—and the darker blue of the Atlantic down below to the west. To our east, the razor-backed peaks of the Pyrenees disappeared in a blue haze that led all the way to the Mediterranean some 270 miles (435 kilometers) away.

From where we were standing we could see the town of Hendaye on the French-Spanish border. It was here in 1659 that the French and Spanish first ministers signed the Treaty of the Pyrenees, which formalized the political border between the two states. Following the line of the coast northward I could see the seaside resort of Saint-Jean-de-Luz, where the sinister French lawyer Pierre de Lancre established his headquarters in 1609 and presided over one of the most lethal witch hunts in European history. Beyond it lay Bayonne, where Napoléon forced the naïve and foolish Spanish king Charles IV to abdicate in 1808 and placed his brother Joseph on the Spanish throne—an act of imperial overreach that ignited one of the most terrible wars in Spanish history.

That war came to an end in the autumn of 1813, when the French were driven out of Spain by a Spanish/British/Portuguese army under the command of Arthur Wellesley, the future Duke of Wellington, in the campaign known as the Battle of the Pyrenees. On November 8, 1813, Wellington had looked down from the same summit where we were standing at the French soldiers building ramparts on La Petite Rhune in a last-ditch attempt to prevent the peninsular army from crossing the Nivelle River. "Those fellows think themselves invulnerable, but I will beat them out, and with great ease," Wellington confidently declared to his skeptical officers. Two days later, British troops stormed the French positions on La Rhune and broke the French defensive line along a 17-mile

(27-kilometer) front stretching from the Atlantic to the Ronces-valles Pass in Navarre.

History was present whichever way I looked down from La Rhune. From the summit I could see the coastal road where I had driven in 1995 with a radio producer on my way to Bayonne to record a radio documentary about the death squads hired by the Spanish govern-ment to assassinate members of the Basque separatist organization ETA (Euskadi Ta Askatasuna) in southern France. Just before the border my producer and I had stopped on that same road and walked off to find the place where the socialist government's mercenaries had once concealed a trunk containing passports, guns, and money. At that time I paid little attention to the mountains overlooking the highway. Now, twenty years later, I had come to La Rhune not simply to look at the view, but to write a book about the Pyrenees and their history.

That decision deserves further explanation. La Rhune was not my first visit to the Pyrenees. In the 1990s I lived in Barcelona and often drove or took the train to Pyrenean towns and villages such as Ribes de Freser, Camprodon, Olot, or Beget, to the Vall de Núria, near the French-Spanish border, or farther afield to the Aigüestortes National Park and the majestic Ordesa Canyon in Aragon. Some-times I went to walk or drive around or spend a weekend in the mountains, but at that time I never imagined writing about the Pyrenees. In the summer of 2014, I found myself in Ordesa for a second time, to research a historical detective novel set in the sixteenth-century Pyrenees. I had not been to the Pyrenees for many years, and whether it was my age or the long absence, it seemed to me that summer that I had not fully appreciated them before, and I was constantly stirred by their beauty and grandeur.

The fascination of these mountains was not due just to the stun-ning natural scenery that was visible everywhere we looked. That did not surprise me. But as we walked and drove past the castles, Romanesque churches, watchtowers, walled medieval towns, and villages that had already begun to feature in my novel, I was constantly reminded of the rich and complex streams of history that had passed through the Pyrenees, and it occurred to me for the first time that this history was worth writing about in a nonfiction book as well.

I was aware that this history had not been told, in English, at least. The history of the Pyrenees tends to reveal itself in a piecemeal and fragmentary way, as an adjunct to the histories of the two great states on either side of them, or as a picturesque embellishment in guidebooks for walkers, climbers, and tourists. But as far as I knew there was no book in the English language that looked at the history and culture of the Pyrenees as a distinctive subject in their own right. My desire to write such a book was not simply intended to fill a gap, however. For many years I have wanted to write a book about a landscape and place and to explore the interplay between the real and the imagined that make up what the Latins called the genius loci—the spirit of a place.

That summer it seemed suddenly obvious to me that the subject of such a book was right in front of my eyes. As Simon Schama has written, all landscapes are "landscapes of the mind," which are defined not just by their physical components, but also by what is thought, remembered, and written about them.[2] The genius loci of the Pyrenees is indelibly bound up with their historical role as a frontier zone between states, cultures, and civilizations. The dominant image of the Pyrenees as a *frontière sauvage*—a savage frontier—is as much a construct of the mind as it is of geography and geopolitics, and it has often obscured and distorted the actual place of the Pyrenees in European and world history. Books about mountains tend to revolve around very similar themes: climbers and climbing, tales of endurance and survival and the conquest of iconic summits—beauty, danger, and physical ordeals that most readers would prefer to contemplate from a safe distance rather than experience for themselves. I have also been one of those readers, but these were not the subjects that attracted me to the Pyrenees. Pyrenean history is not just a history of summits and alpine exploration. It is also the history of wars; of clandestine crossings by refugees and dissidents; of state and civilizational conflict; of the movement of ideas and artistic forms; and of the shifting images and expectations projected onto a mountain landscape that has been imagined as many different things in the course of its long history of human settlement.

These contradictions between the "real" and imagined Pyrenees, between the Pyrenees as border and borderland, were all intrinsically interesting to me as a writer. But if I was honest with myself, I also had a more personal emotional interest in writing such a book. Sei Shōnagon, the eleventh-century Japanese courtier and author of *The Pillow Book*, once compiled a list of "things that quicken the heart." My own such list would definitely include mountains. Some of the happiest and most memorable moments of my life have been spent walking in hills and high mountains.

Robert MacFarlane has written compellingly of mountain climbers who are "half in love with oblivion."[3] That was never part of their appeal for me. I don't climb, and I prefer to avoid exposed paths, abysses, and precipitous drops. But I do love mountains. I love their silence, a silence that is unlike any other silence in the world. I love their physical difficulty, their drama, their beauty, and their fabulous otherworldliness. I love clambering over boulders, crossing mountain streams, walking above a sea of clouds in a world of rock and stone, followed by cool descents through mountain forests at the end of a hard day's hike. I love to have mountains towering over me and I also love to look down from them—though not from too close to the edge. I love the fellowship of the mountains and the conversations with the people who walk in them or live in them.

As far as their relationship to oblivion is concerned, mountains have always instilled a very different response in me. In his essay "On the Fear of Death," William Hazlitt once suggested that dying might seem less terrifying if we dwelt less on our "posthumous existence" and more on the "pre-existent state" that preceded our entry into the world by millions of years.[4] Mountain landscapes are particularly vivid reminders of that "pre-existent state." Forged millions of years before human beings even arrived on earth, they constitute a testament to human inconsequentiality and temporality that I have always found humbling, reassuring, and endlessly exhilarating. "I call these to witness, who have scaled some of the heights of the globe," wrote the great Pyrenean scientist and explorer Louis-François Ramond de Carbonnières, "is there a single person who did not find himself regenerated; who did not feel with surprise, that he had left at the feet of the mountains, his weakness, his infirmities, his cares, his troubles, in a word, the weaker part of his being, and the ulcerated portion of his heart?"[5]

I have never returned from any mountain walk, no matter how difficult, without feeling lighter and more intensely alive than when I set out. In the last few years I have led hiking groups in England and Europe, and I have become increasingly conscious, moving into my sixties, that there will come a time when I will no longer be able to be in mountains, and that one day I will find myself like the seventeenth-century Japanese poet and traveler Matsuo Bashō, "grown old and infirm with hoary frost upon his eyebrows," and no longer able to walk the high trails.[6] So writing about the Pyrenees was not just a chance to write a book: it was also an opportunity to be in the mountains once again and to combine these seemingly contradictory activities, writing and walking, that have become central to my life.

I could not write as Victor Hugo once did, literally scribbling notes as he walked in the Pyrenees. But I could attempt the kind of book that Nietzsche once imagined, removed from the "closed ceilings, cramped spaces," of the library and the writer's study.[7] Because if I was going to write about the history of the Pyrenees, it was logical that I should walk in them as much as possible and try to see and experience what others had seen and experienced. All these different motives and aspirations have made this book possible.

What follows is not a guidebook or a walking companion or a comprehensive history, but a personal exploration of those aspects of Pyrenean history and culture that interest me. In these pages, readers will find walks, mountains, and summits, but they will also find artists and poets; spa towns and concentration camps; shepherds, medieval monks, and feudal lords; the music of Pau Casals (usually known in English as Pablo Casals); the writings of George Sand and Baudelaire; bears and bear festivals; crusaders, witches, and inquisitors; anarchist guerrillas and refugees. In following their footsteps and mine, I hope that readers will gain a better understanding and appreciation of one of the great European landscapes, that they will come to feel the sense of privilege, enchantment, and gratitude that I have often felt on La Rhune and in so many other parts of these astonishing mountains.

PART I

The Perfect Border

As very strong walls and ramparts between kingdoms, sufficient to stop the progress of a conqueror and the armies of the enemy. Such are the Pyrenees between France and Spain, the Alps between France and Italy.

—Père Jean François, *La science de la géographie,* 1652

1

The Land

The causes which would in general be likely to keep a mountain range for long within the realm of fable, such as the absence of low passes, or of longitudinal valleys reaching into the
heart of the chain, its situation away from the lines of communication betwen nations, and the fact of forming a political frontier between them, and lastly the sway of fashion, have
all operated with special force in the case of the Pyrenees.
—*The Geographical Journal*, 1894[1]

In *Perigrinación del mundo* (Pilgrimage of the World, 1680) the
seventeenth-century Spanish missionary Dr. Pedro Cubero Sebastián warns his readers to beware of the "Pyrenean Mountains, so
celebrated amongst the ancient Cosmographers, so harsh to pass
through . . . whose summits appear to be sliding apart so as to fall
on those passing through them; nothing else is to be found there,
except the cadavers of dead men who lost their lives as a result of
the rigorous weather, or because some hard boulder served as their
shroud; there is no doubt that it makes one's flesh creep to cross
them."[2] Cubero's hyperbolic evocation of these horrors was not unusual; mountains were frequently described in similar terms by
European travelers in this period. But his description of the Pyrenees
as a landscape that was "so harsh to pass through" echoed a familiar theme that many writers have evoked in writing about the Pyrenees. For much of their history the Pyrenees have been depicted as
an impenetrable "wall," a barrier to human movement or a strategic

barrier between tribes, civilizations, empires, and states. Such imagery, through constant repetition, has tended to define the Pyrenees as a landscape of desolation, difficulty, and inaccessibility that fully bears out the old French depiction of the mountains as a "savage frontier."

Modern travelers have tended to imbue the Pyrenees with more positive qualities. In his classic memoir of his climbing expeditions in the "enchanted mountains" of the Maladeta massif in the 1950s, the British diplomat Robin Fedden wrote of "that unreality, that sense of a landscape under a spell, which travelers have repeatedly noted in these Pyrenees."[3] To the English politician Harold Spender, who traveled through Andorra and the Central Pyrenees in the late nineteenth century, "There is something almost unearthly about the high mountain landscapes of the Pyrenees. You have no gentle foreground to diminish the savagery of the mountains. . . . You are in the mountains of the moon—on a crust that is already growing cold. It is the fantastic landscape of a dream."[4] In *The Mountain* (1872), the French historian Jules Michelet contrasted "the fantastic loveliness of the Pyrenees . . . those strange and seemingly incompatible sites which are harmoniously bent together by an inexplicable stroke of fairy enchantment," with "the savage horror of the great mountains which lurk in the rear, like a monster hidden beneath the mask of a youthful beauty."[5]

Whether imagined positively or negatively, these evocations of the "savagery" of the Pyrenees are a response to the peculiarities and particularities of the Pyrenean landscape itself, and they are also a reflection of the assumptions that these travelers brought with them, to a mountain range that has been endlessly imagined and reimagined ever since it first began to attract the attention of the outside world. Classical geographers believed that the Pyrenees took their name from Pyrene, the virginal daughter of King Bebryx, who was raped by a drunken Hercules on his way to fight the monster Geryon. In his poetic history of the Punic Wars, the Roman poet Silius Italicus describes how Pyrene flees into the mountains afterward only to be torn apart by wild beasts. When Hercules wakes up from his drunken stupor, he is so filled with remorse that he resolves to find Pyrene's remains and bury them. As the repentant hero gathers Pyrene's mangled limbs, he calls out her name till, "the high mountain-tops, smitten by his cries, were shaken; with loud lament he called Pyrene by name; and all the cliffs and haunts of wild beasts echoed the name of Pyrene."[6]

Other geographers and historians traced the origins of the Pyrenaei Montes to the Celtic word *pyren*, or *pyrn*, meaning "high mountain." Some believed that the Pyrenees took their name from the ancient Greek king Pyrrhus, who supposedly blasted passes through the mountains and burned their forests to clear roads. In *Bibliotheca historica*, written between 60 and 30 BCE, the Greek geographer-historian Diodorus Siculus claimed that the Pyrenees were created by an enormous fire lit by ancient herdsmen that consumed the entire mountain range and left a legacy of "many streams of silver" and "many thick and deep forests" that were still present in his own time.[7]

The location and the extent of the Pyrenees were also disputed. Herodotus believed that Pyrene was a city rather than a chain of mountains. The Greek geographer and historian Strabo compared the Iberian Peninsula to "a hide stretched out in length from west to east, the forepart [neck] towards the east, its breadth being from north to south," and described—inaccurately—how "this chain of mountains stretches without interruption from north to south, and divides Keltica from Iberia."[8] As late as the sixteenth century, Spanish chroniclers traced the origins of the Pyrenees to a man-made conflagration that had covered the mountains with forests and exposed deposits of silver and other precious metals.

The Arab historian of Moorish Al-Andalus Ahmed ibn Mohammad al-Makkari (1578–1632) describes the Pyrenees as "the mountain barriers which there divide Andalus from the continent, where many different languages are spoken. These mountains have several passes or gates, which a Grecian king ordered to be opened in the rock with fire, vinegar and iron, for before his time there was no communication whatsoever between Andalus and the continent."[9]

Even then, al-Makkari was not entirely certain about the geographical location or direction of the Pyrenees, describing their passes as facing Majorca and Minorca, in other words, east rather than south.

Prehistory

It is little more than two hundred years since geologists, geographers, and scientists first began to place the Pyrenees within the overall history of the earth's surface. We now know that the range came into existence as a result of the lifting and folding process that geologists call orogenesis, specifically the Variscan or Hercynian orogeny, which took place between 370 million and 290 million years ago, when the Iberian microcontinent rotated and ground itself against the southwestern promontory of the Eurasian continental plates. Over millions of years these enormous tectonic pressures crushed the softer sedimentary Iberian plate against the harder crystalline rocks that still dominate the Pyrenean uplands, resulting in the emergence of the 500-mile (800-kilometer)-long Cantabrian-Pyrenean chain some 100 million to 150 million years ago, during the Lower Cretaceous period.

Between 35 million and 40 million years ago, a second collision lifted the Cantabrian-Pyrenean chain a second time. This was followed by yet another movement 11 million years ago, which may have added approximately 3,300 feet (1,000 meters) to the Pyrenees over a period of 10 million years. These titanic ructions in the earth's crust created a range of mountains that stretches some 270 miles (435 kilometers) long and 80 miles (130 kilometers) wide at their widest point, which begins almost imperceptibly at the Cantabrian mountains on the Atlantic and continues to Cap de Creus on the Mediterranean coast. In reality the Pyrenees consist of two ranges. The first begins just inside the Atlantic coast and proceeds south and east toward the Val d'Aran, where another begins slightly to the south and tapers off at the Mediterranean. Weathering and erosion have shaped the landscape still further, shaving and wearing the limestone that predominates on the southern side of the range to produce sharp ridges and spiky, razor-like rock formations that can easily slice legs and hands.

Evidence of these convulsions can be found from one end of the mountains to the other: in the piles of boulders tumbling down from mountainsides that the French call *le chaos*; in the epic confusion of rocks crushed together above the Gavarnie Cirque in a mind-bogglingly complicated combination of stratifications, whorls, and fault lines that the nineteenth-century cartographer Franz Schrader once described as a "geological poem"; in the pale limestone karst formations of Navarre and Aragon that have been sharpened, scooped, and hollowed out by wind and water into weirdly other-wordly shapes and forms; in the enormous rocks as high as trees that suddenly loom up in the middle of forests like pieces of mete-orite fallen from the sky.

Though Pyrenean glaciation is part of the same Würm ice sheet that also covered the Alps during the third phase of the Quater-nary Ice Age some seventy thousand years ago, glaciation is less extensive in the Pyrenees. Unlike the Alps, the Pyrenees have few large glacier-fed lakes in their lower valleys, but water is ubiquitous in the mountains, from the rivers, streams, and waterfalls to the small lakes, or tarns, that break up the desolation of the high mountains on both sides of the range. Most of the great Pyrenean waterfalls are on the French side, such as the six or seven streams that con-verge in a boiling, foaming cauldron from all directions beneath the Pont d'Espagne, before crashing downward toward the former spa town of Cauterets. Tectonic activity has also given the Pyre-nees an abundance of thermal waters and underground streams, which have hollowed out some of the largest caves in Europe.

The historic reputation of the Pyrenees as an inaccessible wall is not due to their height. The Pyrenees are smaller than the Alps and smaller than other European mountain systems. Stendhal once called them "pigmy mountains" and joked that he was unable to find them.[10] The highest peak in the range is the Pico d'Aneto, at

11,168 feet (3,404 meters), which is smaller than Mulhacén, at 11,413 feet (3,478.6 meters), Spain's highest mountain, in the Andalusian Sierra Nevada, while the Alps have more than a hundred peaks of more than 13,000 feet (3,962 meters). Unlike the Pyrenees, the Alps have rarely been depicted as a barrier, and such imagery is due partly to topography and partly to geography. Look at a relief map of the Alps and you see a scimitar-like formation curving around from Italy toward Austria and Slovenia in a 750-mile (1,200-kilometer) arc broken by a series of longitudinal valleys and incorporating many different ranges.

The Pyrenees, by comparison, effectively sever the Iberian Peninsula from the rest of Europe, with the exception of a few miles at either end of the range. In between lie dozens of lateral valleys that come out at right angles on their northern and southern sides, like ribs protruding from a spine. Apart from the narrow coastal strips at their western and eastern extremes, these mountains are dissected by dozens of cols, or passes, known as *puertos*—"doors" or "gates" in Spanish—many of which are still difficult to cross in winter. Between these main crossing points there are numerous smaller trails and paths, many of which have been used over the centuries by smugglers, shepherds, and refugees. From a distance, therefore, the Pyrenees can look very much like a giant wall, and this impression is particularly striking from the French side. Approach the mountains from Pau, or farther east from Lourdes and the Ariège, and they cover the horizon, and certainly seem to live up to the French geographer Emmanuel de Martonne's description of the Pyrenees as "the most massive and unbroken barrier on any frontier in France."[11]

The narrow forested valleys that cut into the mountains from the French side do nothing to dispel this impression, as they climb up alongside one of the many rivers, or *gaves*, toward the waterfalls that tumble down sharply from mountainsides and cliff edges. On the Spanish side, the mountains tend to reveal themselves more gradually as the wide plains give way to foothills that lead up past the great Pyrenean rivers of the Segre, the Gallego, the Cinca, and the Aragon. Approach them from the arid lunar landscape between Zaragoza and Huesca, and the high Pyrenees do not even become visible till you have passed through the massive gash of gnarled red rock near Huesca that leads up into the mountains. The historical image of the Pyrenees as a wall has often been confirmed by the proliferation of glacier-formed cirques known as *oules* (porridge bowls), which are a distinctive feature of the Central Pyrenees. Anyone who has seen the great rounded cliffs of Gavarnie or the Cirque de Soasa in the Ordesa Canyon in Aragon will immediately see why the Pyrenees have so often been described as a barrier to human movement.

At first sight, these awe-inspiring and intimidating natural barriers seem to bear out the historical reputation of the Pyrenees as a hostile and inaccessible landscape that human beings cross only at their peril. But the rockier and barren highlands are only one component of a landscape that oscillates easily between the savage and the pastoral. In a single day's walk it is possible to pass from beech and oak forest, through lush valleys filled with sheep and horses, and barren moonscapes scattered with boulders or razor-sharp limestone rocks, before descending vertiginous gorges and canyons that seem incapable of supporting any life at all. Yet just when this desolation begins to feel oppressive and intimidating, you may find yourself walking through grassy meadows and valleys alongside an opalescent stream or mountain lake, enclosed by a cool forest of giant trees.

Once again, these variations are often especially noticeable when crossing from one side of the mountains to the other. On the French side the Pyrenees are generally moist and more verdant, and less directly exposed to the sun, particularly at the western edge of the chain, where the proximity of the Atlantic ensures a generally cooler and moister climate. On the southern side, the impact of Mediterranean winds, or levanters, has created a drier, sun-drenched, and rockier landscape populated by fir trees and mountain pines. Cross into Spain from the French village of Lescun and you begin the day walking through ancient decidious forest, lush green meadows, and rolling pastureland. Within two hours the forest begins to thin out and a steep climb leads past the last shepherd's *cabane* and brings you into a harsh, inhuman landscape of scree and boulders that fully warrant the old seventeenth-century English descriptions of the mountains as "nature's dustbin." From the sharp ridge just below the Petrachema summit, you follow a traverse path into Spain before descending a steep gorge of bleached limestone rock, where everything is sharp, burned, and barren, until finally you emerge back into pine and fir forests that are paler and sparser than their French counterparts.

These differences in climate and terrain have often been evoked by visitors to contrast the "savagery" of the Spanish Pyrenees with the more amenable and domesticated French side of the cain, but such distinctions are not always so clear-cut. Winters are often long and difficult in both the French and Spanish Pyrenees. Until relatively recently, passes on either side of the mountains were regularly blocked by heavy snow, and some of them would once have been impassable for months. Snowfalls, avalanches, and flash floods have long been part of the history of the Pyrenees, which only recently have been tamed by reforestation and the construction of snowbreaks, barriers, and canals. The Pyrenean climate is notoriously unpredictable and unstable, as Edward the Black Prince's army once discovered when crossing through Roncesvalles to invade Spain.

One evening my friend Steve and I arrived at the refuge below the Brèche de Rolande, near Gavarnie. Shortly before reaching it, we crossed a tiny stream that barely reached above our ankles. That night it poured with rain. The next morning the stream had become a foaming torrent, and the wind was so high that we were advised to go back down and enter Spain through the Puerto de Bujaruelo farther west. For most of the day we made our way across one spating stream after another, in winds that were sometimes strong enough to lean into and tore our maps from our hands.

On another occasion I led a group into the Aragonese Pyrenees. We arrived in temperatures of 93 degrees Fahrenheit (34 degrees

Celsius), which had dropped to nearly 43 (6) by the following day, as we walked in thunderstorms and showers of hail.

All these variations and contrasts are part of a mountain landscape that has variously repelled, attracted, and frustrated visitors for thousands of years. Compared with the epic timescales of geologists and paleogeographers, the human presence in the Pyrenees is a minor footnote that can be measured in thousands rather than millions of years. It has been only forty thousand years since the first hunter-gatherers began to settle in the lower Pyrenean foothills, and twelve thousand since their descendants began to shift from hunting game to breeding sheep and cattle at the end of the last Ice Age.

In that short time human beings have transformed the Pyrenees. They have built towns, cities, and villages, roads, bridges, and railway lines. They have constructed reservoirs and channeled mountain lakes and rivers into hydroelectric systems that power some of the great cities on either side of them. They have constructed castles, towns, monasteries, and ski resorts. They have blasted tunnels underneath the mountains and mined iron, copper, and other metals deep inside them and on the surface. Humans have cut down great swathes of forests for timber or firewood, to build ships or open up new pasturelands for sheep and cattle. They have hunted some animals to extinction and introduced new species.

In the course of these long centuries of human settlement, the Pyrenees have also acquired a unique place in European and world history that is not always recognized. "For centuries the Pyrenees have stood aloof from the mainstream of history; a land apart, known only to shepherds, hunters and smugglers," observed a travel piece in the *Daily Telegraph* in 2002.[12] This is the standard image of the Pyrenees that has been handed on to posterity, and which is frequently evoked in order to give the mountains an aura of historical mystery and touristic allure, but it also leaves out a great deal. For one thing, the Pyrenees have rarely, if ever, "stood aloof" from world history. On the contrary, world history has passed through the mountains on repeated occasions. At various times, the fate of nations and empires has been decided by battles and sieges fought in the Pyrenees. Kings have been dethroned and governments have been brought down by armies that have made their way through remote Pyrenean mountain passes. For a few weeks, in the autumn of 1813, the political future of Europe hung on the epic confrontation waged in the Pyrenean mountain passes of Navarre and the Basque Country.

Both the peculiarities of the Pyrenean landscape and the geographical location of the Pyrenees on the periphery of Spain and France have given their history a very particular shape and texture. On various occasions the mountains have constituted a border between life and death for the refugees, heretics, and dissidents who have crossed from one side to the other to escape war or persecution in accordance with the shifting currents of French, Spanish, and European history. For centuries the Pyrenees constituted the physical dividing line between European Christendom and Islamic Iberia—and the main point of entry for the Christian medieval scholars, monks, and pilgrims who passed through them in search of knowledge or salvation.

Far from being a land apart, the Pyrenees belong very firmly to the histories of the two great states on either side of them, and also to the stream of European and world history. Evidence of these interactions can be found all over the mountains: in ancient images painted on cave walls; in cemeteries containing medieval pilgrims along the Santiago de Compostela pilgrimage route; in inscriptions written on tombstones in remote mountain villages; in festivals where villagers dress up as bears and virgins; in the delicate stone carving of two angels carrying the Greek letters for the first two letters of Jesus's name on a twelfth-century Romanesque church built by the people of Assouste for the Santiago de Compostela pilgrimage; in the Royalist fleur-de-lys inscribed in lintels that were hammered flat after the Revolution; in the *Vive* followed by householders' names in Bearnese villages of the sixteenth and eighteenth centuries; in the bizarre sculptures of a man exposing his penis and a woman lifting her skirts that can be found in a church in a village in the Vallée d'Ossau; in abandoned railway lines in the high mountains; in shepherds' huts and remote hermitages; in commemorative plaques, monuments, and "landscapes of memory" that recall dangerous wartime crossings, flights to freedom, battles, wars, and legendary generals.

It is difficult to think of any mountain range in the world that is so steeped in the past and has been visited so often by the currents of world history. Far from being a land apart, the Pyrenees are a mirror of our world, with all its follies, tragedies, cruelties, and absurdities. The history of the Pyrenees is also a case study in the imaginative *creation* of a landscape and the different ways in which human beings have projected their fears, desires, and cultural assumptions onto the natural world—and onto mountain landscapes in particular. Artists, poets, and writers have all responded to the peculiarities of the Pyrenean landscape. Some came to the mountains to sculpt and paint and have left their mark on the landscape in the form of carvings, paintings, frescos, and churches of exquisite beauty. Others brought back images and descriptions to the outside world, which became part of the imaginative reinvention of the Pyrenees from the eighteenth century onward.

In the same period scientists, climbers, and explorers began to penetrate the Pyrenees. Their journeys and explorations broke down the myths, fables, and ignorance that had surrounded the mountains for centuries, and their writings also became part of the "discovery" of the Pyrenees by the modern world. Tourists and travelers; Picasso and Charles Rennie Mackintosh; Leon Trotsky and Rudyard Kipling; visitors to Pyrenean spa towns; Catalan nationalist poets and hikers; French cyclists on the Tour de France; esoteric Nazi researchers in search of the lost treasures of the Cathars; smugglers and shepherds—all these visitors have left the footprints that this book will now follow.

2

The Vanishing Border

As it had been formerly agreed in the negotiations begun in Madrid in the year 1656, upon which this present Treaty is founded, that the Pyrenees Mountains, which anciently divided the Gauls from the Spains, shall henceforth be the division of the two said kingdoms.

—Article 42 of the Treaty of the Pyrenees,
November 7, 1659

Today the physical frontiers until now separated six European countries, among them Spain, disappear. Citizens— Europeans or not—who wish to travel from Portugal to Germany, passing through France, Belgium, Holland and Luxembourg, will no longer encounter any obstacles or long queues that prevent free circulation.

—*El Pais*, March 26, 1995

Situated on the Spanish-French border at the French town of Hendaye on the Atlantic coast, L'île des Faisans (Pheasant Island) is not the most obvious setting for a historic meeting between European heads of state, nor does it have any obvious connection to the Pyrenees. Locating it is hard enough. The island is obscured by the cluster of border shops selling two-liter bottles of vodka, flamenco dresses, and towels bearing images of flamenco dancers. Visitors who make the effort will find an unprepossessing mostly tree-covered clump of land of some 1.7 acres (6,820 square meters) in the middle of the Bidassoa River that barely merits the status of an island. Were it not for the stone slabs lining its banks, Pheasant Island would be even smaller than it is. Both Spain and France are responsible for its upkeep, via the local authorities in Irun and Hendaye, and its management changes hands every six months, as it has done for more than three hundred years, to the general indifference of the local population and the rest of the world.

Visitors aren't allowed onto the island, and there is no obvious reason why anyone would want to visit it. Only a small plaque on the edge of a children's playground on the opposite bank at Hendaye commemorates the island's historic contribution to the "stability of Europe," as a result of the meeting that took place here on November 7, 1659, between Don Luis de Haro and Cardinal Mazarin, the respective foreign ministers of Spain and France. The meeting was part of the negotiations that ended the 1635–59 Franco-Spanish War, and because it was a belated consequence of the Peace of Westphalia, which ended the Thirty Years' War in 1648, its deliberations were keenly followed by European kings and princes. In October that year, the exiled Charles II of England made his way to Zaragoza to meet with the Spanish chief minister, Don Luis de Haro, before the meeting, in what proved to be a vain attempt to enlist Spanish assistance for the Catholic cause. "I am very much deceaved in travelling in Spayne, for by all reports I did expect ill cheere and worse lying, and hitherto we have founde both the beds and especially the meate very good," he wrote. "The only thing I find troublesome is the dust and especially in this towne, there having fallen no rayne on this side the Perineans these 4 months."[1]

Most leaders preferred to observe the negotiations from a distance. The French and Spanish monarchs were very conscious of this attention, and they chose a location between the two countries so that their two chief ministers could meet on neutral ground without either of them losing face. Today it is difficult to imagine the elaborate preparations that preceded this strange encounter. These included the construction of a large wooden palace on the island itself and pontoon bridges on either side to allow separate entry from both sides of the river, which led to a suite of private rooms and an enormous central chamber 56 feet (17 meters) long, 28 feet (8.5 meters) wide, and 22 feet (7 meters) high, where doors on either side allowed Haro and Mazarin to enter simultaneously. Here the two ministers sat in chairs placed on either side of a line drawn on the floor to mark the symbolic dividing line between France and Spain and discussed the territorial arrangements that were formally enshrined in the Treaty of the Pyrenees, also known as the Peace of the Pyrenees.

Historians have depicted the treaty as a watershed moment in Spain's military decline, which confirmed the advent of Louis XIV's France as the hegemonic European superpower. In exchange for French withdrawal from the Catalan territories south of the Pyrenees and an end to French financial support to Portuguese rebels, France obtained the Catalan province of Roussillon and other parts of historic Catalonia north of the Pyrenees, in addition to further territorial acquisitions in the Low Countries. In addition, Spain agreed to the marriage of Philip IV's daughter Maria-Theresa and the twenty-two-year-old Louis XIV with a dowry payment of 500,000 gold crowns, to take place in June the following year in the same location.

In April 1560, the Spanish royal painter Diego Rodríguez de Silva y Velázquez arrived at Pheasant Island, in his capacity as palace marshal, to oversee the preparations on the Spanish side. Velázquez spent seventy-two days decorating the palace and overseeing the royal party's travel arrangements before the infanta was formally given away on June 7. That same day Velázquez contracted tertian fever; he died on August 6, at the age of sixty-one.[2] The meeting between the bride and groom was captured by the French artist Jacques Laumosnier, in a painting that gives some indication of the preparations that may have hastened the great Spanish painter's premature death. In it Philip IV can be seen handing over his daughter to the extravagantly well-dressed Louis XIV, who is wearing stockings and bows on his ankles and is surrounded by equally

The advent of the Pyrenean border: Jacques Laumosnier, *Meeting of Louis XIV of France and Philip IV of Spain in the Isle of Pheasants, 1659.* Note the mountains on the backdrop—possibly painted by Velazquez (Musée de Tessé, public domain, Wikimedia Commons).

foppish and well-turned-out courtiers and officials. The room is draped with carpets, velvet or satin curtains, and a landscape tapestry of the Pyrenees that might have been painted by Velázquez himself.

In fact the infanta had already been married in a church in Fuenterrabía with Haro acting as the Sun King's proxy, because the glacial norms of Hapsburg court etiquette did not allow the young bride to cross the river unmarried, and the French king was not permitted to cross the river to marry her. When the princess had been handed over, the two kings knelt on cushions on either side of the line on the floor, where they kissed the Bible and a crucifix and swore to uphold the treaty's provisions, before Louis swept his bride away to solemnize the marriage in a church in Saint-Jean-de-Luz.

Both kings presented the treaty as a generous and statesmanlike concession to their war-weary subjects, but the "peace" enshrined in the treaty did not last long. Within seven years France and Spain were at war again, in part because the bankrupt Spanish court had not paid the infanta's dowry. If the Treaty of the Pyrenees did not bring much peace, it nevertheless laid the basis for one of Europe's most enduring state borders, whose essential features were to remain unchanged for more than three hundred years. The treaty also confirmed the historic role of the Pyrenees as one of Europe's emblematic "natural" frontiers and its evolution into what the nineteenth-century geographer Élisée Reclus once called "one of the most perfect political boundaries in the world."[3]

The Spanish March

This "perfection" was already evident, long before the French and Spanish monarchs took the first steps toward formalizing their mutual border. In *Natural History*, Pliny the Elder (23–79 CE) notes that "the frontier between the Spanish and the Gallic provinces is formed by the mountains of the Pyrenees, with headlands projecting into the two seas on either side."[4] At that time the mountains constituted an administrative boundary between the two Roman provinces of Narbonnese Gaul to the north and Tarraconensis (Hispania Citerior) in the south, which the Romans sought to regulate and control by establishing fortresses and customs points at the main Pyrenean mountain passes, known as *claustrae* and *clausurae*, or "doors" and "closed passages."

These defenses were initially intended to protect Rome against military incursions from Iberia, particularly from Carthage. During the disintegration of the Roman Empire in the fourth and fifth centuries, the Claustrae Pyrenai assumed a new role as a defensive perimeter that protected Hispania against invasion from barbarian tribes to the north. When Hispania was overrun by the Visigoths in the fifth century CE, the Pyrenees became a dividing line between Visigothic Spain and the Frankish Empire. Following the

Arab-Berber conquest of Visigothic Spain that began in 711, the Pyrenees acquired a new role as a strategic/religious frontier between the Franks and Moorish Iberia. In 732 the emir of Córdoba, Abd-al-Rahman, led a large raiding expedition across the Pyrenees through the Roncesvalles Pass that was halted in a series of engagements at Tours and Poitiers by a Frankish army under the command of the Frankish king Charles Martel "the Hammer"—a victory that the eighteenth-century historian Edward Gibbon and countless others have cited as a decisive event in the history of Europe.

This defeat halted the Moorish advance northward. By 739 the Franks had driven the Muslims from Narbonne, and the Pyrenees became a strategic barrier between Latin Christendom and the emirate of Al-Andalus and was subject to sporadic raiding from both sides. In 778 Charles's grandson Charlemagne (742–814) made a more concerted attempt to push the frontier southward to the Ebro River when he accepted an invitation from the Muslim governor of Barcelona, Sulaiman Yaqzan ibn al-Arabi, to assist a rebellion in Zaragoza against the Umayyad rulers of Al-Andalus. Two Frankish armies converged on Zaragoza, expecting the gates of the city to be opened to them by al-Arabi's fellow conspirators. When the governor of Zaragoza refused to open the city gates, the city was briefly placed under siege, before an anti-Frankish revolt in Saxony forced Charlemagne to march his armies northward once again.

During their retreat, the Franks sacked Pamplona as compensation, and shortly afterward their rear guard was ambushed and destroyed by vengeful Basques at the Roncesvalles Pass in the Pyrenees. In the aftermath of this disastrous campaign, the Franks refrained from further major military incursions and set out instead to create a Christian buffer zone on the southern side of the Pyrenees, governed by an assortment of counts, viscounts, marquises, and monastic orders under Frankish protection.

This zone became known as the Limes Hispanicus—the Spanish Marches. The Pyrenees were only one component of an amorphous march, or border region, that extended from Narbonne and

Montpellier in the north and into Navarre, Aragon, and Catalonia, and its boundaries were rarely stable, as Iberian Christian rulers extended their power across northern Spain and proceeded to drive the Moors southward. Beyond the castles, watchtowers, and fortified towns that guarded the main strategic points and mountain passes lay a "debatable land" over which neither Muslim nor Christian rulers had full control. To the eleventh-century Almoravid rulers of Al-Andalus, the northern *thagr*—march or frontier—was a lawless and godless territory, fit only for the most devout and ascetic holy warriors, known in Arabic as *rabita*, whom they deployed there to defend it against the infidel. Christian rulers often viewed the march in similar terms. In 1057 the monks of Sant Cugat—only 19 miles (31 kilometers) from Barcelona—called for defensive positions to be erected "in barren marches and in solitary places, against the pagans [Muslims]" in a frontier zone they called the *marca última*—a place of "great terror and trembling" inhabited by "perverse and blasphemous men."[5]

By this time most of northern Spain was firmly under Christian control, and the Pyrenees, along with their western extension in the Cantabrian Mountains, had become a base for the Christian resurgence that would ultimately drive Islam from Spain. As early as 870 the Catalan count Guifré el Pelós, or "Wilfred the Hairy," was made Count of Urgell by Charlemagne's grandson and established a powerful independent dynasty in the Catalan march, with its seat of power in Barcelona. In the tenth and eleventh centuries the Pyrenees had essentially lost their strategic significance, as the Christian rulers of Navarre, Aragon, and Catalonia consolidated their control over northern Spain and increasingly asserted their independence against their Frankish protectors.

By the thirteenth century the notion of the Spanish Marches as an Islamic/Christian frontier had become a historical anachronism. Yet it was not until after the unification of the Crowns of Castile and Aragon in the last decades of the fifteenth century, and the fall of the last Moorish enclave of Granada in 1492, that the Pyrenees really began their evolution into the military and political frontier between Spain and France. During the reign of Philip II of Spain (1556–98), the Pyrenees underwent yet another metamorphosis into a "frontier of heresy" between Counter-Reformation Spain and the Huguenot-dominated statelet of Béarn. Even then, the Pyrenean frontier continued to constitute a "debatable" state border. Until 1512 the Kingdom of Navarre straddled both sides of the Pyrenees, with its capital in Pamplona. That year Ferdinand of Aragon sent an invading force into Navarre and began a war that would ulti-mately result in the annexation of all Navarrese territories south of the Pyrenees in 1525. Until 1640, the "composite monarchy" known as the Crown of Aragon—which included the Principality of Catalonia—encompassed territories north and south of the Pyrenees. That year Catalonia rebelled against Castilian rule and appealed to France for military support in what became known as the Reapers' War—a decision the Catalans later had cause to regret, when French troops established a permanent presence in the Cerdagne and Roussillon and proceeded from occupation toward annexation.

Mapping the Border

The treaty signed by Haro and Mazarin at the Isle of Pheasants in November 1659 was intended to formalize these territorial acquisi-tions and establish a more precise and definitive boundary between the two states, with the Pyrenees as its central component. Estab-lishing these divisions proved to be a fraught and complex process. Though Article 42 of the provisional Treaty of the Pyrenees declared that "the Pyrenees Mountains, which anciently divided the Gauls from the Spains, shall henceforth form the division of the two kingdoms," the practical difficulties in implementing this decision were evident in the mutual decision to appoint commissioners who "shall together in good faith, declare which are the Pyrenees Mountains, which . . . should thereafter divide the two kingdoms, and they shall mark the limits they ought to have."[6]

Subsequent attempts to define "which are the Pyrenees Mountains" were not helped by the Spanish negotiators, who were determined to claw back through diplomacy some of what they had lost on the battlefield. In March 1660, French and Spanish commissioners met in the town of Céret in Roussillon, in order to transform the treaty's provisions into an administrative reality. In addition to Roussillon, France also laid claim to the large swathes of the Catalan Cerdagne and other strategic Pyrenean territories in the Conflent, Vallespir, and Capcir Valleys. The Spanish commissioners disputed these claims, and both sides hearkened to classical geographers to support their respective arguments or refute those of their opponents. Pierre de Marca, the erudite commissioner who governed French-controlled Catalonia during the Reapers' War, cited Strabo's and Livy's ancient references to the Limes Hispanicus to assert historic French rights to the Cerdagne, while the Spanish referred to the same sources to counter these claims. At one point the Spanish commissioners even suggested that the border should consist of what "all those who live in the mountains understand as the dividing line" and asked local shepherds, "Where are the Pyrenees?" to support their view that the territories claimed by France were actually located on the Spanish side of the border.

When the French team refused to back down on its claims to some thirty-three villages in the Cerdagne, the Spanish argued that some of these villages were in fact *villas*—towns—and that France therefore had no right to them. These acrimonious discussions were still unfolding even as the French and Spanish wedding corteges were converging on Pheasant Island. At the eleventh hour Spain conceded almost everything France had asked for, and the commissioners now began to reconcile "natural frontiers" such as rivers, streams, and other "watersheds" with centuries-old agreements made by local Pyrenean villages and communities regarding rights of pasturage and access to woodlands and water.

Known as *traités de lies et passeries* (treaties of covenanted entry) in French, or *facerías* in Spanish, these medieval agreements were originally drawn up by individual Pyrenean villages or federations of villages in order to regulate the pastoral economy and eliminate the potential for violent conflict over access to resources and rights of pasturage. In some cases these local agreements were incorporated into the new border, but where this was not possible or strategically desirable, the frontier simply cut through private land and even through buildings. On the Col de Panissars in the Albères massif of Catalonia, for example, the boundary ran straight through a monastery, leaving the church in France and the monks' quarters on the Spanish side.

Situated 10 miles (16 kilometers) inside France in the rich farmlands of the Cerdagne Valley, the Pyrenean town of Llívia was the capital of the Cerdagne during the Roman Empire. Connected by road to the Catalan border town of Puigcerdà in the province of Girona, the town is a popular Catalan mountain resort whose attractions include the oldest pharmacy in the world and a museum containing the skeleton of a Barbary ape dating back to 430 to 600 CE, believed to have been the pet of a prestigious local warrior. For more than three hundred years, Llívia's main claim to fame was its status as a Spanish exclave in France—a categorization that was entirely due to the Treaty of the Pyrenees. It was not included in the French annexation of the Cerdagne because the Spanish commissioners convinced their French counterparts that Llívia was a town, not a village. As a result a special accord was written into the treaty that allowed access to Llívia solely from Puigcerdà, via a single designated road that connected it to Spain.

Long after these negotiations were concluded, the Pyrenean frontier remained a contested border, particularly in the newly annexed Catalan territories, whose inhabitants accepted their new rulers with reluctance. Anti-French rebellions in Roussillon and the Cerdagne were frequent, and French and Spanish armies repeatedly occupied and reoccupied parts of Roussillon during the incessant warring between the two countries. In 1700, on his deathbed, the imbecilic Spanish king Carlos II, the last of the Spanish Hapsburgs, appointed Louis XIV's grandson Philip, the Duke of Anjou,

as heir to the Spanish throne—an announcement that was supposedly greeted by the Sun King with the gleeful observation "The
Pyrenees no longer exist!"

Other European states regarded the "disappearance" of the Pyrenees and the emergence of a new French superstate with alarm
and formed a military alliance to prevent Philip from taking the
Spanish throne. The result was the War of the Spanish Succession
(1701–14, which ended when Philip accepted the Spanish Crown
on the condition that he abandon his claims to the French throne.
The Pyrenees nevertheless continued to be a periodic zone of conflict between the two states until the early nineteenth century. It
was not until 1851 that a French-Spanish commission finally agreed
to draw up a definitive border and began the process of mapping the
boundary that culminated fifteen years later in the Treaty of Bayonne, on May 26, 1866, "fixing definitively the common frontier of
Spain and France." Two more years of work were required before
the commissioners laid the boundary stones that marked this frontier, in accordance with the very precise details contained in the
Final Act of Demarcation, such as the instruction that Border Stone
484 should be placed "following the direction of the same wall,
which forms an angle of 162 degrees with marker 482 of the French
side; and 235 meters away is planted a stone in a bend in the wall."

The Treaty of Bayonne finally ended any remaining ambiguity
regarding the frontier and testified to the new spirit of cooperation
between these two historic rivals that rendered the Pyrenees an
impediment to trade and commerce. In the early 1840s the French
Chamber of Deputies even discussed the possibility of constructing a "canal of the Pyrenees" connecting the Mediterranean to the
Atlantic in order to eliminate the longer passage through the Straits
of Gibraltar. The capital to finance this project was never raised,
and it was eventually made irrelevant by the construction of the
Canal Latéral in 1857, which linked Bordeaux to the Canal du
Midi at Toulouse, thereby allowing boats to cross France from the
Atlantic to the Mediterranean.

In the early twentieth century a new attempt was made to transcend the "natural" Pyrenean border, when French and Spanish engineers began to drill a railway tunnel under the mountains through the Somport Pass. On July 18, 1928, the Somport railway was officially opened at the new Canfranc International Railway Station in Aragon, amid great pomp and ceremony. "To find a parallel to the event one would have to imagine the opening of a tunnel between Calais and Dover," observed the *Manchester Guardian* that day, "for, despite Louis XIV's boastful saying, "The Pyrenees no longer exist,' this chain has always constituted a strategic defence pretty well as formidable as the Channel."

Following the Spanish Civil War, the Pyrenees once again became a militarized frontier, when the Franco regime fortified the mountains in anticipation of an Allied invasion. It was not until 1995 that the Pyrenees effectively ceased to exist as a political border, following the abolition of Spanish and French customs posts and passport controls as a result of Spain's accession into the Schengen Area. In March that year I witnessed that transformation firsthand when I visited the Spanish border town of La Jonquera as a BBC radio correspondent. As part of my report I was asked to drive back and forth across the border to see if anyone stopped me or asked for my passport. No one did. Neither the Spanish nor the French police showed any interest in me or anyone else. Today La Jonquera is a sleazy hypercapitalist entrepôt on the former Roman Via Domitia, dominated by giant hypermarkets, booze shops, and erotic supermarkets selling sex toys.

La Jonquera also has the largest brothel in Europe, the Paradise Nightclub, and sex workers are a ubiquitous presence in and around the town, parading up and down the motorway like modern-day sirens in bikinis, heels, and thongs or taking shelter from the sun under parasols near the enormous truck parks on the Spanish side of the frontier. Despite the abolition of the frontier, there are still sufficient differentials on either side of the border in terms of price, supply, and demand to make La Jonquera a sought-after destination for the thousands of consumers who come here. In 2015, however, the border posts remained as empty as they were when I last saw them.

To all practical intents and purposes, the frontier created by Haro and Mazarin at Pheasant Island has become another of Europe's "dead" borders; it continues to exist only as a line on the map—and in the clichés and metaphorical associations that have been handed down to posterity and that have continued to define the place of the Pyrenees in history.

3

"Africa Begins at the Pyrenees"

When Spain was overrun by the Mohammedan, and when in
the first generation of the eighth century the Asiatic with his
alien creed and morals had even swept for a moment into
Gaul, the Pyrenees became a march: at first the rampart,
later, when they were fully held, the bastion of our civilisation against its chief peril.
—Hilaire Belloc, *The Pyrenees*, 1909

Few borders are entirely "natural," and even the most natural physical frontiers can sometimes have unintended metaphorical associations imposed upon them, so that mountains, rivers, concrete
walls, or wire fences become symbolic frontiers that define or confirm imagined distinctions between the territories on either side of
them. Such distinctions might consist of Christian "bulwarks" against
Islam, like the *Militärgrenze*, or cordon sanitaire, established by the
Hapsburgs along their eastern borders with the Ottoman Turks
in the sixteenth century, or the "iron curtain" invoked by Winston
Churchill. More recently, certain frontiers, such as the U.S.-Mexican
border or the Spanish exclaves in Ceuta and Melilla in Morocco,
have become cutoff points between the first and third worlds.

Historically, the "perfect border" of the Pyrenees has acquired its
own imagined distinctions, most famously embodied in the observation attributed to Alexandre Dumas père in the early nineteenth
century that "Africa begins at the Pyrenees." Whether Dumas
actually said this is not certain, but many of his contemporaries

echoed the same essential distinctions, in identifying the Pyrenees as the dividing line between Europe and an Africanized Iberia. For Stendhal, "Blood, manners, language, way of living and fighting, everything in Spain is African. If the Spaniard were a Muslim he would be a complete African."[1] "It is an error of geography to have assigned Spain to Europe," declared the French diplomat Dominique-Georges-Frédéric de Fourt de Pradt in *Mémoires historiques sur la revolution d'Espagne* (1816). "It belongs to Africa: blood, manners, language, the way of life and making war, in Spain everything is African."[2]

Such imagery has proved to be surprisingly enduring. "Beyond the Pyrenees begins Africa," observed the American anthropologist and racial theorist William Ripley in *The Races of Europe* (1899). "Once that natural barrier is crossed, the Mediterranean racial type in all its purity confronts us. The human phenomenon is entirely parallel with the sudden transition to the flora and fauna of the south. The Iberian population, thus isolated from the rest of Europe, are allied in all important anthropological respects with the peoples inhabiting Africa north of the Sahara from the Red Sea to the Atlantic."[3]

Whether these distinctions were imagined in terms of landscape, race, culture, or religion, the Pyrenees have been cited again and again as the physical dividing line where they were confirmed. It is difficult to think of any mountain range that has so often been depicted in these terms. The Alps, for example, have often been described as a barrier and a physical obstacle for travelers and invading armies, but they have never acquired the same reputation as a cultural and civilizational frontier that has so often been attached to the Pyrenees. This reputation has had a key role in the imaginative construction of the Pyrenees as a "savage frontier," and for this reason we need to look a little more closely at the various ways in which the Iberian "Africa" has been imagined, and see how they became part of the imaginative construction of the Pyrenees themselves.

The Song of Roland

This image has its roots in the eighth-century Islamic conquest of Visigothic Iberia, which severed Spain from the mainstream of Latin Christendom. As a consequence the Pyrenees became another of Europe's *antemurale christianitatis*—bulwarks of Christianity—a role that was confirmed by the defeat of Abd al-Rahman's raiders at the hands of the Franks at Tours and Poitiers in 732, and the subsequent Muslim withdrawal into Iberia. Generations of historians have described the Pyrenees as the crucial defensive barrier that held the Muslims in check in the aftermath of that battle—an assumption that tends to take for granted that the Pyrenees were a sufficient obstacle in themselves to put off any putative invaders.

The Pyrenees first began to acquire these symbolic connotations in the outside world as a result of the medieval poem known as *The Song of Roland*, which was discovered in an Oxford library in 1837. This anonymous poem depicted the famous battle that took place in the Roncesvalles Pass in the summer of 778, when Charlemagne's army was attacked by Moorish troops during its retreat from Zaragoza. Most scholars believe that this classic *chanson de geste* (song of heroic deeds) was written in the eleventh or twelfth century, against the background of the First Crusade, possibly as a compilation or distillation of oral legends and heroic songs told by monks and traveling poets known as jongleurs.

The poem is an almost entirely mythologized account of the battle that allegedly took place at the Roncesvalles Pass on August 15, 778. Very few facts about this battle are known for certain. Even the location is disputed, and some legends claim that it took place farther east, in the Boca de Infierno gorge in Aragon. There is general consensus that Charlemagne's retreating column was attacked by Basques, in revenge for the sacking of Pamplona. Charlemagne's contemporary biographer Einhard declares that it was Basque irregulars, not Saracens, who attacked the Frankish rear guard in the "narrow defiles" in and around Roncesvalles, destroying a Frankish column and a number of knights, including "Roland, prefect of the Breton marshes." In *The Song of Roland*, however, the Basques are replaced by a Saracen horde some four hundred thousand strong— an improbable and almost certainly impossible figure for any army of that time—forewarned by the treacherous Frankish knight Ganelon, which ambushes and annihilates Roland and his cohorts, including the warrior-cleric Archbishop Turpin. In a further departure from the historical record, the poem relates how Charlemagne's vengeful army subsequently returns to Zaragoza after Roland's defeat and crushes the Saracens, before executing Ganelon.

Throughout the poem, Roland and his cohorts are ideal Christian warriors, brave, devout, and self-sacrificing, slaying thousands of Saracens to give Charlemagne's army a chance to retreat. Their Saracen opponents, by contrast, are intrinsically unworthy and despicable. Whereas Roland, Archbishop Turpin, and their fellow soldiers willingly accept martyrdom in exchange for absolution of their sins, the Saracens have no motives except plunder, lands, "gifts of pretty, high-born women," or the "effigies of gold," which they promise to offer to their pagan gods in return for victory. Only the Saracen emir Baligant shows any sign of physical attractiveness or nobility, causing the poet to exclaim, "God what a lord, if he were but a Christian!" as he rallies his troops against the returning Franks, only to meet his death at the hands of Charlemagne himself.[4]

The other Saracens receive no such praise. Not only are they religiously alien, but many of them are also black, a detail that the poem often cites as some kind of explanation for their savagery and depravity. For Roland the sight of this "outlaw race, whose members all are blacker than is ink / and have no white about them, save their teeth," is a terrifying confirmation that he and his comrades will die in the coming battle. They nevertheless sell their lives dearly, killing thousands of Saracens before they are killed themselves. For Roland, Turpin, and their fellow heroes, it is not enough to simply kill Saracens: their swords cleave right through their bodies and even through the bodies of their horses. Heads are split open and blood runs in torrents. The dying Roland is the last to fall.

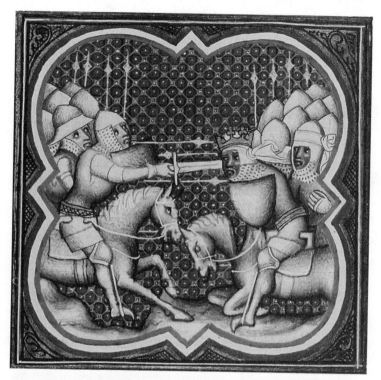

"This outlaw race/whose members all are blacker than is ink." *Battle of Roncevaux Pass*, fourteenth century, anonymous. (Gallica Digital Library, Wikimedia Commons).

Mortally wounded, he tries to break his sword, Durendal, so that the Saracens cannot use it, but the sword has so many sacred relics in its hilt that it cannot be broken, and Roland dies with his weapon in hand, blowing his ivory horn to summon Charlemagne back, before the angels arrive to bear his soul to Paradise.

Roland's sacrifice is redeemed as the Franks and their allies return to massacre the "pagan" population of Zaragoza and Charlemagne kills the Saracen emir Baligant, smashing his bejeweled helmet "with France's sword . . . then cleaves the skull—the brains come spilling out." After Roland's betrayer, Ganelon, is hanged and his corpse fed to the dogs, the angel Gabriel descends and summons Charlemagne forth to new conquests.

The Roland legend captivated medieval Christendom and was disseminated in oral and written versions: through the many illustrations of the battle that appeared in the *Grandes chroniques de France*; through the tenuous connections between the imagined Roland and real Pyrenean places, such as the great portal known as the Brèche de Roland (Roland's Breach) at Gavarnie, which Roland supposedly cut into the rock with his sword, Durendal; through the Santiago de Compostela pilgrimage, on which many pilgrims passed through Roncesvalles to contemplate the scene of Roland's mythical battle before they continued their journey southward.

This, then, is how the Pyrenees first appear in the European literary imagination: as a sacred battlefield between Christian virtue and a Saracen enemy that is religiously and culturally inferior, and already recognizably "African" in its cruelty and savagery; as a hostile wilderness that colludes in Roland's destruction by providing the Saracens with their hiding place, and which constitutes another physical obstacle that Charlemagne's army must overcome as it returns through what the author of *The Song of Roland* calls "those hills, and soaring rocky bluffs / those sunken glades, those harrowing ravines / then leave behind the passes and the wastelands / they've made their way into the Spanish march / and set up camp upon a broad plateau."

Regardless of the assumptions inherent in the poem, the historical period in which the "harrowing ravines" of the Pyrenees acted as a "bulwark" and a "rampart" was relatively short. As early as the ninth century, Spain was already sufficiently Christianized for pilgrims to make the pilgrimage to Santiago de Compostela. For much of the Middle Ages the Pyrenees constituted a physical barrier between rival Christian kingdoms, rather than between Muslims and Christians. Yet even after Islam had been definitively removed from Iberia, Spain continued to be perceived as a land apart that was distinct from the rest of Europe and tainted by its Moorish past, and the Pyrenees were cited again and again as the dividing line between one civilization and another.

"Spain Is Different"

Such imagery was not due simply to the military threat—whether real or imagined—of Islam, but to assumptions and conclusions about the cultural and even racial impact of the Muslim presence in Spain. Medieval Christian travelers often commented with astonishment about and disapproval of the popularity of Moorish food, music, and fashion in Iberian Christian courts. Even after the unification of Spain under Christian rule, sixteenth-century Protestant propaganda tracts depicted Spain as a suspect country that was fatally corrupted by its Moorish and Semitic past.

Spain's "African" and "Oriental" qualities were frequently cited by French veterans of the Peninsular War. Napoléon allegedly observed that "Spain is different" after the French defeat at the Battle of Bailén in 1808, and many French soldiers echoed this conclusion. The Swiss-born Albert de Rocca, a *sous-lieutenant* in the second regiment of French hussars, arrived in Spain from more congenial occupation duties in Germany and found that "with regard to knowledge and the progress of social habits, Spain was at least a century behind the other nations of the continent. The distant and almost insular situation of the country, and the severity of its religious institutions, had prevented the Spaniards from taking part in the disputes and controversies which had agitated and enlightened Europe during the sixteenth century."[5]

One French financier described his passage into Spain as a journey from "a country where all traces of the past had disappeared" to a country in which "I was finding myself thrown back several centuries. . . . The monastic costumes mixed in with the people . . . it was a representation of the seventeenth century; it was history in action." Many veterans saw confirmation of these distinctions in the guerrilla tactics adopted by the Spanish. "At that time one had to travel to Spain in the same way as one did in Arabia: woe be to he who strayed from the caravan," wrote one former soldier of the guerrilla tactics used by the Spanish. "The Spaniards, in whose veins were still to be found some drops of African blood, became veritable Bedouins: motivated more by love of pillage than patriotic duty."[6]

Napoléon's soldiers were not the only occupying army to attribute their defeat to the barbarousness of their enemies. Nevertheless, the image of Spain as an anachronistic outpost of religious fanaticism and ancien régime reaction was echoed by other commentators. In her account of her nineteenth-century Spanish grandmother Pepita's native land, Vita Sackville-West wrote of "that proud, aloof, and ruthless nation [which] still dwelt self-contained behind the barrier of the Pyrenees; the expression *cosa de España* (a thing peculiar to Spain) really meant something quite indigenously different from any other part of Europe; the reserve, the austerity, the streak of Oriental secrecy in the Spanish character set them apart even more effectively than the frontier of their mountains."[7]

For some nineteenth-century travelers, the differences between Spain and the rest of Europe were confirmed by the landscape itself. Returning from a journey to Spain via Le Perthus Pass in the 1780s, the English traveler Arthur Young compared "the natural and miserable roads of Catalonia" with the "noble causeway, made with all the solidity and magnificence that distinguish the highways of France," on which he and his companions found themselves: "Instead of beds of torrents you have well-built bridges; and from a country wild, desert, and poor, we found ourselves in the midst of cultivation and improvement."[8]

In his memoirs, Louis-Gabriel Suchet, the governor of Aragon during the Peninsular War and one of the most intelligent of Napoléon's commanders, evoked a Spanish landscape that was familiar to many French soldiers, with its "constantly burning sun, high lands devoid of culture, of which no animated object ever breaks the uniformity."[9] For many soldiers—and the nineteenth-century touristic travelers who later followed in their wake—these differences were immediately evident on crossing the Pyrenees. Writing in the 1840s, the English traveler Richard Ford observed that "while the French slope is full of summer watering-places, social and civilised, the Spanish side is still the lair of the smuggler, and of wild birds and beasts."[10]

Such differences were not entirely inaccurate, but nor were they universal. In the Western and Central Pyrenees there is often little difference in the vegetation or climate between the French and Spanish sides. Drive south of Toulouse, Montpellier, and Narbonne and you will find sun-bleached corrugated fields and palm trees that are no less Mediterranean and "African" than the landscape on the other side of the border. But actual distinctions in landscape, terrain, and levels of development were often secondary to the imagined differences and assumptions imposed on the Spanish "Africa" that were sometimes steeped in disgust and at other times inspired a romantic fascination.

"Lovely Spain"

For most nineteenth-century travelers, the differences in landscape and terrain on either side of the Pyrenees merely confirmed certain notions that they had already brought with them. For the American diplomat and congressman Caleb Cushing, the Pyrenees were "still the great national barrier between the neighbouring kingdoms" in 1832 as they had always been, and the Spanish people were "as unlike the French, as unlike the other nations of Europe, as they were when Cortes and Pizarro ravaged America, or when Philip II reared the sombre masses of the Escorial among the snows and tempests of the Guadarrama."[11] Inspired by Spanish resistance to the Napoleonic occupation, a number of British writers developed an infatuation with what Lord Byron called "Lovely Spain! Renowned, romantic land!" in *Childe Harold's Pilgrimage*. In her narrative poem *Blanche of Castile* (1813), Mary Russell Mitford hailed "Romantic Spain! . . . Fancy's faery land." In 1825, the poet and novelist Letitia Elizabeth Landon described Spain as the

"Land of the olive and the vine / The saint and soldier, sword and shrine!"

François-René de Chateaubriand, Théophile Gautier, Prosper Mérimée, and Washington Irving all depicted Spain as an exotic aberration at the foot of Europe, inhabited by proud women in mantillas, fiery gypsy dancers, bandits, smugglers, and Quixotic dreamers driven by quaint but antiquated notions of honour, passion, and chivalry. In the preface to his collection of poems *Les Orientales* (1829), Victor Hugo praised the fact that "Spain is still the Orient; Spain is half Asiatic." In 1822, the future French prime minister Adolphe Thiers traveled around the Cerdagne as a journalist to report on the violent spillover from Spain's short-lived conflict known as the Liberal Triennium (1820–23), between supporters of the 1812 constitution and the autocratic Ferdinand VII.

At a camp of Royalist supporters near Mont-Louis in the Cerdagne, Thiers expressed his astonishment at the sight of "these monks, these guerrillas, in short, that picturesque people who resemble a migration of Asiatics in the midst of Europeans" and compared these "Asiatic" warriors to a mediocre Europe, which "is almost all softened down into general uniformity by the progress of civilization, and shows only a tolerably happy and tranquil state of society. In the mountains of Spain, is especially to be found that dramatic and original barbarism . . . which arouses the imagination, and offers it grand features to study."[12]

Other writers echoed similar sentiments. "[The traveller] crosses the Pyrenees, too weary of the bore, commonplace, and uniformity of ultra civilization," wrote Richard Ford, "in order to see something new and un-European; he hopes to find again in Spain . . . all that has been lost and forgotten elsewhere."[13] For Jules Michelet, the Pyrenees constituted an "austere, formidable, unbroken rampart . . . the barrier between Europe and Africa,—that Africa which men call Spain," where the traveler experienced "an absolute and direct divorce, for which no graduation prepares us . . . if you have started from Toulouse over the Pyrenees, and descended their rapid southern slope to Saragossa, you have crossed a world."[14] Like

Ford and Thiers, Michelet described the Pyrenees as a gateway to the "unknown which lay beyond" the mountains and "the land of romance and improbable adventures."

Perhaps not surprisingly, Spaniards have not always been flattered by such descriptions. "The apothegm that Africa begins at the Pyrenees remains commonplace in Europe," lamented the Spanish novelist and diplomat Juan Valera in 1868."[15] "The ignorance of what we were and what we are seems incredible. . . . I have been asked by foreigners if we hunt lions in Spain; they have explained to me what tea is, supposing that I have never taken it or seen it." Spanish liberals of the nineteenth and early twentieth centuries were often frustrated by these representations of Spanish difference, whether it was imagined in positive or negative terms.

In the early 1960s the Franco regime's minister for information and tourism, Manuel Fraga Iribarne, astutely transformed Napoléon's observation at Bailén into a catchy slogan for Spain's booming tourist industry. Posters in English proudly proclaimed, "Spain is different: Visit Spain," accompanied by images of sandy beaches, flamenco dancers, bullfights, and Holy Week processions.

Today the notion of Spanish "difference" has lost most of the negative connotations that it once had, and the age of air travel has long since eroded the image of the Pyrenees as an imagined "rampart" or "gateway" between cultures and civilizations. Few of the thousands of visitors who travel overland through abandoned Pyrenean customs posts each year, or take the high-speed train from Paris to Barcelona, are likely to see the Pyrenees as a civilizational dividing line or the point of entry to a backward and culturally retarded "Africa." The "imagined" Pyrenean frontier has vanished along with the political border itself. But historical clichés often acquire an afterlife of their own. As late as 1999, the *Encyclopedia Britannica* described the Pyrenees as a historic "barrier to human movement" that "rise abruptly from the flanking plains of France and Spain with only steep gorges and steep-walled natural amphitheaters that lead to almost impassable lofty summits. . . . The French peasant's adage, 'Africa begins with the Pyrenees,' is not without a large measure of truth in emphasizing the historic significance of the Pyrenees as a barrier in the development of Spain."

The Pyrenean Borderland

Such observations give the Pyrenees more metaphorical weight than any mountain range can bear, and they also tend to obscure and overlook a great deal. Every year, on July 13, French villagers from the Barétous Valley in the Bearnese Pyrenees hand over three cows to a Spanish delegation from the neighboring Roncal Valley, chanting the ritual refrain "pax avant, pax avant, pax avant" (peace first). The "Tribute of the Three Cows" dates back to the fourteenth century, when the inhabitants of the two valleys met to put an end to a long and sometimes violent conflict between them. As a result of these negotiations, it was agreed that pastoralists from Barétous could take their cattle to pasture in the Roncal Valley for twenty-eight days a year, on condition that they did not remain overnight. To ensure that these pledges were kept, the inhabitants of the Barétous agreed to hand over three cows with identical horns, teeth, and coats to their Spanish counterparts each year.

Perhaps not surprisingly, this quaint relic of the Middle Ages has become a minor tourist attraction, but the Tribute of the Three Cows is also a testament to cross-border interactions that have rarely been acknowledged in the imaginative construction of the Pyrenean "wall." Such anomalies are not unique to the Pyrenees. The distinctions imposed on national or historical borders often seem clearer with hindsight or when viewed from a geographical distance, and these distinctions are inevitably hazier on closer inspection. The Pyrenean border, like all borders, is an artificial line that dissects a broader and more multidimensional geographical and cultural space, whose inhabitants often have more in common with one another than they do with their respective countries. To many of the peoples who have actually lived in or near the mountains, the

Pyrenees have not been a border between Europe and Africa, or even between France and Spain, but a shared borderland, with affinities and allegiances that reach across the mountains and transcend the reality of the border.

The agreement between the villagers of the Roncal and Barétous Valleys is only one of many *traités* that long preceded the advent of the Spanish-French border and continued after it was formalized. At the height of the War of the Spanish Succession, in 1712, when French armies were locked in battle with Spanish and Allied armies in Spain, the *intendant* of Béarn wrote to his superiors to request permission to allow Bearnese cattle breeders to sell their animals in Aragon, reminding them that "the inhabitants of the French and Spanish mountains will do anything to conserve their union, which has never been interrupted even by the bitterest of wars."[16]

In this war, and in many others, Spanish and French military commanders were often frustrated by the reluctance of Pyrenean mountain communities to fight or even support their own national armies. In some cases, villages or federations of French and Spanish villages collectively refused to participate in the wars fought by their respective states and even warned one another of the arrival of invading armies. In 1910, nearly half a century after the signing of the Treaty of Bayonne, the French historian and geographer Henri Cavaillès found that many Pyrenean villages on either side of the border were still observing reciprocal agreements and *traités* that dated back to the Middle Ages. In 1952, the Spanish legal scholar Victor Fairén Guillén noted the existence of a "great international Pyrenean community of men and social groups, united by an extensive system of common interests [which] has been unjustly forgotten"—a system that was still, even then, in existence, centuries after it had first been established.[17]

This coexistence should not be exaggerated. There have been periods in which Frenchmen and Spaniards in the Pyrenees have hated each other and sometimes fought each other with the same ferocity as their fellow countrymen. But even then, their conflicts were not necessarily explained by their real or imagined cultural differences. In his classic study of the fourteenth-century Pyrenean Cathar village of Montaillou, Emmanuel Le Roy Ladurie describes the Catholic, Cathar, and Saracen migrant shepherds of Mount Vézian, near Flix in Catalonia, whose members "cooked and shared garlic-flavoured pies, mingling together as brothers regardless of their different opinions."[18] For Le Roy Ladurie these freewheeling shepherds were part of a common "community of culture, at once Moorish, Andalusian, Catalan and Occitan," that reached across both sides of the Pyrenees.

Today, the abundance of Catalan flags and the prevalence of the Catalan language in the French Pyrenean towns and villages of the Cerdagne and Roussillon are a historical reminder of the *Països Catalans*—Catalan heartlands that once reached across both sides of the Pyrenees. Similarly, the Western Pyrenees divide the Spanish Basque provinces from the three French territories that form the Basque provinces of Soule, Labourd, and Lower Navarre, which many Basques regard as the Iparralde—the northern part. Each year thousands of Basques take part in the 1,293-mile (2,080-kilometer) relay race known as the Korrika through the seven historic Basque provinces to promote and celebrate the Basque language on both sides of the border.

Such affinities are not unique in themselves. State boundaries often dissect territories whose inhabitants have more in common with their counterparts closer to the border than they do with those of their respective capitals. Many borderlanders speak each other's languages and share certain cultural and historical markers, and the closer one examines them, the more one finds contradictions and anomalies that do not fit with the expectations placed upon the border itself. But these cultural connections are too often ignored in the depictions of the Pyrenees as a harsh and forbidding dividing line between countries and civilizations—a dividing line that has tended to be imagined in binary, either/or terms. Too often the "savagery" of the Pyrenean landscape is invoked as a confirmation of the cultural assumptions that have served to distinguish the backward and exotic Spanish "Africa" from the modernity embodied by

France and the rest of Europe. Not only are these assumptions questionable in themselves, but they have also tended to reduce the history of the Pyrenees to their role as a border, and too easily present the mountains as an uninhabited wilderness. Yet the mountains are, and always have been, only one component of a wider borderland and a mosaic of cultures, languages, and political arrangements that have never been fully encompassed or acknowledged by the French-Spanish frontier—or by the historical representations of Spain's "African" qualities.

In looking to the "savage" Pyrenees to confirm such distinctions, too many historians and commentators have forgotten that people were living in the mountains long before the border came into existence, and they have also obscured the historical role of the Pyrenean borderland as a cultural bridge, rather than a barrier between Iberia and the rest of the continent, and a transmission belt through which many different exchanges have taken place.

PART II

Pyrenean Crossings

When Louis XIV accepted the offer of the last Hapsburg King of Spain to bequeath his crown to a grandson to the Grand Monarque, a Spanish ambassador at Versailles exclaimed joyfully, "Now there are no more Pyrenees!" But those gloomy masses stood their ground as an obstinate barrier to French *lumières*, and as a symbol of the resistance that would meet the attempt of a dedicated few to Europeanize the Spanish mind.

—Will Durant and Ariel Durant, *The Story of Civilization*[1]

4

Scholars, Pilgrims, and Troubadours

> Since it is proper that those who have drunk of any philo-
> sophical nectar love each other, and that anyone who might
> have anything rare, precious, and useful which is known to
> others, should impart it generously . . . [we] have been zeal-
> ous to investigate if we had anything of this sort, which we
> might present to you, who test through experience, as some-
> thing sweet and delicious.
>
> —Petrus Alphonsi, *Epistola ad peripateticos*[1]

The Marxist sociologist Henri Lefebvre (1901–92) is more widely
associated with his pioneering studies of everyday life and urban
spaces than with mountains or the Pyrenees. But even though
Lefebvre spent much of his working life in Paris, he was born in
Hagetmau near Pau, in the Pyrénées-Atlantiques, and died at his
mother's house in the village of Navarrenx in Béarn. In addition to
two doctoral theses on the Pyrenees, he also wrote a book, *Pyrénées*
(1965), in which he acknowledged his intellectual debt to "this region, in which I endured heavy clerical conformism, [which] had
nourished and sustained all the heretical currents: From Arianism
brought by the Visigoths to Albigensian and Cathar heresies to
Protestantism to Jansenism."[2] For Lefebvre, the Pyrenees did not
refer merely to the mountains themselves, but to a broader "meridi-
onal" space encompassing a wide swathe of southern France and
reaching as far south as Barcelona. This "heretical periphery" was a
crucial component of his intellectual formation and an identity
that he defined as "Occitan, that is to say, peripheral—and global."

Lefebvre's celebration of his Pyrenean borderland heritage might seem idiosyncratic to some, but his invocation of a "peripheral" space that was also connected culturally and intellectually to the wider world is in many ways a more accurate depiction of the actual place of the Pyrenees in history than the endless references to "gloomy masses" and impenetrable barriers that have so often been attached to them. Consider the Benedictine monastery of Santa María de Ripoll, in the foothills of the Catalan Pyrenees. Established around 879 by Wilfred the Hairy, the Count of Urgell and the "founder of Catalonia," the monastery is one of the great ecclesiastical buildings of the early Spanish March. It is most famously associated with the formidable scholar-statesman Abbot Oliba Cabreta of Ripoll (971–1046). Among his many intellectual achievements, Oliba was one of the promoters of the Peace and Truce of God movement, which resulted in the agreement by the Latin church to impose limits on feudal violence in 1027—one of the first attempts in history to impose rules and conducts on the treatment of "civilians" and noncombatants in war.

Oliba also presided over the expansion of the Ripoll monastery's library and scriptorium. At its peak in the late tenth and early eleventh centuries, the scriptorium contained a number of Arabic translations of Greek and Latin manuscripts that were being translated back into Latin by local monks. In the second half of the tenth century a precocious French monk named Gerbert of Aurillac came to the monastery to study there. Gerbert went on to become one of the great intellectuals of Dark Ages Europe, and his remarkable interaction with the intellectual culture of "Saracen" Iberia suggests a very different role that the Marca Hispanica once played in European history than the one that the Pyrenees have traditionally been associated with.[3]

The Mathematical Pope

Gerbert's Iberian journey began in 967, when the abbot of the local monastery in Aurillac in south-central France entreated a Catalan nobleman named Count Borrell II of Barcelona to take Gerbert back to Catalonia to find "men proficient in the arts." Gerbert would have been only around twelve years old then, but the novice monk's prodigious grasp of Latin, logic, philosophy, and mathematics had already outstripped his teachers' knowledge and abilities. The abbot of Aurillac clearly believed that new intellectual horizons were more likely to be found south of the Pyrenees, and Borrell accepted his request. As a result Gerbert was placed under the tutelage of Atto, (died 971) the warrior-bishop of Vic in Catalonia, where he quickly immersed himself in the vibrant polyglot culture of the Marca Hispanica, with its fusion of Arab, Jewish, and Christian influences. The young monk also became acquainted with the stream of translated classical Greek, Roman, Persian, and Sanskrit manuscripts that were making their way into the Umayyad caliphate of Córdoba from Damascus and Baghdad.

Gerbert's studies in Catalonia had a decisive impact on his intellectual development, particularly on his understanding of the four disciplines pertaining to the quadrivium—arithmetic, geometry, astronomy, and music. In addition to discovering the nine Arabic numerals and zero for the first time, he also became familiar with the calculating device called the abacus. Gerbert may have learned how to use the astrolabe—a spherical device for calculating time and position developed by Arab scientists—which became the main navigational device until the development of the compass.

In December 970 Gerbert traveled to Rome with his mentors Count Borrell and Bishop Atto, where the Holy Roman emperor Otto I assigned him as tutor to his son. In 972 Gerbert took up a new post at the cathedral school of Reims, where he began to disseminate some of the mathematical and astronomical theories he had imbibed in Catalonia to a wider audience. Gerbert soon established a reputation as an innovative teacher, with a penchant for ingenious pedagogical devices in the classroom such as the monochord, a single string over a sounding box, which he used to demonstrate the mathematical relationship between musical harmonies and different pitches. He revamped the old Roman abacus, with a smaller and simplified version that incorporated Arabic numerals for the first time in Europe.

In addition to writing a textbook on geometry and demonstrating the use of the astrolabe, Gerbert also created a six-note musical scale, invented a water-powered church organ, and devised mathematical poem puzzles, such as the *carmen figuratum*, or "figurative poem," which he gave to his former pupil and friend Otto II. These innovations were not always favorably viewed in a Christian world where the spirit of intellectual curiosity was still encircled— and to some extent policed—by dogmatism and superstition. Some clerics regarded Gerbert as a necromancer and claimed that his inventions were the result of magic rather than science. Others alleged darkly that he had consorted with Saracen magicians and witches in Iberia. In the twelfth century, William of Malmesbury claimed that Gerbert had "surpassed Ptolemy with the astrolabe, and Alcandraeus in astronomy, and Julius Firmicus in judicial astrology" in Iberia, where he also learned "what the singing of birds portended; there he acquired the art of calling up spirits from hell: in short, whatever hurtful or salutary, human curiousity has discovered." In the course of these travels, the English historian claimed that Gerbert had sold his soul to the devil, who helped him steal a book from a mysterious Saracen philosopher and escape to France where he learned to cast "the head of a statue" that could supposedly predict the future.[4]

Such accusations did not deter the Holy Roman emperor Otto II from appointing his former tutor Pope Sylvester II in 999. The appointment proved to be short-lived. In 1002, Gerbert and his mentor were driven from office by the Roman populace. Gerbert died the following year, on May 12, 1003, revered by his friends and students, but still subject to dark rumors regarding the forbidden knowledge that he had acquired south of the Pyrenees, whose repercussions can still be felt by generations of mathematicians and computer programmers.

Translators

Both the reasons for Gerbert's journey to Iberia and the ideas and knowledge that he brought back with him suggest that the Spanish March did not always signify to contemporary Christians what it later came to symbolize for generations of historians. In the centuries that followed, many Christian scholars followed his footsteps to Spain in search of books, manuscripts, and ideas that were not available elsewhere in Europe. These journeys were part of the cultural and intellectual diffusion that led, as the historian Philip Khuri Hitti puts it, "from the portals of Toledo through the Pyrenees . . . through the Provence and the Alpine passes into Lorraine, Germany and Central Europe as well as across the Channel into England."[5] This movement of ideas reached a peak in the twelfth century, according to the medievalist John Tolan, when "a wave of Arabic texts, swept north through the Pyrenees, changing the intellectual map of Europe,"[6] and European scholars from across the continent traveled to Iberia to work at the translation school established by Archbishop Raymond in Toledo in 1126. These scholars included men like Gerard of Cremona, Adelard of Bath, Hermann of Carinthia, Daniel of Morley, and Robert of Ketton, all of whom traveled to Iberia and brought back translations of Arabic manuscripts or Greek and Latin treatises on algebra, medicine, and philosophy that had been translated into Arabic.

Many of them crossed the Pyrenees to reach their destinations, and such journeys are often ignored or forgotten, not only because there is a general reluctance to accept that Islam may have played a positive role in Europe's intellectual development, but also because the representations of the Pyrenees as an "impassable" barrier against the movement of ideas do not allow for the possibility of interactions of this kind. For many of these scholars, however, the Pyrenean frontier was not a barrier between civilization and savagery, but a gateway to an Arab/Islamic cultural milieu that was more conducive to the spirit of scientific inquiry than the countries they came from.

Such sentiments were not universal. The Huesca-born Jewish convert to Christianity Moses of Huesca, better known as Petrus Alfonsi (ca. 1062–1110), became court physician to Henry I, the son of William the Conqueror. Alfonsi also wrote the bestselling *Priestly Tales*, a compilation of didactic stories that some scholars believe constituted the template for *The Canterbury Tales* and *The Decamaron*. Born in Huesca, a town that had been under Muslim control only ten years before his baptism in 1106, Alfonsi received an Arab/Jewish/Islamic education before his conversion, but he remained bitterly hostile to Islam and Judaism and wrote two influential tracts condemning both faiths that were widely read in Christian Europe.

One of their readers was Peter the Venerable, the abbot of the powerful monastic order of Cluny, who traveled to Castile and Galicia through Navarre in 1141 to receive a donation and endowment of two monasteries for his order from King Alfonso VII. Peter's Iberian journey also had a more unusual purpose. Inspired in part by Petrus Alfonsi's diatribes, he commissioned a team of learned Latin scholars in Castile "with entreaty and high fee" to translate a number of Arabic texts, including the Koran.[7] These efforts were intended not to promote interfaith dialogue but to combat a religion that Peter regarded as intrinsically abhorrent. His efforts nevertheless resulted in Robert of Ketton's annotated Latin translation of the Koran, which Peter's secretary took back with him to France, thereby providing Christian Europe with its first translated version of the Koran and its first analysis—however jaundiced—of its essential precepts.

Scientists in the twenty-first century might recognize kindred spirits in men like Gerard of Cremona, Adelard of Bath, Muhammad al-Khwarizmi, or Maimonides. But others will struggle to remember that there was once a time when Christian and Jewish scholars made their way through lonely Pyrenean mountain passes carrying translations and manuscripts in their baggage, their heads full of algebraic formulae and philosophical questions that they were unable to answer in their own countries. We have no descriptions from these scholars of their Pyrenean journeys, but some of them, like Peter and his secretary, would have made their way through the same mountain passes that have so often been described as inaccessible or impassable barriers to the movement of men and ideas, and they would have stayed at the inns, monasteries, and guesthouses established along what had already become one of the great institutions in the Christian religious calendar.

The Way

The origins of the pilgrimage to Santiago de Compostela date back to the ninth century, when a trickle of European pilgrims first began to make their way southward to Galicia to pay homage to the shrine of Saint James. According to the eleventh-century *Historia Turpini*, or *Pseudo-Turpin*, one of the five books that make up the *Liber Sancti Jacobi* in the archive of the Cathedral of Santiago de Compostela, Saint James appeared to Charlemagne in a dream and revealed the road to his tomb at the end of a field of stars. There is no evidence that Charlemagne ever went to Galicia, but thousands of the pilgrims who made their way to Santiago de Compostela believed that he had. By the twelfth century, thousands of men and women from all walks of life undertook the difficult and often perilous journey to Santiago de Compostela, which could cover between 1,250 and 3,700 miles (2,000 and 6,000 kilometers) and last the best part of a year.

Some traveled as members of pilgrimage fraternities and societies. Others went at their own behest to do penance or gain remission for their sins, or in the hope of achieving a miraculous cure for themselves or a relative. Kings and queens, merchants and prostitutes, and condemned prisoners, peasants, and serfs all took part in this arduous and sometimes dangerous journey, whose principal routes led through the Pyrenees. The majority crossed the mountains through the "French route," from Saint-Jean-Pied-de-Port to the Cize Pass and Roncesvalles in Navarre, or via the "Aragonese routes," across the Somport or Portalet Pass.

For many of these pilgrims, mountains were already places to be dreaded, and the Pyrenees would have been a daunting and even terrifying ordeal. In his twelfth-century pilgrim's "guidebook" known as the *Codex Calixtinus*, the French monk Aimeric de Picaud describes the Cize Pass as a "very high mountain" whose "height is such that it seems to touch the sky: to him who climbs it, it seems as if he was able to touch the sky with his hand."[8] The mountains were not the only obstacle the pilgrims faced. The *Codex* frequently condemns the ferrymen and toll keepers along the pilgrimage route, who charged extortionate fees for transporting pilgrims across rivers and streams in overloaded boats. Those who refused to pay were beaten with sticks, and some ferrymen even stripped the clothes and possessions from unfortunate travelers who drowned while making these crossings.

Not surprisingly, the *Codex* is lavish in its praise of the clerics, monarchs, and "roadmen" who built bridges, restored and maintained roads, or paid for their construction, thus enabling pilgrims to avoid such predators. Artfully promoted by the Catholic Church and the powerful Cluniac monastery, the pilgrimage helped restore and consolidate the connections between the Mozarabic Church and Latin Christendom, and it also became another instrument of cultural transmission and diffusion, as pious rulers and monastic orders commissioned churches, monasteries, sanctuaries, and hospices along the main pilgrimage routes, all of which attracted artists and craftsmen from across Europe.

The Christian Pyrenees

Evidence of their work can still be found all over the Pyrenees: in the cemeteries of medieval pilgrims who died of plague while crossing the Somport Pass; in the delicate stone carving of two angels carrying the Greek letters for the first two letters of Jesus's name on a twelfth-century Romanesque church built by the people of As-souste for the Santiago de Compostela pilgrimage; in the Roman-esque capitals on the San Juan de la Peña monastery that was built into an Aragonese mountainside in the early Middle Ages; in churches, chapels, monuments, and sanctuaries that were built even in the most remote settings, such as the Abbey of Saint-Martín-du-Canigou, in the present-day *département* of the Pyrénées-Orientales in southern France.

Perched on a steep mountain in the shadow of Mount Canigou, only a few miles from the Spanish border, the abbey is reached either by a stomach-churning drive in a jeep up the dirt road that wraps its way around the mountain or by a steep walk up through pine forest. Those who make the walk will be rewarded by the splendid little complex of two Romanesque churches and a clois-ter, whose stone walls rise like an extension of the rock face on which it was built, offering panoramic views of the crags and for-ests of the Canigou massif. The abbey was founded in 1009 by Wilfred Count of Cerdanya (970–1050). In 1035 Wilfred became a monk and retired to the monastery, where he lived until his death fifteen years later. The following year his fellow monks sent one of their number on a special journey to solicit prayers for his salvation. The anonymous emissary recorded his journey on a parch-ment, on which representatives of more than one hundred monas-teries and churches wrote pious tributes to the abbey's deceased founder.

As a result we know that the monk walked through many of the valleys of the Eastern Pyrenees before turning northward toward Carcassonne. He then continued onto Poitiers, Tours, Orléans, and Paris, walking onward to Maastricht, Aachen, Coblenz, and Metz, before finally turning back toward Canigou and Saint-Martín. Even in their isolated mountain retreat, the monks of Saint-Martín-du-Canigou were able to send one of their members more than 1,000 miles (1,600 kilometers) from his Pyrenean home, knowing that he would be received en route by people who understood his language and his concerns, and confident that he would afterward be able to return safely to the savage frontier that, even then, was far closer to the rest of Europe than historians have often claimed.[9]

The Christianization of the Pyrenees was not limited to the main Pyrenean pilgrimage routes. As Christian rulers and religious institutions extended and consolidated their control over the Spanish March, they also set out to stamp their mark on the Pyrenees themselves. At first sight there is little to distinguish the Vall de Boí, in the Alta Ribagorça region of Catalonia, from many similar Pyrenean valleys. To the north, the valley is dominated by the serrated peaks of the high Pyrenees that separate Spain from France. Most visitors approach it from the south through a wild Arizona-like landscape of rust-colored canyons, turquoise rivers, and flat-topped rugged hills, dotted with the high-walled medieval villages and fortresses that testify to the region's previous significance as a frontier zone.

The main point of attraction in the Vall de Boí lies in the nine Romanesque churches that were built up and down the valley in the eleventh and twelfth centuries with the help of artists and builders from Lombardy, which have transformed the valley into a World Heritage Site. This sought-after designation is a tribute to what UNESCO calls the "profound cultural interchange across medieval Europe, and in particular across the mountain barrier of the Pyrenees" in this period. These small mountain churches are exquisite constructions, built with the simplicity and lack of ostentation that distinguish Romanesque churches from the overbearing Gothic churches and cathedrals that would later come to dominate so many Spanish towns and villages. The Church of San Clemente in the village of Taüll is one of the finest in the valley, with its rounded stone walls and its rectangular bell tower layered with narrow arched windows and the blind arches known as Lombard bands.

The apse at San Clemente once contained a fresco painted by the anonymous artist known as the Master of Taüll around 1123. Like many Romanesque frescos, the original is in the National Museum

Sant Climent de Taüll (Photo by Xavigivax, September 9, 2007, Wikimedia Commons).

of Catalan Art in Barcelona, but the church projects a skillful remapping of the fresco onto the walls for visitors. One afternoon I watched these bare stone walls lit up by the gloriously expressive image of Christ Pantocrator surrounded by saints and angels, in a sumptuous blaze of purple and terracotta. It wasn't necessary to be religious to be moved by this display, or to admire the Master of Taüll and his fellow artists who left such beautiful images and buildings in places where very few people at the time would have been able to see them.

It is not known why so many artists left the Italian lakes region to work abroad in this period, or what led them to these remote mountain valleys, but the most logical explanation is that there was work available. There was clearly a market for their skills in what the Burgundian chronicler and historian Rodolfus Glaber (985–1047) once called the "white cloak of churches" that spread over "all the earth, but especially in Italy and Gaul" in the early Middle Ages.[10] In commisioning such buildings in the Pyrenees, Christian rulers and clerics not only demonstrated their own piety; they also demonstrated the power of the church over the mountains themselves, and these efforts were not limited to chapels, churches, and sanctuaries. As the *Codex* suggested, the building of bridges was regarded as a pious and a practical endeavor, which the religious and secular authorities were often eager to associate themselves with. One of the most eminent bridge builders of the Catalan March was Hermengaudius, later Saint Ermengol, who first enters history as archdeacon of the diocese of Urgell in 1002.

In the course of his relatively short career, Ermengol performed a number of what his biographer calls "hydraulic miracles" along the Segre River. On one occasion the Segre was spating after heavy rain and threatening to overflow, whereupon Ermengol fell down on his knees "begging Christ that the force of the river might turn away from the Virgin Mother" and crying out, "O water, do you dare to perform this sacrilege so that you might break up the estate of the church because you are bored with your usual path? Desist from this crime, violator, I challenge you in the divine name to hear my prayer."[11] The next day the waters subsided, and Ermengol was able to continue the construction of a bridge across the Segre. In 1035 the then bishop of Urgell was less fortunate when a bridge that he was helping to build across the same river collapsed at a place called Bar on the banks of the Segre, and Ermengol fell into the river and cracked his skull on a rock and died. The bridge was not built until 1076, but it lasted until its final collapse in 1985.

Songs of Love

The cultural traffic across the Pyrenees during the Middle Ages was not simply a by-product of religion. Secular cultural influences also made their way across the mountains, often by the most unlikely routes. Today there is little to distinguish the dusty Aragonese city of Barbastro, in the Pyrenean foothills beneath the Sierra de Guara, from many other Spanish cities. The surrounding landscape is mostly concealed by anonymous blocks of flats and traffic-bound streets that give little indication of the ancient origins of a Celtiberian city that preceded the Roman Empire. According to some literary scholars, however, this dusty, nondescript city may have played a peripheral role in one of the great European literary movements of the Middle Ages. In *The Arabic Role in Medieval Literary History* (1987), the late Cuban American medievalist María Rosa Menocal argued that the troubadour poetry that flourished in Provence between 1095 and 1295 was inspired by the Arabic musical and literary culture of Al-Andalus, and that the word "troubadour" originated from the Arabic word *taraba* (to sing) or *tarab* (song).

Menocal found precedents for troubadour song in the *muwashshahas*, or "ring songs," of Moorish Iberia, which fused classical Arabic verses with refrains or choruses sung in colloquial Arabic or even Hebrew and Mozarabic Latin. Like other proponents of the "Arab origins" theory of troubadour poetry, Menocal cited an obscure episode that took place in Barbastro in the summer of 1064, when a Catalan-Aragonese army, supported by a contingent of Norman, Burgundian, and French knights, laid siege to what was then one of the last remaining Moorish redoubts in the Spanish March.

There is some debate among historians over the purpose of this assault. Some scholars contend that it was a "crusade before the crusades," carried out with the approval of the papacy; others describe it as a routine border raid in search of plunder. Whatever its motivations, the siege had dire consequences for the inhabitants of Barbastro. After negotiating a truce that allowed the population to leave, the Christians reneged and proceeded to massacre the male inhabitants before embarking on a spree of rape and pillage. Some French knights then "went native" and proceeded to dress and eat like Moors. According to the Moorish chronicler Ibn Hayyan (987–1075), the besiegers of Barbastro "received a house with all that it contained, women, children and furniture," and a Jewish emissary sent to the city to ransom some of its more prominent captives found one "crusader" in Moorish dress seated on a divan and surrounded by Moslem waiting girls, one of whom played the lute and sang to entertain their guest.[12]

This "waiting girl" was most likely one of the singing girls, or *qiyan*, who had become a fixture of Muslim courts in Iberia and were also popular with Iberian Christian rulers. Such entertainers were trained to sing and dance, and they were also expected to play what the historian Roger Boase has called "the role of the courtly beloved . . . coquettish and modest, demanding and deceptive, raising hopes but rarely fulfilling them."[13] Between five hundred and five thousand of these slave girls may have been carried back across the Pyrenees from Barbastro as slaves by the marauding Christians, and many of them went on to become lute-playing singers at courts in southern France. Some of these *qiyan* ended up at the court of William VIII, Duke of Aquitaine and Count of Poitiers (1025–86), one of the Christian commanders at Barbastro. William's son William VII (1071–1127) became the most famous early proponent of the Provençal troubadour boom that spread through southern Europe between the late eleventh and thirteenth centuries, and which reached its apotheosis in the "courts of love" established by William's great-granddaughter Eleanor of Aquitaine (ca. 1122–1204) in Poitiers. Ezra Pound referred indirectly to this episode in his Canto VIII: "And Poictiers, you know Guillaume Poictiers / had brought the song up out of Spain / With the singers and viels."

Whether or not the "song" really made its way across the Pyrenees from Barbastro in this way, the troubadour culture of Languedoc and Provence subsequently made its way into Spain. Troubadours were extremely popular in medieval Aragon and Catalonia, where many of them found patrons following the papal crusade against the Cathars in the thirteenth century. One of them was Guiraut Riquier (1254–92), the jaded and disillusioned "last troubadour," who fled his devastated and occupied homeland in Languedoc and rediscovered the "way of true love" first in "joyous Catalonia" and then at the court of King Alfonso the Wise of Castile, where he spent ten years. Riquier and his fellow troubadours were a clear influence on the lyrics and illustrations in the Castilian king's beautiful song cycle *The Canticles of Holy Mary*, in which the Virgin Mary becomes the unattainable object of love for a troubadour-protagonist seeking salvation, who may have been Alfonso himself.

All these transactions are part of a movement of ideas in the Middle Ages that once enabled the Hispanophile historian Marcelin Defourneaux to describe the Pyrenees as "not a barrier but a zone of permanent contacts."[14] The Pyrenees continued to play this role in the centuries that followed, and they often did so in spite of the intentions of the rulers on either side of them. In the late sixteenth century Philip II attempted to transform the Pyrenees into a cordon sanitaire in order to incubate Counter-Reformation Spain against the Lutheran heresy, by preventing the entry of censored books and unwanted people, but the anti-Lutheran repression carried out by the Inquisition within Spain itself was always a more effective barrier to the spread of unwanted religious doctrines than the mountains themselves.

For much of the sixteenth and seventeenth centuries Spain simply lacked the resources to prevent the movement of shepherds, smugglers, and migrant workers across the Pyrenees. In 1626 the Spanish royal secretary Fernández de Navarrete lamented the fact that "all the scum of Europe have come to Spain, so that there is hardly a deaf, dumb, lame or blind man in France, Germany, Italy or Flanders, who has not been to Castile."[15] Many French migrants who settled in Aragon and Catalonia found themselves under suspicion by the Inquisition *after* they had crossed the mountains because of their real or suspected political allegiances.

Such distinctions are important to acknowledge, because it is too easy to cite the physical barrier of the Pyrenees as a pseudo-explanation for the differences between the societies on either side of them. In Friedrich Schiller's *Don Carlos*, Queen Elizabeth of Spain tells her daughter, "We must look beyond the Pyrenees to find upholders of the justice of our cause" when her tyrant husband Philip II refuses to recognize her child. Three years after the play's first German performance, the reactionary Spanish foreign minister the Conde de Floridablanca declared his intention to set out to "put a cordon on the frontier, as for a plague," to prevent French revolutionary ideas from entering Spain.[16]

For both Schiller and Floridablanca, the Pyrenees were an ideological frontier where ideas could be kept in or kept out, but the mountains were always an imperfect means of achieving such aspirations. Even in the "closed" Spain of the sixteenth and seventeenth centuries, Spanish plays and novels were popular in Northern Europe, where they were translated into French and English. In the eighteenth century, Spanish science students, known as *pensionados*, continued to study in Paris, Germany, and Central Europe, despite the subsequent suggestions by historians such as the Dunants that the "gloomy masses" of the Pyrenees helped to seal Spain off from the influence of the Enlightenement.

Even real walls rarely achieve such aspirations, and the "natural" border of the Pyrenees was always more porous and accessible than it seemed in retrospect. From the French Revolution to the Spanish Civil War and beyond, Spanish social and political reformers continued to take inspiration from beyond the Pyrenees. If their efforts were sometimes thwarted or slow to take effect, this was due not to the Pyrenean "wall," but to the prevailing political and social conditions within Spain itself, and to the relationships between the two great states on either side of the mountains, which have often brought violence and conflict across the Pyrenees and into the very heart of them.

5

The Zone of War

Put on my espadrilles, give me my beret, give me my rifle,
For I'm off to kill more Reds than the month of April has
flowers.
                    —Carlist marching song, Spanish Civil War

Situated in a typical narrow Navarrese valley, the village of Lesaka
is one of the five villages known as the "Cinco Villas" in the mountains of northern Navarre and lies less than a mile (1.6 kilometers)
from the Bidassoa River, which marks the Spanish-French frontier.
Its tall and stolid white stone houses block out much of the surrounding greenery and give the village a dark and slightly claustrophohic
feel, even in summer. In the autumn of 1813, the Allied Peninsular
Army under the command of Arthur Wellesley, then Marquis of
Wellington, established its headquarters here, in preparation for
the invasion of France. That September, John Malcolm, a British
officer in the Forty-Second Regiment of Foot, walked into the hills
above Lesaka and later wrote a lyrical description of the surrounding landscape: "To the west the ocean spread like a sheet of fire,
beneath the descending sun. Around me were a congregated train
of mighty hills, towering over rocks and ravines, and mantled with
forests, then touched with the waning tints of October; while the
more distant and gigantic mountains were covered with snow, but
flushed to a rose-tinge in the glow of the evening sky."[1]

From his position overlooking the village, Malcolm observed
"various French, British and Spanish regiments, at their evening

parade—their arms glancing in the setting sun, and the martial or mournful strains of their native lands, performed by their bands of music, rising amid the calm, and mellowed by distance, came floating up the mountain-glens like strains of Fairyland." Malcolm had only recently come to Spain and had not yet seen action. It was not until October 6 that his regiment was told that it would be crossing the Bidassoa the next day. After the usual stormy night that so often preceeded Wellington's major battles, Malcolm's unit formed up before dawn, accompanied by a drum roll, and marched to its staging point by the river. At the sound of the bugle, the British waded into the water and scattered the French pickets on the opposite bank, before driving up through the mountains just beyond them. From the top of a pass Malcolm looked down on a smoke-covered combat zone, in which "long lines of bayonets would suddenly jet up from gorge and glen—flash their light upon the eye, and then as suddenly disappear, as if swallowed up by the earth."[2]

Malcolm also encountered a number of casualties, including a French soldier "lying stretched on his back, but exhibiting symptoms of life in the quivering of his limbs, and the convulsive startings of his feet. I approached, and, looking down upon him, beheld a large aperture in his head, exhibiting a frightful mass of blood and brain." Malcolm's shock and disgust were sharpened by the surrounding landscape. "The evening was bright and calm," he recalled, "and the birds were singing in their bowers; but at that moment the serene aspect and the glad voice of nature seemed shocking; for they impressed the painful feeling, that she had no sympathy with man; that her smiles are shed alike on his festal hour, and his dying agony; and that her roses bloom equally bright in his bridal garland, and on his mouldering tomb."[3]

More than seventy years since the Pyrenees were last visited by a major conflict, it is difficult to imagine the scenes that Malcolm once described with a nineteenth-century romantic's pen. Today this attractive corner of northeasten Navarre is more fit for shepherds and tourists than for soldiers, but Lesaka is only one of many places up and down the mountains where the "serene aspect

and the glad voice of nature" have been violated by war and
bloodshed.

Invaders

In military terms, the significance of the Pyrenees derives primarily
from their historic role as a stategic barrier between warring armies
or as a gateway for invasion. As a result, the military history of the
mountains tends to revolve around Roncesvalles, Maya, Le Perthus,
Somport, Portalet, and other crossing points. Generations of schoolchildren have learned that the Carthaginian general Hannibal
Barca crossed the Alps during the Second Punic War in 218 BCE.
Fewer know that Hannibal first took his army of fifty thousand
infantry, nine thousand cavalry, and thirty-six elephants across the
Pyrenees in July that same year. Hannibal chose the more difficult
mountain crossing rather than the Mediterranean coastal road in
order to avoid a premature confrontation with Roman troops. Before entering the mountains, he detached a force of ten thousand
men under the command of his general Hanno to put down resistance and protect his rear guard before he brought up the bulk of
his army in three columns.

It is not known which routes the Carthaginians took. The scholarly consensus is that they crossed via the Col de Perthus, though
some Catalan historians have argued that Hannibal's troops took a
more arduous route along the Segre River through Andorra and
across the Cerdagne before reuniting at Illiberis (Elne, near Perpignan), where they continued their march toward the Alps. According to Livy, Hannibal's soldiers were so overawed by the sight
of the Alps that they refused to go any farther, but Hannibal reminded them that they had already fought their way across "the
passes of the Pyrenees, which were held by most warlike tribes"
and that the Alps were therefore nothing to be afraid of. "What do
you imagine the Alps to be other than lofty mountains?" Hannibal
declares in the speech that Livy gives him. "Suppose them to be

higher than the peaks of the Pyrenees, surely no region in the world can touch the sky or be impassable to man."[4]

Hannibal eventually cajoled his men into making the crossing for which he was more famous. Long after his army had been driven out of Italy, Roman armies continued to cross the Pyrenees in the opposite direction to wage war on Romans. In 76 BCE Pompey the Great led an army across Le Perthus to suppress the rebellion of Quintus Sertorius in Hispania, leaving a victory monument four years later. In 49 BCE Hispania became a battleground between Pompey's supporters and Julius Caesar. In spring that year, Caesar ordered three legions under the command of his legate Gaius Fabius to seize the main Pyrenean mountain passes and engage Lucius Afranius and Marcus Petreius, Pompey's lieutenants in Hispania, while he besieged the town of Massilia (modern Marseille), which had taken Pompey's side.

By the time Caesar's forces reached the Pyrenees, Fabius's legions had failed to achieve their objective, and Caesar's armies proceeded to pursue them across the wild, mountainous terrain between the Cinca and Segre Rivers. Caesar conducted this campaign with his customary resolution and aplomb. At one point his soldiers built rafts from timber and hides to get across the flooded Segre River and constructed a bridge for the rest of the army to cross. Finding the road to the Ebro River blocked by the Pompeians, Caesar described how his soldiers encircled them through "extensive and difficult valleys. Craggy cliffs, in several places, interrupted their march, insomuch that their arms had to be handed to one another, and the soldiers were forced to perform a great part of their march unarmed, and were lifted up the rocks by each other."[5] In this way Caesar was able to secure the surrender of Pompey's exhausted, demoralized and half-starved armies near the Ebro while losing only seventy of his own men—an astonishing achievement that earned him the title of dictator following his return to Rome.

Many other armies followed in his footsteps. In 409 CE, an alliance of Germanic tribes led by the Suevi poured into Hispania through undefended Pyrenean *claustrae* and unleashed an apocalypic storm of violence that reduced much of northern Spain to starvation and cannibalism. In 415 Visigothic warriors from southern Gaul entered Hispania through the Eastern Pyrenees and defeated the Suevi to establish a new Christian kingdom in Hispania that would last until the eighth century. The Moorish raiders defeated by Charles the Hammer at Tours/Poitiers in 732; Charlemagne's failed expedition to the Spanish March in 778; the Norman knights who joined the "mini-Crusade" at Barbastro in 1064; the French invaders who ravaged Aragon in 1285—all these invading and marauding armies marched back and forth through the same Pyrenean passes on foot, on horseback, or in carts from one side to the other until as late as the nineteenth century.

Even English armies have made their way across the mountains. In 1367, more than six centuries after Charlemagne's legendary fighting retreat at Roncesvalles in 778, Edward the Black Prince of Wales (1330–76), then recently invested as ruler of Aquitaine, led three divisions of soldiers and "free company" mercenaries through the same pass to assist the incumbent King Pedro the Cruel of Castile in a civil war against Enrique of Trastamara. The chronicler Jean Froissart was undoubtedly thinking of Charlemagne's and Roland's campaigns when he described the passage of Edward's army in freezing winter conditions through "the ravines and canyons of Navarre, which are most dangerous to pass through, for there were a hundred places among them where a whole army could be held up by thirty men."[6] The fourteenth-century *Chronicle of San Juan de la Peña* describes how the armies of Philip III of France attacked Aragon in 1285 during the War of the Sicilian Vespers, where they "marched through the valley of Pintano, reaching Bailó and Arbués, which they burned. Entering the valley of the Aragón, they came to the town of Berdún and destroyed it by fire."[7]

Between 1512 and 1529, Castilian, French, and Navarrese armies marched back and forth through the Maya and Roncesvalles Passes in a war of conquest and reconquest, before the Spanish annexation of Iberian Navarre was confirmed at the Treaty of Cambrai. In

1592, eight hundred troops from the Huguenot viscounty of Béarn attempted to invade Aragon through the Somport Pass in the hope of inspiring a rebellion against Castile and recovering Navarre. After occupying the villages of Sallent de Gállego and Biescas in the upper Valle de Tena, the Bearnese spent eleven days looting and desecrating churches before they were defeated by Castilian troops at the gorge that is now known as the "Ravine of the Lutherans."[8]

From the seventeenth century onward, the Pyrenees became a constant battleground or invasion route in the incessant warring between Spain and France, in the Reapers' War (1640–52), the War of Devolution (1667–68), the Dutch War (1672–78), the Nine Years' War (1688–97), and the War of the Spanish Succession (1701–14). In 1793 Spain invaded Roussillon as a member of the first counterrevolutionary coalition. The following year the French Convention hastily raised an army in the Eastern Pyrenees that drove the Spanish back into Catalonia, while the French Army of the Western Pyrenees marched through Roncesvalles yet again and forced the Spanish back into Navarre.

These clashes were dwarfed by the catastrophic confrontation that unfolded in the spring of 1808, when French troops occupied Madrid and other Spanish cities as part of Napoléon Bonaparte's attempt to install his brother Joseph on the Spanish throne. Five years of bloody warfare were required before the war finally came to an end and the French were forced out of Spain, and in the summer of 1813 northern Navarre became the scene of the greatest battle in Pyrenean history.

"Full Bludgeon Work": The Battle of the Pyrenees

The campaign known as the Battle of the Pyrenees was actually a series of battles that began when Napoléon placed Marshal Nicolas Jean-de-Dieu Soult in command of the Army of Spain, following the rout of his brother Joseph's army at the Battle of Vitoria on June 21, 1813. Tasked with launching a counteroffensive to prevent

Wellington's forces from entering France, Soult hastily organized some 85,000 battered troops and prepared to go into action against the 100,000-strong allied army. This confrontation was more evenly matched than it seemed. Despite their numerical superiority, Wellington's forces were in the midst of two simultaneous sieges in San Sebastián and Pamplona, spread out across a difficult theater of operations that extended some 40 to 60 miles (64 to 97 kilometers) wide and encompassed a militarily complex landscape of "peaked mountains, narrow craggy passes, deep watercourses, dreadful precipices and forests," as the historian Sir William Napier described it.[9]

The confrontation began on the morning of July 25, 1813, when 21,000 French soldiers attacked 7,000 troops from the British Second Division in the Maya Pass, under the command of Major General William Stewart. The British were drawn up along the ridge overlooking the village of Maya between the Rock of Aretesque and Mount Alcurrunz, when the assault began. One British officer recalled how "the enemy's numbers . . . covered the country immediately in front of us and around us. The sinuosities of the mountains, the ravines, the water courses were filled with them in overwhelming force."[10] The French advance was halted by four hundred Gordon Highlanders in a lethal twenty-minute exchange of musketry in which more than half the defenders were killed or wounded. "They stood there like a stone wall," remembered one officer, "overmatched by 20 to 1, until half their blue bonnets lay beside those brave northern warriors. When they retired, their dead bodies lay as a barrier to the advancing foe."[11]

The fighting continued until the late afternoon, when reinforcements enabled the beleaguered defenders to push the French back. The day might have ended with a British victory, had it not been for events at nearby Roncesvalles, 20 miles (32 kilometers) away, where a simultaneous French assault had forced its 13,000 British defenders to retreat toward Pamplona in order to prevent encirclement. Stewart's men were obliged to follow suit to avoid being cut off themselves, and both armies withdrew to the village of Sorauren, less than 10 miles (16 kilometers) from Pamplona. When Wellington heard the news, he immediately realized that Soult intended to split his armies, and he rode off to rally his troops, accompanied only by his aide-de-camp, and hastened toward the tiny Navarrese village that now found itself at the epicenter of the great European war.

Today Sorauren is a whitewashed village overlooking the main road between Pamplona and the Maya Pass that is barely worth a second glance. On the afternoon we visited it, it was baking hot, and the village was deserted except for the children playing beneath the old stone bridge that leads across the Ulzama River. On July 27, 1813, Wellington dismounted at the same bridge and observed the combined armies from Maya and Roncesvalles nervously camped out above the village, in expectation of an attack by a French force of more than twice their number that was still gathering on the other side of the narrow ravine just below the village.

Wellington quickly assessed the situation and leaned on the parapet of the bridge to write out a dispatch ordering his troops to concentrate on the 2-mile (3-kilometer)-long ridge that divides Sorauren from the village of Oricáin just behind it. He then rode up to the pilgrimage chapel above the village, where he was greeted with such rapturous cheers from his troops that Soult believed that reinforcements had arrived. Looking through his telescope, Wellington saw his opposite number consulting with his officers. Calculating that the notoriously cautious Soult would not attack until late the following morning, he summoned reinforcements from Pamplona.

The next day the French columns began to form up in what one of Wellington's officers described as "the most imposing masses I ever beheld. . . . The enemy's grenadiers in their bear-skin caps with red feathers and blue frock coats appeared the most warlike body of troops possible. As they moved on they threw out their skirmishers, which were met by the British light troops, and thus the work of the bloody day began. . . . I never remember to have witnessed so tremendous an onset."[12] It was nearly noon before the indecisive Soult finally threw the full weight of his columns into the battle. By this time Portuguese reinforcements had begun to arrive from Pamplona, and the French suffered horrific casualties as they charged out of the narrow ravine and up the scrub-covered slopes toward the Oricáin heights, where they were driven back by musket fire and bayonet charges in what Wellington drily described as "full bludgeon work."

Early the next day Soult tried to regain the initiative by detaching a section of his army to march on San Sebastián instead of Pamplona, but Wellington immediately redeployed troops farther to the northwest to block the maneuver. At daybreak on July 30 British troops charged down from the Oricáin ridge and drove the French from the ravine below Sorauren. "We followed them close to their heels and soon got them on a small level, [where] they soon got huddled together like a flock of sheep," recalled Private William Wheeler of the Thirty-First Light Infantry. "As we were galling them with sharp fire, they summed up resolution to turn on us and threatened us with a taste of steel. . . . Now the tug of war began . . . many were the skulls fractured by the butts of firelocks."[13]

By midday Soult's army was in headlong flight toward the French border, as Wellington's troops attacked from Sorauren and farther north at the village of Lizaso. Thus ended Napoléon's "Battle of the Bulge" counteroffensive, and the last possibility that the emperor might gain time by negotiating a peace with some of his more hesitant opponents who were marching on France from the north. With the fall of San Sebastián on August 31, the way was now clear for the invasion of France itself, and the next phase of the campaign that would lead to Napoléon's exile and ultimately to his final defeat at Waterloo.

There is no monument in Sorauren to these events, and the hermitage where Wellington had once observed his opposite number no longer stands, but as I clambered up the slope to where I thought it would have been, it was difficult to imagine how any French soldiers could have charged up the steep, stony slopes and sharp

William Heath, *Battle of the Pyrenees, July 28, 1813* (1814–15). The date suggests Sorauren, but neither the fighting nor the landscape bear much relation to the actual battle, and the artist appears to fuse various battles into a single generic portrait of the campaign (City Library of Toulouse, Wikimedia Commons).

foliage into the waiting guns and bayonets. Such actions are often described as "gallant" in military histories, but I felt more sorrow than admiration as I contemplated the young men who had charged up to their deaths on that harsh, stony ground, and I felt relieved as I returned to my wife and child slumped in the hot car and drove away past the laughing children who were still playing beneath the Ulzama bridge.

The Fortress-Mountains

Such large set-piece confrontations were relatively rare in this mountainous region. Most Pyrenean wars have consisted of route marches from one side to another, or sieges or assaults on the fortresses and

fortified towns designed to prevent such incursions. Evidence of this history can be found all over the Pyrenees, in the castles, watchtowers, and fortified towns and cities overlooking strategic mountain passes, or farther back along the main roads leading down from them. Some of these fortifications date back to Roman times. Some were built by Moorish and Christian rulers during the centuries of the Spanish March. Others were built more recently. In the last decade of the sixteenth century, Philip II commissioned the Italian military architect Tibúrcio Spannocchi to design a defensive system in the Aragonese Pyrenees in the event of a French invasion. Spannocchi's most outstanding achievement was the great citadel in Jaca, whose pentagonal shape and thick sloping walls would subsequently provide Napoléon's troops with their most enduring base during the Peninsular War.

In the late seventeenth century, Louis XIV's great military architect Sébastien Le Prestre de Vauban (1633–1707) visited southern France on a number of occasions to inspect the defenses along the Pyrenean frontier. These visits resulted in a series of fortifications along the Atlantic coast and in the newly annexed French territories in Roussillon, where Vauban designed a series of elegant fortresses and strongholds stretching from the town of Prats-de-Mollo-la-Preste on the Spanish border to Collioure on the Mediterranean coast. Vauban's Roussillon fortresses, such as Fort Liberia above Villefranche-de-Conflent, Mont-Louis, Fort Lagarde at Prats-de-Mollo, and Bellegarde in Le Perthus Pass all followed the new Italian Renaissance designs of angular sloping walls built to resist artillery, tunnels, and galleries, and they were also strategically located to block the main routes between the Segre and Tet Valleys.

Other fortifications were built away from towns and villages in the heart of the mountains themselves, such as the eighteenth-century Spanish fort overlooking Canfranc in the Coll de Ladrones, or the French fortress of Portalet built in the same period in the Vallée d'Aspe. These defenses were essential strategic objectives for armies crossing the mountains. Puigcerdà, the gateway to the Spanish Cerdanya through the Coll de la Perxa, was besieged by

French armies on numerous occasions. In May 1678, two thousand Spanish troops and two hundred Catalan peasants defended the city for a month against a French army of twelve thousand commanded by the Duc de Noailles. After thirty-three separate assaults, the defenders finally surrendered and the French destroyed the city's fortified walls.

The Catalan fortress-village of Castelciutat, now a "wellness center" within the boundaries of the town of La Seu d'Urgell, overlooks the main route into Catalonia from the Cerdagne and Andorra. Castelciutat has been besieged several times, most famously in September 1713, during the War of the Spanish Succession, when defenders under the command of the Catalan general Josep Moragues surrendered to a Franco-Bourbon army after running out of food and ammunition. French Pyrenean fortresses were also subjected to assaults and sieges. In 1793 two thousand French soldiers at Fort Bellegarde in Le Perthus resisted a two-month siege against twelve thousand Spaniards. That same year Spanish troops briefly seized Villefranche-de-Conflent, the town known as "la bien gardée"—the well guarded, because of its walls and its Vauban fortress—before the town was retaken by a French army under the aristocratic revolutionary general Dagobert de Fontenille.

Some of these fortifications were never used for their original purpose. The elegant elliptical rifle tower known as the Tower of Fusiliers, which overlooks the current N-330 road to Canfranc, was built in the last years of the nineteenth century in the event of a French invasion that never came. In the aftermath of the Spanish Civil War, the Franco dictatorship attempted to transform the Pyrenees into an impregnable fortress, through the construction of a series of bunkers, machine-gun nests, and hidden arms depots under the direction of the military engineer Colonel José Vallespín. Work on Franco's "Maginot Line" intensified in 1944, as the war turned in the Allies' favor, and continued into the 1950s, and some of these fortifications can still be found, particularly in the Catalan Pyrenees, where forest fires in 2011 revealed many of them for the first time.

Guerrillas and Resisters

If the Pyrenees did not favor large-scale confrontations, they were eminently suitable to the "raids and ravages of partisan warfare" that John Lynn has identified as a characteristic of Louis XIV's Pyrenean campaigns, where French armies often struggled to make headway against "small forces, rugged terrain, sparse population, limited supply and restricted roads."[14] This kind of warfare has a long pedigree in the Pyrenees that reaches back to the wars between Celtiberian tribes and the Romans and the Frankish campaigns of the eighth century. During the War of the Spanish Succession, Catalan Fusellers de Muntanya (Mountain Fusilliers) and light infantrymen known as *miquelets* waged desperate hit-and-run warfare against the Franco-Spanish Bourbon armies in the mountains and gorges of the Pallars Sobirà and the present-day location of the Aigüestortes National Park in an attempt to relieve the siege of Barcelona.

Wearing their trademark brown woolen jackets and peaked caps or uniforms captured from the enemy, armed with two pistols, a dagger, and the long hunting musket common to the Pyrenees known as the Espanyola, these Catalan irregulars earned themselves a reputation that remained nearly a century later, when the 1798 *Dictionnaire de l'académie française* defined "miquelet" as "a type of bandit who lives in the Pyrenees. The miquelets are strongly to be feared by travelers" (my translation). Guerrilla bands, or *partidas*, sprung up across the Pyrenees to resist what many Spaniards regarded as an invasion by Napoléon's "Godless heretics" in 1808. Some of the earliest bands were formed in the mountainous regions of northern Navarre, such as the "Land Corsairs" led by the eighteen-year-old Xavier Mina, "El Estudiante" (the Student), and subsequently taken over by his uncle Francisco Espoz y Mina in 1810.

In the Eastern Pyrenees *miquelets* and local militias called *somatenes* attacked French columns and stragglers, blockaded forts and garrisons, cut French supply lines, and even carried out raids into the

Quico-Sabaté mural, Yeza, 2007. The image was taken from a famous photograph of Sabaté and the caption reads: "Bandit capitalism. Terrorist state. The Anarchist Resistance will never surrender" (Commons: Licensing Spain).

Cerdagne, stealing sheep and cattle and extorting money from the local population. The French governor of Aragon, Marshal Louis-Gabriel Suchet, later recalled how "on the approach of our troops, these bands withdrew without fighting, so that they made their appearance at every spot we did not occupy, and offered no opportunity for making a serious attack upon them in any position."[15] One of the largest and most effective guerrilla bands of the Peninsular War was formed in Aragon in 1809 by two Spanish army officers, Miguel Sarasa y Lobera and Mariano Renovales, and based at the iconic monastery of San Juan de la Peña, near Jaca.

The monastery had been built to replace the older medieval monastery that had been destroyed by fire in 1675, and it was here that

Sarasa and Renovales's men established their base in the summer of 1809, blockading the French garrison at the nearby Jaca fortress and shutting down one of the main supply routes for the French army through the Somport Pass. After various attempts to relieve the garrison, Suchet sent a large force under the command of General Louis François Félix Musnier to dislodge the guerrillas from "the palladium of their independence" at San Juan de la Peña.

On August 25, Musnier's forces attacked and burned the new monastery. Sarasa and Renovales were able to escape, and Musnier's men proceeded to carry out a series of punitive counterinsurgency operations in the Hecho, Ansó, and Roncal Valleys farther north, where the guerrillas enjoyed widespread support. Today Hecho is a picture-postcard Aragonese village, tumbling gracefully down terraced fields by the edge of the Subordán River. Only the blackened traces on its cathedral walls testify to the events of August 28, 1808, when units from the French Army of Aragon burned two-thirds of the village to the ground and shot seven of its inhabitants, before proceeding to leave a similar trail of misery and devastation throughout the surrounding valleys.

This grim dynamic of guerrilla warfare and counterinsurgency is a recurring feature of the irregular wars of the Pyrenees. Froissart describes how the Black Prince's mercenary "free companies" terrorized and pillaged the villages around Lourdes before their intervention in the Castilian civil war. During Castile's conquest of Navarre in 1512, the Duke of Alba's Castilian troops occupied the fortress of Saint-Jean-Pied-de-Port and destroyed crops and cut down apple and other fruit trees in order to starve the local population into submission. In 1794, French revolutionary armies occupying the Spanish Cerdanya burned villages and churches and confiscated food and livestock from the local population.

During World War II French *résistants* in the Pyrenees faced similar reprisals when waging guerrilla warfare against the Nazi occupying army and their Vichy collaborators. Their ranks included many former Republican soldiers from the Spanish Civil War. Some of the first Resistance fighters in southern France were recruited by the Spanish Communist Party among Spanish Republican prisoners in French internment camps, who were used as forced labor in the Pyrenees as woodcutters, agricultural workers, and dam builders. Isolated in their Pyrenean *chantiers* (construction sites), these former internees forged alliances with Spanish and French charcoal burners in the mountains and formed the nuclei of the armed groups that would subsequently be incorporated into the XIV Corps of Spanish Guerrillas.

Many Spaniards fought with the maquisards who established themselves around Mount Canigou in southern France. About an hour into the route from Vernet-les-Bains to the Canigou summit, a simple stone monument bearing the inscription "To the Glory of the Maquis Henri Barbusse FTPF. Battle of 28 June 1944" commemorates the events that unfolded in the summer of 1944, when a combined force of Vichy paramilitaries and German border police attempted to encircle the twenty-strong group of maquisards operating from a refuge in the Canigou massif. After a pitched battle, most of the maquis retreated into the mountains to their base at the present-day Courtalets mountain refuge. On July 7 the refuge was attacked by German parachutists, but once again the maquisards managed to escape before the refuge was burned down.[16]

Unable to capture or destroy the maquisards themselves, the Germans and their Vichy allies punished their civilian supporters. On 1 August 1944, a combined force of some 620 Wehrmacht, SS, German frontier police, and the Vichy paramilitary Milice attacked the village of Valmanya, on the slopes of Canigou, in response to an attack by French and Spanish *francs-tireurs* on the Gestapo headquarters in the town of Prades two days previously. Though six maquisards held off the attackers long enough for the majority of the population to escape, the Germans killed and tortured four of the inhabitants who remained and burned much of the village to the ground.

Similar reprisals were carried out elsewhere in the mountains. In June 1944 units from the SS Das Reich division attacked a French/

Spanish maquis base near the village of Rimont on the road between Saint-Girons and Foix in the Ariège, and deported the entire population. These methods failed to accomplish their objectives.
Between the Allied landings on June 6 and the liberation of France
in August, the Fourteenth Corps of Spanish Guerrillas attacked
German convoys across the Ariège and liberated various towns and
villages, including Foix. In August 1945, Spanish and French partisans came down from their mountain hideouts and waged open
war with the occupiers, in what rapidly became a general uprising.

On August 19–20, 1944, the Pyrénées-Orientales became the
first *départment* in France to be liberated by Resistance forces
without the help of the Allied army. Many of these fighters had spent
much of the war in the Pyrenees. On August 24, some three thousand Spanish anarchists, communists, and republicans paraded
with General Philippe Leclerc's Ninth Armored Division, known
as "la Nueve" in the streets of Paris, many of whom saw the liberation of France as a prelude to the liberation of their own country.

Uncivil Wars

The wars of the Pyrenees have not only been wars between states.
The French Wars of Religion (1562–98) were fought with particular viciousness in the Western Pyrenees. In 1569 the queen regnant
of Navarre Jeanne d'Albret's Huguenot army, under the command
of Count Gabriel de Montgomery, burned towns and villages
across Béarn, killing Catholics and members of the clergy and
destroying or desecrating churches, convents, and monasteries. In
July 1570, a combined force of Royalist troops and Catholic Béar-
nois under the command of Henry III's savagely anti-Huguenot
marshal Blaise de Monluc (1502–77) laid siege to the Huguenot
town of Rabastens, 45 miles (72 kilometers) west of Pau, now the
site of one of the largest cattle markets in southern France.

In his memoirs Monluc describes how he instructed his troops to
massacre the population, because "the men who are in this place are
those who with the Count of Montgomery destroyed your Churches

and ruined your houses. . . . If we carry the place, and put them all to the sword, you will have a good bargain for the rest of Béarn."[17] In the course of the five-day siege, Monluc was shot in the face with an arquebus and was so badly wounded that he was obliged to wear a leather mask to hide his shattered nose for the few remaining years of his life. His soldiers nevertheless took their revenge, forcing fifty "heretics" to jump to their deaths from the tower of the town's château. Similar scenes were enacted during the Huguenot rebellions against Louis XIII in the early seventeenth century, when government armies set out to subjugate the Huguenot territories of Béarn, Navarre, and Foix. In 1625, seven hundred inhabitants of the Pyrenean village of Le Mas-d'Azil in the Ariège held out for a month against a ten-thousand-strong Catholic/Royalist army, by manufacturing grenades and musketballs from recycled metal. The Huguenots sheltered from artillery bombardments in the giant cave near the village and eventually obliged the besiegers to withdraw after suffering five hundred casualties.

Two decades after the Peninsular War, the Spanish government found itself at war with some of the same *guerrilleros* who had once fought Napoléon, during the first of Spain's three civil wars known as the Carlist Wars (1833–39). Support for the reactionary, ultra-Catholic contender for the Spanish throne, Carlos, was particularly strong in the Basque Country and Navarre, and much of the fighting took place in the northern Navarrese highlands, where government troops waged an asymmetrical war with Carlist insurgents under the command of the gifted Carlist general Tomás de Zumalacarrégui. Though government forces were able to control the lower Navarrese mountain valleys, they were unable to dislodge the Carlistas from the ridges and heights that many Navarrese peasants and farmers were already familiar with as smugglers or bandits.

Edward Bell Stephens, a pro-Carlist English correspondent for the *Morning Post*, spent six months observing "the most stirring scenes of the mountain strife" in Navarre and Guipúzcoa, and attempted to counter his own government's support for the Spanish government with praise for the "hardy, honest, generous, intelligent and noble people" he encountered fighting in the mountains, "in whom the love of liberty and the contempt of death in its defence, seem instinctive."[18] The British army officer Charles Frederick Henningsen also fought with the Carlists and presented his readers with a romantic image of the "wild, proud, and intractable" partisan fighter of Navarre that had changed little since the Peninsular War, with his red beret, cartridge belt, sandals, and light knapsack, sleeping on the hoof with his musket and "ready at the word to march fifty miles." Henningsen's purple prose also presented his readers with a landscape that was as wild and picturesque as its inhabitants, where "bold and fantastic masses, high above the pathway, terminated sometimes in points and pinnacles; at others, seemed piled one above another, menacing the traveller below."[19]

The Carlist war was far more brutal than it appeared in such romantic accounts. Both government troops and rebels burned villages and killed civilians who opposed or did not support them and freely traded reprisals and atrocities. In Andorra in 1835 the Scottish traveler James Erskine Murray passed through a village that had only recently been burned and looted by Carlists in response to the killing of four Carlist officers by Christino soldiers, who had entered the neutral republic illegally the previous day.[20] In the Val d'Aran, Murray found the population in the process of transporting their worldly goods into France in anticipation of a Carlist assault.

The Pyrenees played only a peripheral role in the most destructive of all Spain's civil wars, which began in July 1936, when Nationalist troops under the command of Francisco Franco attempted to overthrow the Spanish Republic. For much of the war, the Pyrenees were a static front that was removed from the main battlegrounds in the conflict. Carlist militias, or Requetés, helped the Nationalists seize control of Navarre. In Aragon, the Nationalists seized all the main cities in the province from Huesca in the north to Belchite in the south, and also took control of the border town of Canfranc.

Outside the cities, Republican forces, bolstered by Catalan anarchist militias, controlled a broad swathe of territory that reached from the mountainous Spanish-French border to the Ebro River in the south. Though some Catalan and Aragonese mountain villages took part in the anarchist-led agrarian collectives that embraced more than a million people before their suppression by the Republican government in June 1937, support for the Republican or Nationalist cause often varied from one town or valley to the next.

The Republican government regarded the defense of the Pyrenean frontier as a key objective and established specialist mountain units in Aragon and Catalonia, some of which had their own particular political affiliations. In 1936, the president of the Generalitat authorized the creation of a Catalan mountain militia, the Regiment Pirinenc núm.1 (Number 1 Pyrenean Regiment of Catalonia), known as "Maisortum" (We Shall Never Leave). The new unit was the brainchild of Josep Maria Benet i Caparà, a former Boy Scout and hiker and a fervent Catalan nationalist, and his unit was dispatched by the Catalan regional government to the Cerdanya (Catalan: Cerdagne), equipped with skis, snowshoes, light machine guns, and specialist mountain clothing, charged with preventing the flow of men and weapons across the frontier.

Benet refused to accept the authority of the anarchist administration in the Cerdanya, headed by the notoriously acquisitive smuggler Antonio Martín Escudero. In March 1937, dozens of his soldiers were arrested by Escudero's men in the chalet town of La Molina and removed from the sector. The following month Escudero was killed at the town of Bellver, apparently by locals who were tired of his depredations.

It was not until the spring of 1938 that the war really began to reach the Pyrenees, when the Nationalists launched an all-out offensive across a 150-mile (241-kilometer) front in Aragon. Within a few days the Republicans lost 1,500 miles (2,414 kilometers) of territory as the Aragonese front collapsed. From April 1938 to January 1939 close to three hundred thousand Nationalist and Republican troops were locked in a titanic battle up and down the Segre River, as the Republicans attempted to halt Franco's advance into Catalonia. That year, Franco's forces opened the Pyrenean dams along the Segre and the Noguera Pallaresa Rivers and flooded the Ebro, where the Republicans had launched a counteroffensive, and German and Italian planes began bombing the Pyrenean hydroelectrical power stations on which Barcelona depended for its electricity.

Bolstered by specialist mountain troops and local volunteer militias, Franco's armies fought their way across upper Aragon and Catalonia. From April 14 to June 15, 8,000 members of the Republican Forty-Third Division under the command of Antonio Beltrán, known as "El Esquinazau" (the Dodger) because of his family's smuggling past, fought off an aerial and ground assault at the town of Bielsa in Huesca Province by some 14,600 Nationalist troops. Though much of Bielsa was destroyed by Nationalist bombing, the "Bielsa pocket" enabled some 4,000 refugees and most of the division itself to cross the French border to safety.

Volunteers

The Carlist volunteers were not the only fighters to use the Pyrenees as an illegal entry route into Spain's wars. Many of the 59,380 foreign volunteers who fought with the International Brigades in defense of the Spanish Republic crossed the mountains to avoid the Non-Intervention Committee's ban on foreign fighters in the civil war, which came into force in January 1937. For many of these volunteers, the Pyrenees were the first test of their commitment and physical aptitude. In the summer of 1996 I interviewed the late Bill Alexander, the last commander of the British International Brigade, for a BBC radio documentary. I still have the tape in which Alexander describes in his thick Hampshire brogue how he came to Spain in 1937 as a member of the British Communist Party, after traveling to Paris as a tourist. From there, the French Communist Party organized his transport to the South of France, where Alexander and his comrades were smuggled across the Pyrenees at night with the help of local guides. Alexander remembered that some members of his party became "extremely distressed" during the climb to the point when they were "literally down on their knees" by the time they reached the whitewashed boundary stones along the Spanish border.

Many of the volunteers who fought with the International Brigades made these nocturnal crossings. One British volunteer later remembered his first sight of the Pyrenees at night, lit up by "long lancing pencils of light from searchlights which were placed every couple of miles apart as far as the eye could see." George Wheeler, a wood machinist from a Labour Party background in London, crossed the Pyrenees in the summer of 1838 with a group led by the future Transport and General Workers' Union leader Jack Jones. In his memoir, Wheeler describes how he and his comrades were taken from a bus en route to Perpignan to a farmhouse, where they ate a communal meal and were introduced to their guides. After the meal they were issued with the standard *alpargatas*, rope-soled sandals worn by Spanish peasants, and led past the French frontier guards and their dogs in a group of fifty across the Catalan Pyrenees.[21]

It was, he recalled, "a marvellous night and, being young and fit, I really enjoyed the climb. . . . Dawn was just breaking as we neared the summit, and a spectacular view opened up before us. Mountain mists swirled around high crags, forming strange and spectacular shapes, while rays from the rising sun bathed them in vivid colours." Not all of Wheeler's party found the climb so enjoyable. Four men had to be carried to the top, before the group was ready to descend "with light hearts and singing lustily" to meet their Republican contacts, where they were greeted by Catalan landworkers with a clenched-fist salute and "*¡Salud, camaradas!*" and taken to Republican outposts.

These nocturnal climbs feature again and again in the memoirs and writings of the International Brigades. "You had to feel your way from ledge to ledge, clutching hold of the gorse," recalled David

Haden-Guest, a mathematics lecturer from Southhampton University. "When daylight came you were amazed that you managed to scale such precipitous heights in the dark."[22] The British volunteer Walter Gregory described his terror of "falling into gullies and ravines, of damaging ankles, arms and legs and of being shot by border patrols." The future Hollywood screenwriter Alvah Bessie, an American volunteer with the Abraham Lincoln Brigade, described a horrendous six-hour ascent in which he and his group were caught in a storm that quickly soaked the meagre possessions they carried in brown paper parcels. Many of Bessie's fellow volunteers had bleeding feet from walking through the rocky terrain in espadrilles, as they moved through the dark with "one hand outstretched before [them], like elephants in a circus procession holding on to each other's tails."[23]

By the time they reached the border, the face of one of Bessie's companions was covered in blood, another had to be carried by two of his companions, and most members of the group were limping. Steve Nelson, another volunteer with the Abraham Lincoln Brigade, recalled how he and his group followed their guide through the dark "like spavined horses." Nelson was a tough Philadelphia slaughterhouse worker. He nevertheless wrote how "the muscles in my thighs danced wildly, uncontrollably, as they had danced for hours; there was a slimy, sour taste in my mouth and my throat and my lungs were on fire, my blood was roaring in my ears."[24] This ordeal ended when their guide stopped by a cairn and performed a little dance, shouting "España!" and Nelson and his companions made their way down to the Republican transport trucks.

These dawn sightings were also part of the Pyrenean rite of passage. Many hikers have looked down on Spain with the same sense of euphoria after a difficult climb, but few have felt what these brigadiers felt as they contemplated the country they had come to fight and die for. Alvah Bessie remembered how "the brilliant light hurt our eyes . . . you could feel the grit in the corners of your eyes . . . the men's clothes were the colour of the earth." The British volunteer Jim Brewer described the "enormous panorama of colour in the sky. It was just like a Van Gogh landscape."[25] These moments of rest were followed by a knee-crunching descent to their pickup points, where the Brigadiers were greeted by the Republicans who had been assigned to take them to their base. Not all volunteers got this far. Some turned back before reaching the crest of the mountains. The British volunteer Frank McCluster remembered a party of four Americans and a Briton "carrying typewriters and things like that" who vanished on the trail and were never seen again.[26]

In December 1937 the English writer Laurie Lee walked across the snow-covered Pyrenees alone with the intention of fighting for the Republic—a decision that he later recalled as "one of a number of idiocies I committed at the time." After crossing the Eastern Pyrenees into Catalonia, Lee was taken by a shepherd to a pro-Republican farm in the mountains, where he was fed and put up for the night. The next day he was handed over to Republican militiamen in the nearest town, who arrested him for espionage. His interrogators refused to believe that a lone Englishman with a rucksack filled with books, cameras, and a fiddle had come to fight, and took Lee for a German agent. Lee spent nearly a week awaiting execution, before he was released and taken to Figueres and then to the International Brigades barracks at Albacete. Epileptic and physically frail, Lee was not considered suitable military material and was sent back to England eleven weeks after entering Spain.[27] Some 9,934 Brigadiers never returned from the country they saw for the first time from the high peaks and steep arêtes of the Eastern Pyrenees that had nearly broken so many of them.

The Last War of the Pyrenees

Many of the Spaniards who fought with the Resistance believed the liberation of France would be followed by the liberation of their own country. During World War II the Spanish Communist Party established an umbrella organization to unite anti-Francoist forces in southern France and even established a radio station called Radio España Independiente (Spanish Independent Radio), known as "La Pireneica" (the Pyrenean), even though it was broadcast from Moscow, not the Pyrenees, to rally the opposition inside Spain itself. In October 1944, Republican fighters operating under the rubric of the Agrupación de Guerrilleros Españoles (Group of Spanish Guerrillas) attempted to liberate their country themselves. On October 19, 1944, between five thousand and seven thousand Republican fighters took part in Operation Reconquest of Spain and entered Spain through the Val d'Aran, Roncesvalles, Hecho, and other Pyrenean mountain passes in an attempt to establish a foothold between the Cinca and Segre Rivers.[28]

The Communist Party hoped that this "invasion" would ignite a national uprising and provide a base from which to liberate the whole country, but these expectations quickly unraveled, as Franco deployed regular army, Civil Guard, and police units, backed up by some forty thousand Moroccan troops, to the Pyrenees. The Republican offensive was concentrated on the Val d'Aran, a beautiful but remote *comarca* (district) in the Catalan province of Lleida that is politically part of Spain even though it juts into France. Today the valley still feels remote and cut off from the rest of the country, despite the heavy trucks that now roll through the recently opened tunnel connecting it to France. Until 1948, when a tunnel was cut out of the mountains to connect the main town of Vielha to the Alta Ribargorça, the valley could be reached only by a single pass, which was often inaccessible in the winter.

This was the unlikely setting for the doomed offensive that features in Guillermo del Toro's *Pan's Labyrinth*. On October 19, members of the Republican Army of National Unity opened fire on the Civil Guard headquarters at Vielha. Though the Republicans succeeded in occupying towns and villages across the Pyrenees, they failed to take Vielha and were forced to retreat across the mountains, after some four hundred men had been killed or captured. Following this debacle, General Charles de Gaulle ordered the Republican resistance in France to stay 12.5 miles (20 kilometers) from the border, but these orders were not obeyed. In Aragon, ex-members of the Forty-Third Division from the "Bielsa pocket" formed a resistance group around Canfranc and Somport, using the rocky outcrop known as the Peña Montañesa as their base of operations, and carried out assassinations of local officials and acts of sabotage on local towns and villages. In response, the Civil Guard created their own "contrapartidas" (fake maquis) to flush out collaborators and track the guerrillas in the mountains.[29]

By 1956 armed resistance to the dictatorship had been extinguished from the Aragonese highlands. In Catalonia, the resistance lasted much longer. For nearly two decades after the war, small groups of anarchists continued to cross the mountains in order to wage their own war on the Franco regime. The most famous of these post–World War II resisters was the Catalan anarchist Francisco Sabaté Llopart, known as "El Quico" (1915–60), the model for Gregory Peck's die-hard Spanish Civil War veteran Manuel Artiguez in Fred Zinnemann's movie *Behold a Pale Horse* (1964). A committed anarchist and proponent of direct action from his teenage years, Sabaté went on to fight during the civil war with the CNT-FAI Young Eagles Column on the Aragon front and then with the legendary Durruti Column. During World War II he fought against the Nazis, and when the war ended he turned his attention to Spain, crossing the border to smuggle weapons, rob banks, assassinate Francoist officials or police informers, and disseminate anarchist propaganda.[30]

From his base less than a mile from the Spanish border, just outside the village of La Clapère, near Prats-de-Mollo-la-Preste, El Quico recruited fellow anarchists to cut wood and farm the land in order to maintain the pretence that he was establishing a libertarian commune, and crossed the mountains repeatedly, narrowly avoiding capture on numerous occasions. Other members of his family were less fortunate. In 1949 his younger brother Manuel was arrested during an operation in Barcelona and executed. That same year his older brother José was killed in Barcelona in a police ambush. Sabaté continued to fight on, even after the principal anarchist organizations in exile had begun to distance themselves from his operations.

In December 1959, El Quico's luck ran out when the Spanish authorities received information that the regime's "public enemy number one" and four companions were preparing to enter Catalonia from Sabaté's latest farmhouse base near Coustages. Sabaté and his comrades were tracked to a farmhouse near Girona. After a prolonged gunfight, the anarchists took advantage of nightfall to try to escape. Three of them were shot dead and Sabaté was badly wounded, but he still managed to crawl through the circle of Civil Guards. For nearly a week he evaded his pursuers. At one point he hijacked a train and then abandoned it to avoid arrest. Starving and in great pain, he hobbled through the Montseny mountains in an attempt to reach Barcelona. On January 6, 1960, officers from the Civil Guard and the Catalan militia caught up with him in the town of Sant Celoni, where he was trying to find a doctor. Sabaté refused to surrender and reached for the submachine gun that had accompanied him on so many of his mountain crossings, wounding one of his pursuers before he was shot to death.

A photograph of El Quico's corpse was published by the Franco press, which gleefully celebrated his death. Other members of his group continued to *echarse al monte* (go to the mountains). One of them was an anarchist named Ramon Vila Capdevila. Born in 1908 in the Catalan village of Peguera, Capdevila was badly scarred as a child by lightning, which also killed his mother and earned him the name Caraquemada—Burntface. During the Civil War he was a member of the anarchist Tierra y Libertad (Land and Freedom) column and went on to fight with the French Resistance under the nom de guerre Captain Raymond, during which he established a reputation as an explosives and sabotage expert. Powerfully built, fearless, and soft-spoken, he commanded the Anarchist Libertad battalion, and after the war he continued to lend his skills to the anti-Francoist cause, regularly crossing the border into Spain to carry out robberies and acts of sabotage. On the night of August 6–7, 1963, Capdevila was on his way back to France after blowing up an electricity pylon, when he was ambushed by a Civil Guard and police patrol near the village of Castelnou. In the ensuing gunfight Capdevila was shot dead, and with his death the Catalan anti-Franco resistance was over; so, too, was the last "war" in Pyrenean history.

The Wars of Pau Casals

No history of the wars of the Pyrenees would be complete without mentioning some of the pacifists and opponents of war who once made their homes in the mountains. This history can be traced back to the Peace and Truce of God movement promoted by Abbot Oliba in the eleventh century. More recently it includes the English Quaker and relief worker Edith Pye, who bought a derelict farm at La Coume in 1933 at the village of Mosset in the foothills of the Eastern Pyrenees. The following year Pye loaned the farm to Pitt and Yvès Krueger, two refugee-intellectuals from Nazi Germany, who turned La Coume into an international peace and education center and a colony for children.[31]

During the 1930s La Coume attracted a number of foreign visitors, including the future British chancellor of the exchequer Denis Healey, and it also became a home for orphans and refugees from the Spanish Civil War. The Andalusian pacifist Professor José Brocca, a member of the War Resisters' International (WRI), in 1938 established a refuge at Prats-de-Mollo-la-Preste near the French-Catalan border for Spanish children, orphans, and widows. Brocca crossed the border on various occasions to rescue both Nationalist and Republican children trapped in the conflict, and he remained at the refuge until 1939, when he was arrested by the French authorities and placed in the nearby internment camp from which he later escaped to Mexico.

In the last weeks of the Spanish Civil War the Pyrenees became home to one of the twentieth century's most famous pacifists, the Catalan cellist Pau Casals, who came to Prades in the Tet Valley, with his "life companion" Francesca Vidal de Capdevila, during the chaotic Republican exodus that followed the fall of Barcelona in January 1939. Following the fall of France in June 1940, Casals was ordered to leave the country by the Vichy government, and he would have gone into exile had the ship that was supposed to take him to South America from Marseille not struck a mine. Though he had influential friends who could have helped him to leave the country, the sixty-three-year-old cellist chose to return to Prades so that he could remain close to his country and to the Spanish refugee population in the South of France.

This decision was not without risks. High-ranking Spanish army officers talked of bringing Casals back to Spain to "break his arms," and the Vichy authorities regarded him as a politically suspect "Red." The prospect of repatriation to Spain became more likely with the extension of the Nazi occupation to the south. On one occasion three Nazi officers visited Casals in Prades and invited him to play for Hitler in Berlin. Casals politely refused. When the officers asked him to play for them on the spot, he pretended that he was suffering from rheumatism. Casals spent the rest of the war living in these precarious circumstances in the house on the outskirts of Prades that he and Capdevila shared with his friend the Catalan poet Joan Alavedra and his family. Visitors can still see the house on the outskirts of Prades where Casals composed his "oratorio for peace" *El Pessebre* (The Crib), a nostalgic evocation of Catalan Christmas traditions, in the shadow of Mount Canigou, the great symbol of Catalonia.

Following the liberation of France, Casals began to perform local benefit concerts to raise money for victims of the war. In 1945 he performed a series of concerts in London in the belief that the British government would act against "the villainous Franco." By December 1946 it had become clear that the Allies had no intention of doing any such thing, and Casals took the radical decision, at the age of seventy, to withdraw from public performances in protest. Instead he continued to assist Spanish families in France from

Prades and gave occasional classes to the stream of cellists who turned up at his house from around the world. In 1949 Alavedra and his family returned to Spain, and Casals moved into a new house in Prades. That year the Lithuanian violinist Alexander Schneider, a member of the Albeneri Trio in the United States, interrupted a European tour to visit him there. After trying in vain to persuade Casals to play in the United States, Schneider offered to organize a Bach festival in Prades to commemorate the bicentennial of Bach's death, under Casals's direction.

Casals accepted, and on June 2 he performed one of his most celebrated pieces, the Prelude to Bach's Cello Suite in G Major, in the Church of Saint-Pierre, to a gathering of musicians, dignitaries, reporters, and music critics from across the world, before conducting the Bach Festival Orchestra in a performance of the Second and Third Brandenburg Concertos. For the next seven years this Bach "festival in exile" became an annual ritual. In 1957 Casals left Prades to live in Puerto Rico, and the administration of the Prades festival was taken on by his brother Enrique Casals. In 1966, Casals returned to Prades for the last time as part of the celebrations for his ninetieth birthday, where a group of string players from the Barcelona Symphony Orchestra serenaded him with Mozart's "Eine kleine Nachtmusik." On October 22, 1973, he died of a heart attack, and it was not until 1979 that his remains were returned to a democratic Spain.

Apart from two interruptions, the Pau Casals Festival has continued to take place in Prades every year, in honor of the man who once declared that "everything is more important than music when it comes to human pain." One evening we drove up to the monastery at Saint-Michel-de-Cuxa on the slopes of Canigou, just above Prades, where Casals had played so often. France was still under a state of emergency because of the risk of terrorism and the police swarming the parking lot near the monastery were another reminder of the seemingly endless "wars" of the early twenty-first century. Casals loved the monastery, and its grass-covered cloister, rows of arched marble pillars, and Romanesque capitals constitute one of the great legacies of the early medieval Catalan march.

Inside the vaulted chamber where Casals had once performed, we listened to a concert of chamber music, and as the sound of cellos and violins echoed playfully around the great stone walls and tall pillars of the ancient monastery, I thought of the little bald man in glasses sitting down in his house who had played there so often. I imagined him beginning his daily practice with his beloved Bach, as he did almost every day during the wartime years. For Casals, music and peace were inseparable, and in those years the prospect of ever playing in front of an audience must have seemed as difficult to imagine as it is for our generation to believe that there may come a day when we will look back on the barbarism of our own era with the same incomprehension.

6

Safe Havens

After the barbed wire, the countryside, the road, and there, eating away at the sky, the Pyrenees. We walk stamping the ground, trying to feel the soles of our feet.
— Max Aub, "Vernet, 1940"[1]

The history of war is not just the history of armies, campaigns, soldiers, and battles, but the history of civilians and noncombatants who have been victims of these conflicts. From the catastrophic invasions of the Suevi to the Napoleonic Wars, civilians in the Pyrenees have found themselves directly in the path of war, while their long history as a frontier zone between warring states has also given the mountains a unique place in the history of Europe, as an escape route from state violence or persecution. Some crossed the mountains alone or in small groups; others fled en masse in search of safety and refuge.

The largest episode of forced emigration in Pyrenean history took place within living memory. A few streets away from the main thoroughfare at the Spanish border town of La Jonquera, an unusual boxlike building of glass and red metal stands out glaringly against the shops, nightclubs, and hypermarkets and bears the unlikely title of Museu Memorial de l'Exili (Memorial Museum of Exile). This museum commemorates the grim events that unfolded in La Jonquera in January 1939, in the last month of the Spanish Civil War, when tens of thousands of panic-stricken Republican refugees fled toward the French border to escape the Nationalist advance on

Barcelona, pursued by planes that bombed and strafed the fleeing columns.

Thousands of these refugees crossed the Pyrenees at La Jonquera. "Every side road, every field, and even the hills are swarming with unhappy thousands who are gradually finding their way to La Junquera," observed the *New York Times* correspondent Herbert L. Matthews. "It was not just an army fleeing, not only families, but entire villages, complete cities with everything they could take, and entire people, one was surprised the earth itself did not follow them."[2] In 2007, the Catalan regional government established a commemorative museum at La Jonquera to remember these events. A permanent exhibition of photographs, testimonies, and music recalls the often-forgotten story of the Catalans interned in French and Nazi concentration camps at the end of the civil war. The museum invites visitors to reflect on the universal phenomenon of forced migration that reached its peak in the twentieth century, and it also touches on a recurring theme in the history of the Pyrenees, in which the mountains constituted a boundary between freedom and persecution, life and death, and an often grueling physical obstacle that refugees, dissidents, and exiles were obliged to cross from one side to the other.

Flight and Expulsion

The Pyrenees had already begun to play this role long before the advent of the political border. As far back as the eighth century, Spanish Christians fled to the mountains of Cantabria, Asturias, and the Pyrenees to escape the Moorish invaders. The *Chronicle of San Juan de la Peña* relates how "three hundred Christians who had escaped the hands of the Saracens" established themselves in the mountains near Jaca where the monastery was later built. The nineteenth-century Aragonese political economist Ignacio de Asso wrote of the Christian settlers who created "an almost incredible multitude of places" in the mountains around Jaca in the centuries that followed the Moorish invasion.[3] In the thirteenth century, the Pyrenees became an escape route for Cathars fleeing papal persecution from southern France. Some took refuge from the war in mountain caves, while others fled southward into Catalonia and Aragon to escape the Inquisition.

In the fourteenth century it was the turn of Jews from southern France to cross the Pyrenees in search of sanctuary, when Philip IV of France expelled one hundred thousand Jews from his realms, most of whom settled in Navarre, Catalonia, and Aragon. In 1315 the Jews were invited back into Languedoc by King Louis X. Five years later thousands fled southward once again to escape the pogrom perpetrated by the Shepherds' Crusade in their violent rampage from Paris to southern France. Even then the Pyrenees provided only temporary sanctuary, as the *pastoureaux* followed these refugees into Iberia, carrying out further massacres in Jaca, Montclus, Monreal, and other Pyrenean towns and villages.

From the late fourteenth century onward the tide of refugees across the Pyrenees began to move in the opposite direction. In 1391 Sephardic Jews who had lived in Catalonia for centuries fled northward into France following the wave of anti-Jewish violence that spread across Spain that year, in which Jews were forced to convert to Catholicism or killed. In 1492, Ferdinand and Isabella ordered all unconverted Iberian Jews to convert to Christianity or leave the country. Most of of these Jews went by ship to North Africa, but others made their way into southern France. In 1497 King Manuel I of Portugal ordered all Portuguese Jews to convert or leave the country, and tried to prevent Jews from leaving by ordering all Jews who refused to convert to leave their children behind. Once again many Jews smuggled their children into exile in France, where they settled in places close to the Pyrenees such as Saint-Jean-de-Luz, Bayonne, Bordeaux, and Montpellier.

In the last decades of the sixteenth century, Muslim converts, or Moriscos, bore the brunt of Spanish state persecution; many found refuge in the Protestant viscounty of Béarn, where small Morisco communities were established in Pau, Oloron, and other towns and cities close to the frontier. Moriscos were not allowed to leave Spain, and many of these refugees escaped across the Pyrenees through the Somport Pass, or via more inaccessible routes, sometimes with the help of Spanish and French smugglers. When the Spanish king Philip III took the decision to expel all Moriscos from the country between 1609 and 1614, the Pyrenees acquired a new role as an instrument of one of Europe's early episodes of "ethnic cleansing," as thousands of Moriscos were driven across the Pyrenees into France.

In June 1610, 5,000 Aragonese Moriscos were left stranded in the Pyrenees for weeks on the border with Béarn, when French and Bearnese officials refused to allow them to enter. Eventually they were allowed to cross the frontier and continue their journey into exile. That same year 14,000 Aragonese Moriscos were force marched to the border town of Canfranc, where they, too, were refused entry by the French authorities and obliged to undertake a grueling forced march to the Mediterranean coastal port of Los Alfaques that killed many of them before they even arrived. In the summer of 1612, 22,000 Aragonese Moriscos were taken across the Pyrenees under armed escort. The anti-Morisco priest Pedro Aznar Cardona described their progress "bursting with grief and tears, in a great commotion and confusion of voices, laden with their women and children, their sick, the old and young, covered in dust, sweating and panting."[4]

The expulsion of the Moriscos was then the largest single example of forced migration in Spanish history, but it was not the last time that unwanted people were driven across the Pyrenean border. Thousands of pro-French Spaniards known as *afrancesado*s followed Napoléon's defeated armies into France in 1813. In 1822 Adolphe Thiers encountered entire families of Royalist supporters camped out on the French side of the border near Prades. Thiers expressed his horror at the sight of "twelve or fifteen hundred poor creatures, men, women, children . . . stretched upon the ground, with their baggage spread out; some were lying on a little straw, others added their clothes, and endeavoured to make beds of them."[5]

The following year Spanish liberals were obliged to seek sanctuary in France, following the French-backed restoration of Ferdinand VII. One of these exiles was Francisco Goya, who crossed the Pyrenees at the age of seventy-eight, accompanied by his maid, Leocadia, and her five-year-old daughter, and settled in Bordeaux, where he died four years later. The Carlist wars saw a new movement of refugees and exiles northward. In 1840 thirty thousand Carlist refugees poured into France, and the Baltimore journal *Niles' National Register* warned that "fresh dissensions in the government of Spain . . . may engender another civil contest, and send across the Pyrenees swarms of refugees of new denominations, all destitute, and vastly more eager than grateful for French hospitality."

Non-Spaniards also used the Pyrenees as an escape route. In September 1879 the Cuban nationalist writer José Martí escaped from a Barcelona prison and made his way across the Pyrenees to Paris and then to New York, where he continued to agitate for Cuban independence until his death in battle fighting Spanish troops in Cuba in 1895. In 1896 another Cuban, Fernando Tarrida, professor of mathematics and engineering director at the Polytechnic Academy of Barcelona, smuggled letters and documents across the Pyrenees detailing the savage police torture of dozens of prisoners in the Montjuïch fortress in response to an anarchist bombing in the Catalan capital that same year. These documents subsequently became a book, *Les inquisiteurs d'Espagne: Montjuich* (1897), which provoked widespread anti-Spanish protests across Europe.

Spain's long history as a country of exile, persecution, and forced migration reached a peak during the Spanish Civil War. In the first year of the war fifteen thousand refugees crossed the Pyrenees, most of whom were Republicans fleeing the fighting in the Basque Country and Nationalist repression in Navarre and Aragon. Some Francoist supporters were also obliged to cross the Eastern Pyrenees in order to escape from Republican territory into France in order to reenter Nationalist-held Spain. On July 22, 1936, the parish priest at the sanctuary of Núria, Bonventura Carrera (or Mossèn Ventura as he was known locally), removed a Romanesque statue of the Virgin Mary from the sanctuary after hearing that anarchists had burned the church in nearby Puigcerdà. Father Ventura carried the statue in his rucksack through the Coll de Finestrelles and placed it in a Swiss deposit box, where it remained until it was returned to Spain in 1941. In November 1937 the pro-Franco priest Josémaria Escrivá de Balaguer (1902–75), the future saint and founder of the ultraconservative Opus Dei movement, hiked across the Andorran Pyrenees with seven companions from Barcelona. Walking for up to sixteen hours a day, Balaguer and his companions reached France via a route that has since become a pilgrimage route for Opus Dei followers, and reentered Nationalist Spain via Hendaye.

Nationalist refugee crossings in the Pyrenees were rare. Most exiles and refugees who crossed the mountains during the civil war were Republican victims of Francoist violence and terror. By the autumn of 1937 between fifty thousand and sixty thousand Republican refugees had already entered France, most of whom walked through the Central Pyrenees from Aragon or western Catalonia. These numbers increased in April 1938, when thousands of Republican soldiers and civilians fled northward into France, following the Nationalist capture of Lérida. Some ten thousand men, women, and children crossed the Pyrenees to escape the Nationalist onslaught, four thousand of whom reached France through the Port de Benasque and other snowbound mountain passes. "Not all found the haven they sought," reported the *Chicago Daily Tribune.* "Some perished in snowbanks, unable to keep pace with their trudging companions. At least 15 plunged to death in canyons. Four literally fell into France and to their death at the same time."

These numbers paled beside the vast exodus that took place in the last week of January 1939, when hundreds of thousands of refugees fled the devastating Nationalist offensive in Catalonia to La Jonquera, Le Perthus, and other Catalan border posts. The French

Spanish Republican women fleeing through the Pyrenees toward the French border, probably through Catalonia in 1939 (Alamy stock image).

authorities were reluctant to give safe haven to a population it regarded as politically suspect, and they closed the border. It was not until January 27–28 that the right-wing Daladier government reopened the frontier. Over the next two weeks, nearly half a million Spaniards poured into France, doubling the population of the Pyrénées-Orientales. Appalling scenes unfolded as these refugees struggled to obtain food and shelter in freezing mountain conditions, amid the general indifference of the French authorities. On the road between Le Perthus and Perpignan, the French communist Jean Bénazet observed Spanish women prostituting themselves to French border guards in exchange for bread, and young children lying by the roadside in the snow under piles of straw, sacks, blankets, and tarpaulins. Over the next few months, tens of thousands of Spanish refugees found themselves subjected to the new forms of internment that had already begun to define the mid-twentieth century.

Pyrenean Gulag

For governments on either side of the frontier, the Pyrenees have often provided a conveniently distant and remote place of imprisonment. During the Napoleonic Wars, French prisoners of war in Catalonia were held on the "natural prison" of Capolatell in the Sierra de Busa in the Pre-Pyrenees. Separated from the rest of the Busa plateau by cliffs as high as 377 feet (115 meters) and accessible only by a single metal bridge, this "island" became a literal death trap for hundreds of French soldiers, who were abandoned there and left to starve. In 1848 Henri IV's former château at Pau was used as a temporary prison for the Algerian resistance leader the emir Abd-el-Kader, who fought the French invasion of Algeria for the best part of twenty years before his surrender in 1847.

Abd-el-Kader had surrendered on condition that he be allowed to retire to Egypt, but the terms of the agreement were broken and he was taken to Toulon and then Pau—a betrayal that inspired an ode from William Thackeray to the "wild hawk of the desert . . . borne away to France." In 1848 the British writer Sabine Baring-Gould visited Abd-el-Kader in the Pau château, where he found the resistance leader and his wives in gloomy exile, "all insensible to the stateliness of the castle and the glorious panorama from the windows. They lounged about the rooms silent and smoking, sulky, without occupation and without interests. Their habits were so dirty that the tapestries and rich furniture had all to be removed."[6]

Abd-el-Kadr and his wives were eventually allowed to retire to Damascus, but other Pyrenean prisoners never left the mountains. Hundreds of Republican prisoners were imprisoned after the civil war in the isolated Coll de Ladrones fortress built under Philip II to guard the Somport Pass; many were executed within its walls. In the wake of the Republican *retirada* (retreat) of 1939, the French authorities established a chain of camps along the southern Mediterranean coast and closer to the Pyrenees, where Spanish refugees were interned. Tens of thousands of men, women, and children were herded by the local authorities into compounds with little or no shelter and inadequate food, guarded by gendarmes and troops with orders to shoot anyone who tried to escape. As many as fifteen thousand Spaniards may have died of exposure and hunger between February and September 1939 in camps that have long since become beach resorts and holiday destinations.

Following the outbreak of World War II, many of these camps were used by the Vichy regime to imprison political dissidents and unwanted foreigners. They included the Hungarian writer Arthur Koestler, who was interned at the Pyrenean camp of Le Vernet in the Ariège as an "undesirable alien" from October 1939 to January 1940, and the Mexican-Spanish novelist Max Aub, who was imprisoned in the camp on two separate occasions. Le Vernet also housed many former International Brigadiers, some 350 of whom were interned in the "Leper Barrack" in what Koestler described as a "horrifying revelation of the abjectness and misery to which men can be reduced."[7]

The largest of these Camps du Mépris (Camps of Scorn) was located at the village of Gurs in Béarn. Nowadays a visit to the village requires a complicated car journey from Orthez through a pretty Bearnese landscape of cornfields, forest, medieval villages, and old stone barns. Just outside the village there is a short stretch of railroad track, about fifty yards long, that connects an enclosed barbed-wire compound to the memorial that commemorates the former Centre d'Accueil (Reception Center), established by the French authorities for Spanish Republican refugees in 1939. Until the 1960s, much of this 1,998-acre compound was covered in forest, which had been planted since the war to conceal its original purpose. Various nations cofunded the clearing of the forest to make way for an official memorial to a camp where men, women, and children from more than fifty-two nations were interned between 1939 and 1945.

The first prisoners at Gurs were Spanish Republicans and members of the International Brigades who arrived in the winter of 1939. From 1940 onward, German Jews, French political prisoners, and other "undesirables" in Vichy France were sent there, including the Jewish political scientist and philosopher Hannah Arendt. During the Vichy roundups of Jews in 1942, thousands of French Jews were placed under house arrest in Pyrenean villages, to await transportation to concentration camps, and many of them were also sent to Gurs. Even after its official closure in 1943, Gypsies and other "undesirables" were still being brought to the camp. Strictly speaking, Gurs was an internment camp where detainees were held before being transferred to somewhere worse, but the spartan and primitive conditions ensured a high death toll. In the winter of 1940–41, more than a thousand inmates died of cold, hunger, and illness. In 1940 most of its inmates were women, one of whom described her arrival at "Gurs—the old Spanish camp," where she was confronted by the sight of "a miserable cohort of women . . . saw something resembling a grey swamp, three kilometres long, barracks lined up against each other, behind the barracks other barracks as far as they eye could see. Not a tree, not a spot of green. How to live in this desolated universe?"[8]

Some women survived by prostituting themselves to the camp guards in exchange for food for themselves and their children, who were imprisoned with them. Others died of hunger, exhaustion, and infections and were buried in the cemetery, which is filled with Jewish names like Kaufman, Dreyfuss, and Stein. Many of the names on the roll of the dead were in their seventies and eighties and would have died very soon after their arrival. Near the entrance to the camp, a small hut remains, the only original building still standing from the "city of wood," where the Swiss Red Cross nurse Elsbeth Kasser, known as the Angel of Gurs, tended to inmates. Now a memorial trail leads through the woods that were planted to conceal this sordid chapter in French history, and houses with verandas look over the railroad track that symbolizes the journey to Auschwitz taken by four thousand of the camp's Jewish detainees. At the education center, a copy of an inmate's painting shows famished, shrunken men and women behind barbed wire with the snow-capped Pyrenees in the background.

It is a mournful but essential monument to one of the most shameful chapters in French history, and the largely forgotten role that the Pyrenees once played in the twentieth century's detention universe. Arthur Koestler has written how "the scale of sufferings and humiliations was distorted, the measure of what a man can bear was lost," during this period of twentieth-century history, to the point when "in Liberal-Centigrade, Vernet was the zero-point of infamy; measured in Dachau-Farenheit it was still 32 degrees above zero."[9]

Something similar could be said of Gurs and the other Pyrenean camps, which the collaborationist government of Marshal Pétain continued to fill with new categories of prisoners throughout the war. In August 1945, Pétain himself was briefly imprisoned at the military fortress of Portalet in the Somport Pass, following his conviction for treason, only an hour's drive from the camp where so many of the men and women imprisoned by the Vichy authorities had suffered and died.

The Mountains of Freedom

By this time, the Pyrenees had become an escape route for many of Pétain's own countrymen for the first time since the expulsions of the Jews in the Middle Ages, as a refugee population that included French and foreign Jews, stateless "undesirable foreigners," Frenchmen hoping to fight with the French army in North Africa or flee forced-labor conscription programs, and Allied airmen and soldiers made their way southward into Spain. In the summer of 1940, thousands of people streamed southward to escape the German advance through northern France. "All France was on the move. All France was in flight, and in all directions, madly, at random," remembered the German-Jewish novelist and internee Lion Feuchtwanger. "All railways and all highways in southern France were crowded with fugitives—Hollanders, Belgians, millions of French from the North . . . plodding along the roads in endless throngs, under the torrential rains, toward the Spanish border."[10]

For most of these refugees, Francoist Spain was not a safe haven in itself but a transit route to the United States or South America. Thousands arrived by train from Toulouse and crossed the border with forged papers or official exit visas at Puigcerdà, Latour-de-Carol, or Cerbère. Those unable to obtain these documents were forced to make their way across the mountains with the help of shepherds, charcoal burners, and woodcutters who were sympathetic to them or willing to act as guides in exchange for a fee.

On September 13, 1940, the sixty-year-old Alma Mahler-Werfel, the widow of Gustav Mahler, made her way up the steep path through the Albères hills beyond Cerbère, carrying a bag of jewelry and the manuscript of a Bruckner symphony, accompanied by her husband, the novelist Franz Werfel, Heinrich Mann and his wife, and his brother Golo Mann. All of them owed their escape to the American literary journalist Varian Fry, the "American Schindler," who arrived in Marseille as a representative of the Emergency Rescue Committee in June 1940, tasked with helping writers and artists reach the United States. Many of the two thousand–odd refugees helped by Fry's network were Jews, whose numbers increased following the mass roundups of Jews in France between October 1942 and January 1943.

For many Jews placed under house arrest or in internment camps in or near the Pyrenees, crossing the mountains was the only way to escape transportation to the concentration camps of Eastern Europe. Some paid shepherds and smugglers to guide them across the mountains. Others were helped by local sympathizers. Between twenty thousand and thirty thousand Jews are believed to have crossed or attempted to cross the Pyrenees in the course of the war. Not all of them survived these journeys. Some froze or fell to their death. Others were robbed and sometimes killed by their escorts in the mountains to steal their money. The French historian Émilienne Eychenne has estimated that 226 refugees died trying to cross the frontier between 1939 and 1945, mostly after being repatriated from Spain, while the Confédération Nationale des Anciens Combattants Francais Evadés de France estimates that 450 were killed through accidents or repatriations or died in Spanish concentration camps.[11]

For some of these refugees, politics transformed the Pyrenees into an impassable barrier. On a summer's day you can see the hazy bluish outline of the Pyrenees from the village of Boeil-Bezing, on the Bearnese plain between Pau and Lourdes. At the rear of the cemetery just behind the village church, a marble headstone bears the inscription in French: "To the memory of Carl Einstein, Poet and Art historian, Fighter for Liberty, Born 26 April in Neuwied Germany, who committed suicide on the 5 July 1940 to escape Nazi persecution." The nephew of Albert Einstein, Einstein was a novelist, scriptwriter, and art critic whose circle of friends included Picasso, Georges Braque, and the avant-garde writer Georges Bataille. He was also a committed anarchist and anti-facist who fought as an anarchist militia commander during the Spanish Civil War and delivered the funeral oration of the Aragonese anarchist Buenaventura Durruti.

Following the Republican defeat, Einstein returned to France, where he was briefly interned before escaping to Paris, and then interned once again as a German national in a camp near Bordeaux. In June 1940 he was separated from his wife as they fled the German advance, and he found himself in Béarn, in the shadow of the Pyrenees. For Einstein, the former anarchist commander, the Pyrenees offered no possibility of escape or refuge. On June 26–27 he cut his wrists and was taken to the monastery at Lestelle-Bétharram near Lourdes to recover, and ten days later, on July 5, he drowned himself in the Gave de Pau.

No Way Out: The Last Journey of Walter Benjamin

Einstein was one of six writers in the dedication of Arthur Koestler's *Scum of the Earth* who committed suicide because they were unable to find a safe haven in this period. These dedicatees include the German-Jewish writer and literary critic Walter Benjamin, whom Koestler met in Marseille in the autumn of 1940. Benjamin was hoping to reach New York via Lisbon, and he had Spanish and Portuguese transit visas. But the Vichy authorities were refusing to give exit visas to German émigrés, and so he was obliged to walk across the Pyrenees. Benjamin knew that this was his last hope of survival, and he told Koestler that he had brought thirty morphine tablets, which were "enough to kill a horse," in the event that he failed to find safe passage.

On September 25 he turned up without warning at the house of Lisa and Hans Fittko, two German anti-fascists and members of Varian Fry's team, who had established themselves with false papers in the seaside town of Banyuls-sur-Mer, where they continued to escort refugees across the border. Benjamin was accompanied by a woman named Henny Gurland and her teenage son, Joseph, and he asked Lisa Fittko to take him and his companions across the mountains. Fittko's husband was away, and she was immediately struck by Benjamin's old-fashioned "Spanish court etiquette" and the "intellectual scholar's head and the searching gaze behind thick lenses," which led her to describe him affectionately as *Der alte Benjamin*—Old Benjamin.[12] She agreed to help him, and that afternoon she led Benjamin and his two companions on a trial walk up a former smuggling route called *la route Lister*, named after the Spanish Republican general Enrique Lister, which led up into the Albères, at the point where the Pyrenees drop down toward the Mediterranean. Fittko intended to take her party up the 2,198-foot (670-meter) Querroig peak, in order to avoid the French border guards at the Col de Cerbère, and the route that she followed has now become a commemorative trail in Benjamin's memory.

On a hot, blustery morning, I set out on the Chemin Walter Benjamin from the Banyuls town hall, past the French soldiers patrolling the main road to protect the crowded beach from an attack by Daesh/Islamic State. The heat was only partially relieved by the wind that whipped across the hills as I made my way up through a succession of terraced vineyards along the route that Benjamin and his companions had taken. Apart from the heat, it was not a particularly hard walk: Fittko herself described it as a "ramble," but it would nevertheless have been a daunting prospect for a forty-eight-year-old asthmatic writer with a heart condition. Once again, Benjamin had weighed up his prospects of survival and calculated that he needed to stop for a minute every ten minutes in order not to strain his heart.

He carried with him a leather briefcase containing a manuscript that he described to Fittko as "more important than I am, more important than myself." After three hours, the party reached a small clearing by a large boulder, where Fittko proposed that they return to Banyuls and continue the following day. To her amazement, Benjamin announced that he was going to spend the night where he was. The next morning Fittko and the Gurlands returned to find Benjamin waiting for them, and they continued the climb at his slow stop-start pace. It took me about an hour to reach the point where I thought Benjamin must have spent the night. To my left I could see the high ridge climbing up toward Querroig from the Col de Cerbère. Below me I could see Banyuls, where my wife and daughter were spending the day on the beach. As I stood by the large boulder, listening to the pylon line above my head humming like a distant carousel, I thought of Benjamin, the flaneur and connoisseur of urban spaces, sitting up there alone with his precious manuscript and his morphine tablets, and I wondered what thoughts had gone through his mind as he lay propped up on the hard, rocky slope with the high ridge looming above him from the south that separated France from Spain.

The climb up toward the ridge was much steeper than the first part of the walk. Gurland later remembered how "we had to crawl part of the way on all fours."[13] At one point Fittko lost the way, and Benjamin helped her find it. At two o'clock Benjamin's party reached the top of the ridge, where Fittko later described the view: "Far below, where we had come from, the deep-blue Mediterranean was visible; on the other side in front of us, steep cliffs fell away to a glass sheet of transparent turquoise. . . . Behind us, to the north, the semicircle of Catalonia's Roussillon, with its Côte Vermeille, the Vermilion Coast, an autumn landscape with innumerable hues of red and yellow-gold. I gasped for breath—I had never seen such beauty before."[14]

Fittko had no papers herself and was not able to continue into Spain. She told Benjamin and his companions to make their way down to the Coll de Rumpisa and present themselves to the first Spanish border post. Today this pass bears a plaque that marks the beginning of the Catalan side of the Walter Benjamin route and its incorporation into one of the Espais de Memoria (Places of Memory), which the Catalan regional government has established throughout the Catalan Pyrenees. For some reason, Fittko does not mention the Austrian-Jewish refugee Carmina Birman, who had reached the Coll de Rumpisa with her sister and two friends earlier that day. In a short memoir that was published in 2006, Birman describes how she and her party were joined by "an elderly gentleman, a younger female and her son. The gentleman, a German university professor named Walter Benjamin, was on the point of having a heart attack. The strain of mountain climbing on an extremely hot September day, together with the anxious endeavour to escape German arrest was too much for him."[15]

Birman and her companions found Benjamin some water, and he was eventually able to continue with them toward their common destination at the seaside town of Port Bou. Even in my walking boots I found the stony path hard going, and the sharp, prickly bushes that scratched at my clothes and skin fully merited every description of the Pyrenees as a savage frontier. It would have been agony for a sick man wearing ordinary shoes and carrying a briefcase, who had nearly died of a heart attack. From time to time I passed commemorative plaques of Benjamin, containing the famous photograph with his chin on his hand and quotations from his books.

Both the photograph and the quotations were an incongruous sight in this harsh, unforgiving terrain—a reminder of the world of books and ideas that was waiting for Benjamin in New York. It wasn't until I reached flat ground that the first signs of cultivation began to appear and the track widened past the railway station and into Port Bou. It was a relief to sit in a bar on the pier and contemplate the little bay and the crowded stony beach, where families were still sunbathing and playing in the sea. When Benjamin saw the town, it was still partly destroyed by the Nationalist bombing during the civil war. According to Birman, their party accidentally missed the first Spanish customs post, and they were arrested at the second on suspicion of illegal entry and taken to a "special police hotel," the Fonda de Francia, in Port Bou, and told they would be returned to France the next day.

While Birman's sister tried in vain to bribe the hotel owner and the police officials, Birman tried to console Benjamin, who was sitting on his hotel bed "in a desolate state of mind and in a completely exhausted physical condition," staring at a "very beautiful big golden grandfather watch with open cover on a little board near him." When Benjamin hinted to Birman that he had some "very effective poisonous pills" with him, she tried to convince him to "abandon the idea of suicide." Henny Gurland also tried to persuade him not to kill himself, before going to bed. These efforts appear to have been in vain. At seven the next morning Gurland returned to Benjamin's bedside, where he told her that he had taken morphine during the night and asked her to say that he had fallen ill.

Benjamin gave her a letter to pass on to his friend Theodor Adorno, who was working at the New School in New York. Gurland committed its words to memory before destroying it: "In a situation presenting no way out, I have no other choice but to make an end of it. It is in a small village in the Pyrenees, where no one knows me, where my life will come to an end."

She then called a local doctor, who diagnosed an embolism and refused her request to take Benjamin to hospital. Benjamin died that morning. Later that day, the local police reversed their decision and the rest of Benjamin's party was allowed their journey to Portugal. Benjamin was buried with Catholic rites under the name Benjamin Walter to hide his Jewishness, in a ceremony by Mosen Andreu Freixa, without altar boys or a procession, in lot 563 in the local cemetery. In 1949 Benjamin's remains were moved to a common grave in another part of the town, and his manuscript was never found, though an official document refers to unknown papers in his possession at the time of his death.

On October 7, 1940, the German-Jewish refugee newspaper *Aufbau* reported that "Professor Walter Benjamin, a well-known pyschologist," had committed suicide at Port Bou. Today, outside the whitewashed cemetery, a haunting installation in Port Bou built by the Israeli sculptor Dani Karavan commemorates Benjamin's doomed Pyrenean journey. Entitled *Passages* after Benjamin's unfinished magnum opus, *Passagen-Werk*, or *Arcades Project*, the monument consists of a metal gateway leading down a flight of steps to a glass window looking out over the foaming sea, where visitors can read Benjamin's own words: "It is more difficult to honour the memory of the nameless than of the well-known. Historical construction is dedicated to the memory of the nameless."

Benjamin was not one of the nameless, and that is one reason why his doomed Pyrenean crossing is remembered when the names of other Jews who failed to find a route to safety through the mountains have gone unremembered and unrecorded. Like them, Benjamin chose to die on his own terms rather than allow himself to be sent back to the certain death that awaited him. Having shown immense courage and resourcefulness in overcoming the physical obstacle of the Pyrenees, he became a casualty of an international system that still prevails, in which "paper walls" can open and close in a single day, and transform themselves from a route to safety into the walls of a trap.

Escape Lines

Refugees were not the only ones to cross the Pyrenees during World War II. For thousands of Allied soldiers, airmen, and Frenchmen, the Pyrenees were not just a route to safety, but an opportunity to return to the war. Britons, Canadians, Poles, Romanians, Czechs,

Bulgarians, Austrians, French, Greeks, and Americans all crossed the Pyrenees in the course of the war to escape imprisonment and live to fight again. In May 1941 Andrée "Dédée" De Jongh, a young female Belgian Red Cross volunteer, and a thirty-two-year-old Belgian cinema technician named Arnold Deppé established an underground network from Belgium to Saint-Jean-de-Luz, near the French-Spanish border, known as Operation Comet, which smuggled Allied airmen into Spain and onward through Spanish ports or the Portuguese "Lisbon route" to North Africa or their own countries.

More than seven hundred British, Canadian, and American fliers returned to combat through this route, most of whom were brought by train from Paris to the Atlantic coast, where Basque guides took them across the Western Pyrenees by night—a trek that could last from five to sixteen hours. Dozens of "escape lines" were established in other parts of the Pyrenees, where soldiers and airmen, Free French resisters or ordinary Frenchmen fleeing Nazi forced-labor programs, were transported to the embassies or consulates in Bilbao, Barcelona, and Madrid, that facilitated their onward journeys.

Until November 1942 the German army and units of the Grenzschutz—border police and customs—controlled only the western part of the frontier from Hendaye on the Atlantic coast to Roncesvalles, while the Vichy government exerted a more relaxed vigilance over the remaining section of the border. With the extension of the German occupation to the whole of France in 1942, the entire Pyrenean frontier was declared a forbidden zone 9.5 miles (15 kilometers) deep, and border security was reinforced by units of Gebirgsjäger alpine corps. As a result, escapees were obliged to try to get to Spain through more inaccessible and dangerous routes into Catalonia, Andorra, or Aragon.

One of the most famous World War II escape lines was the Pat line, established by the Special Operations Executive (SOE) agent Captain Ian Garrow of the Seaforth Highlanders, and named after Lieutenant-Commander Pat O'Leary, the nom de guerre given to the Belgian cavalry officer and British intelligence operative Albert-Marie Guérisse, who was recruited by Garrow. Like many escape lines, the Pat line worked closely with Spanish Republican refugees in southern France, such as the Spanish anarchist and teacher Francisco Ponzán Vidal (1911–44), who collaborated closely with SOE and MI6, as well as the French and Belgian secret services.[16] In addition to organizing safe houses for Allied escapees in Perpignan, Toulouse, and Foix, Vidal also arranged guides to take them across the Pyrenees. One of his most well-known "parcels" was the future conservative parliamentarian Airey Neave, one of the few British soldiers to escape from Colditz, who crossed the Pyrenees with a group of escapees in April 1942, led by a Spanish guide who wore white boots to keep himself visible as they walked from Port-Vendres into Spain through freezing winds and a rainstorm.

Facilitating such escapes was generally punishable by death or transportation to a concentration camp. Vidal was arrested in April 1943 and shot the following year. Some 155 members of the Comet line were arrested, including Dédée De Jongh, who was arrested trying to cross the Basque Pyrenees in January 1943, and tortured before going on to survive the war in Ravensbrück and Mathausen camps. The guides, or *passeurs*, who collaborated with these networks were driven by a range of motivations. Some were smugglers who took their "parcels" across the Pyrenees in order to make a living. Others acted out of political or religious conviction. The Comet line relied heavily on a Basque hunter and smuggler named Florentino Goikoetxea, who led hundreds of refugees and escapees to safety through the Basque and Navarrese Pyrenees. The Catalan anarchist Joaquim Baldrich Forné (1916–2012) fled to Andorra following the Republican defeat and became a smuggler out of economic necessity, before forming an escape line that transported British servicemen across the Pyrenees and delivered them to the very doors of the British consulate in Barcelona.

Unlike the Alps, which played a similar role for refugees and escapees seeking to reach neutral Switzerland during World War II, the *évadés* who reached Spain found themselves in a country that was formally neutral but sympathetic to the Axis powers. At the beginning of the war, men of military age who crossed the border illegally were liable to be imprisoned in the border town of Sort or taken to concentration camps such as Miranda del Ebro and Nanclares de la Oca, before they were handed over to their embassies. Between 1942 and 1944 the Franco regime adopted a harder line in response to German pressure and began sending escapees and refugees caught within 3 miles (5 kilometers) of the French frontier back to France. As the war turned against the Axis powers, Franco became more willing to allow evaders and escapees to reach their respective embassies and consulates. Altogether some fifty thousand men, women, and children were arrested by the Spanish authorities, according to the Catalan historian Josep Calvet, and estimates of the overall numbers of soldiers, refugees, and *résistants* who crossed the Pyrenees in the course of the war vary from thirty thousand to one hundred thousand.[17]

The Chemin de la Liberté

Today some of these Pyrenean escape routes are remembered through the commemorative walking trails that have been established in the mountains in recent years. On a muggy evening in mid-July 2015 I stood with a small crowd of British and French spectators at the site of a former Nazi command post by a large rock at Kercabanac, in the Couserans area of the Ariège, while French and foreign soldiers and members of the British Legion, many of them holding their regimental standards and in full uniform, paid tribute to these escapees and the *passeurs* who had guided them across the mountains. During World War II, Kercabanac marked the beginning of the *zone interdite* (the forbidden zone) alongside the Spanish frontier.

A plaque now commemorates the Spanish and French men and women who defied these regulations, and every year, walkers, veterans, and local dignitaries gather here at the beginning of the annual trek known as the Chemin de la Liberté (Road of Free-dom), which follows one of the toughest of these wartime escape routes. I was one of a group of more than fifty men and women who had come to walk the *chemin* from Saint-Girons to the Catalan village of Esterri d'Aneu in Spain. We stood to attention while bouquets were laid at the monument and the strains of a bagpipe echoed through the thickly forested hills, and a retired French air force colonel hailed "those who thought their future could be dreamed differently, all those who acted so as to change their present and thanks to whom ours can be enjoyed peacefully."

The following morning more than sixty-five of us assembled at the site of the former railway bridge in Saint-Girons, where escapees coming by train were once alerted by the drivers and jumped off to begin their trek. Our group included a former British consul-general in Barcelona, a serving Royal Marine Commando, a former RAF wing commander with the word for "peace" emblazoned on his T-shirt in more than fifty languages, a team of NATO soldiers on a personal development course, fund-raisers for the British Legion, a Welsh furniture upholsterer who kept fit by dancing to salsa music, a former Cardiff rugby team second row forward, a young punk-jazz musician, and numerous soldiers and veterans. All of us carried packs weighing an average of twenty-six pounds, containing supplies of food and equipment that were not available to wartime escapees. British airmen in World War II were issued "escape boxes" that included silk maps, compressed food, and six tablets of Benzedrine to help them make their way across the Alps or the Pyrenees, but some escapees had only a crust of bread or a chunk of cheese to tide them over. One British serviceman had walked this route wearing a slipper on one foot and a shoe on the other.

In 1943, Nancy Wake, the New Zealand–born French Resistance courier known to the Gestapo as the White Mouse, crossed the Pyrenees with the assistance of two Spanish guides, a man and a woman connected to the Pat O'Leary line. Wake made five failed attempts to find guides to take her from Perpignan across the

12-mile (20-kilometer) forbidden zone along the French frontier before she succeeded on her sixth. Accompanied by a Frenchman, two Frenchwomen, and two American airmen, the guides, and their dog, Wake walked for forty-seven hours, often in deep snow, stopping every two hours for ten minutes' rest. As was the custom, the party wore espadrilles and were under strict orders not to speak during their journey. Despite a blizzard and the near exhaustion of some members of the group, the party reached Spain, and Wake returned to England via Barcelona, from where she subsequently returned to France as an agent for the Special Operations Executive.[18]

The American fighter pilot and future test pilot Chuck Yeager, the hero of Tom Wolfe's *The Right Stuff,* crossed the mountains in even more challenging circumstances. On March 5, 1944, Yeager was shot down near Bordeaux and taken by the local maquis to the Pyrenees with a group of Allied airmen. Yeager and a B-24 navigator named Pat Patterson left the main group and soon got lost in the mountains after climbing 7,000 feet (2,134 meters). "The Pyrenees make the hills back home look like straight-ways," Yeager recalled in his autobiography. "The climb is endless, a bitch of bitches."[19]

After three days in the mountains the two airmen encountered a German patrol and Patterson was shot in the leg before they managed to escape. After amputating his leg at the knee, Yeager carried his wounded companion toward the frontier. On reaching Spain, Yeager pushed him over a ridge and rolled him down to the road, in the hope that a passing car would pick him up. Patterson was found by the Civil Guard shortly afterward and survived the war, and Yeager also made it back to Britain and resumed the war.

All of us were conscious of this history as we trudged across the Mont Valier massif in temperatures of 95 degrees Fahrenheit (35 degrees Celsius), on a four-day trek that was unlike any walk I had ever done. Before leaving Saint-Girons, one of the walk coordinators warned us that there were "multitudinous ways to seriously hurt yourselves" en route, and these warnings were not exaggerated. Within two hours of leaving one woman had broken her collarbone. By the end of the walk eleven people had been forced to retire from exhaustion and heatstroke. The first two days we walked mostly through grassy meadows and shaded woodlands, sweating our way upward in a long snaking line through fern-lined paths and forests, under the vigilance of the French *accompagnateurs* in their lime-green T-shirts, toward the high peaks that revealed themselves only intermittently.

Our rest breaks were invariably preceded by speeches from the ubiquitous French air force colonel who had greeted us on the first day, followed by renditions of the haunting resistance anthem, the "Chants des Partisans," with its fulsome tributes to bombs, grenades, machine guns, and snipers. Few of the British walkers knew the words, and most of us merely hummed along, but it was a stirring spectacle to watch former Resistance fighters and their descendants singing this sombre paean to resistance and patriotic killing with their hands on their hearts. On the first afternoon we gathered outside a barn where the young *passeur* Louis Barrau—a local shepherd—refused to surrender to a Nazi/Vichy patrol. Barrau's father and uncle had already been deported to a German labor camp for similar activities, and neither of them survived the war. When the soldiers set fire to the barn, Barrau tried to make a break for it but was shot dead on the spot. These were the episodes that we had come to remember. History, war, and survival were recurring subjects in our conversations as the forest began to thin out and we found ourselves clambering up stony paths and over high boulders. On the second day we camped out in the open next to a shepherd's hut, where a plaque dedicated the *chemin* to "the evaders of France, to the beauty of memory and the peace of the heart" (my translation).

That night our French *accompagnateurs* sang and danced joyously and passed around the wine, and I went to sleep that night beneath a sky that was filled with more stars than I had seen in years. The next day we hiked up and down two peaks of more than 7,000 feet

(2,134 meters) between them. It was a punishing but exhilarating experience to walk above cloud level through a corrugated, weatherworn moonscape of limestone rocks and great piles of boulders, toward the jagged ridge that the locals call Le Dinosaur. The only signs of life were a few scattered Méren horses, Napoléon's old workhorses during the invasion of Russia, and the occasional shepherds with their dogs and cattle. In the morning we passed the wreckage of a Halifax bomber whose seven-man crew had all died when their plane crashed into the mountainside in July 1945. One of my companions, a former wing commander, commented sadly on the "waste of men and machinery" before the names of the crew were solemnly read out one by one.

Even then, despite the pieces of broken metal, and the tributes to the dead from the British Legion, it was difficult to reconcile this history of destruction, death, and escape with the beauty of the Pyrenees, as the sun slowly began to emerge above the sea of clouds that completely obscured the world below. Wartime escapees had once traveled at night across the same terrain, sometimes running down the same vertiginous slopes that we gingerly descended, with German patrols in pursuit. Some members of our group would not have been alive had their parents or grandparents not made these crossings. Jaz, a sixty-three-year-old retired head teacher, had come to honor his Polish father, a former airman with the RAF, who had escaped twice across the Pyrenees.

For all its associations with war, danger, and hardship, the *chemin* was by no means a gloomy experience. On the last day of the trek, we trudged for forty-five thigh-burning and nerve-wracking minutes up a precarious glacier made up of tired, worn-out old snow that seemed ready to crumble beneath our feet at any moment. At one point a female member of the group began humming "La vie en rose," and the whole group joined in. For a few moments the anxiety and exhaustion were gone as the sound of our voices echoed in the silence above the steep gulley. Finally we emerged on solid ground once again at the narrow ridge at the Col de la Pale de Clauère that looked down toward Spain.

Here the NATO soldiers passed around a bottle of whisky to mark the occasion, and we shook hands, embraced, and congratulated one another as we looked down over the pine-covered mountains stretching out far below us. In that moment there could have been few members of our party who did not feel something of the exhilaration that so many escapees had once felt at having gone this far. One member of our group, an amateur escape-line historian named Keith Janes, scattered the ashes of Dot Collins, the widow of the RAF pilot Maurice Collins, who had taken this same route as a wartime escapee in 1942. In 2007 Janes had scattered her husband's ashes at the same spot. Now we watched in solemn silence as he scattered the ashes of Collins's widow, and I felt once again the invisible presence of those men and their guides who had once looked down from the pass with us, before we began the long descent, exhausted, triumphant, and exhilarated, into the Noguera Pallaresa Valley, toward the road that led down from the mountains and back to a world where freedom was too often taken for granted.

PART III

The Magic Mountains

Nature here is beautiful and majestic. The mountains surround me, reaching up to the heavens, so peaceful, so impassive, so joyful! They do not play the slightest part in our daily lives or partisan struggles; they are close to insulting us with their hideous insensitivity—but perhaps that is only their rigid outer face.

—Heinrich Heine, Letter from Cauterets, 1841[1]

7

Pioneers: The "Discovery" of the Pyrenees

Where are the scientists when the Pyrenees offer such beautiful objects of meditation? In the name of science, where are they and how have they forgotten them? I find them on the ice of Mont Blanc, on the basalt of Antrim, on the lava of Etna . . . They are everywhere, but I find myself alone here, and on Monte Perdido I have not seen anyone else.
　　　　　　　—Louis-Ramond de Carbonnières, 1797[1]

At 9,439 feet (28,777 meters), the Pic du Midi de Bigorre is one of the most visited mountains in the Hautes-Pyrénées, and this is largely due to the cable car that connects the summit to the ski resort of La Mongie about 3,300 feet (1,000 meters) down below. Every summer thousands of tourists ride up to the summit from the commercial complex of La Mongie, and those who can afford to do so can spend a night looking at the stars from the astronomical observatory on the summit. The summit was not always so accessible. In August 1776 an English traveler named Henry Swinburne arrived at the nearby hamlet of Tremes-Aigües in search of a guide to take him on what he believed to be a first ascent. Swinburne came from a wealthy Northumberland landowning family, but he was more interested in European travel than in his estates.

The previous winter he had left his family in Tarbes and crossed the Pyrenees into Spain, a journey that produced the bestselling *Travels in Spain: In the Years 1775 and 1776*. On returning to his wife and children, he embarked on a 350-mile (563-kilometer) horseback tour of the Pyrenees, which he later described in a supplement to his Spanish travelogue. It was in the course of these explorations that he came to climb the Pic du Midi. Swinburne initially struggled to find a guide, but he eventually hired a local shepherd boy to take him to the summit. About a third of the way up they reached a place where "not a trace of man or his improvements was to be discerned; no tree, no paths, no animals; all dreary, silent, and savage."[2] At this point the young guide refused to go on, saying that no one had ever been any farther. Swinburne continued alone in his "espartilles or packthread shoes," despite the heat and the absence of any water except what he was able to scoop from the occasional brackish puddle.

Eventually he reached the summit in a state of exhaustion, where he "strove to enjoy, as much as possible, the charms of the most extensive and superb view the imagination can conceive, or the eye admit," before making his descent. Swinburne's account of his Pyrenean journeys was one of the first English-language texts to bring the mountains to the attention of the gentleman traveler, and many of his readers would have been surprised by his depiction of the Pyrenees as a "grand style of landscape" where "nature exhibits her boldest features. Here every object is extended upon a vast scale, and the whole assemblage impresses the spectator with awe as well as admiration."[3]

This was not how the Pyrenees were generally perceived in the second half of the eighteenth century. When Swinburne undertook his horseback tour, the mountains were rarely visited and little was actually known about them. Their summits had not been climbed or measured, and many had not even been named. More than a century after the signing of the Treaty of the Pyrenees, the mountains had yet to be definitively mapped and the few maps of the Pyrenees that did exist were basic and often left out much more than they included. Contours were generally absent, and cartographical depictions of the Pyrenees consisted mostly of one-dimensional profiles or "horseback rider" perspectives. Beyond their main passes and crossing points, therefore, much of the Pyrenees remained essentially a terra incognita.

Much of this applied to the Alps, too, but the Alps enjoyed a very different reputation in the eyes of the outside world, as a daunting but nevertheless essential destination on the aristocratic Grand Tour, through which travelers endured the discomforts of carriages and sedan chairs in order to gain access to the cultural glories of classical civilization in Italy. The Pyrenees, by contrast, continued to constitute a remote and forbidding periphery on the southern fringes of Europe, a route to an Iberian world that few travelers except the religiously devout were inclined to visit.

In the century that followed Swinburne's solitary ascent of the Pic du Midi, all this began to change, as a stream of scientists, explorers, climbers, and adventurers made their way to the Pyrenees and presented the outside world with new information about the mountains. It was in this period, in which the Pyrenees were drawn ever-more closely into the orbits of their respective states and the wider world, that they were "discovered" for the first time as an object of scientific scrutiny, as a cultural and historical landscape and a travel destination in their own right. This "discovery" was not simply a consequence of the accumulation of information and scientific facts; it also resulted in an imaginative reinvention of the savage frontier that would make the outside world increasingly familiar with the "grand style of landscape" that Swinburne described.

Scientists and Explorers

The advent of modern science in the Pyrenees was driven by a number of overlapping factors. The intellectual curiosity unleashed by the Enlightenment and the mania for classification and exploration that accompanied it certainly played a part. So, too, did the strategic and military considerations of Spain and France, which sought to map the Pyrenees and exploit their resources in terms of minerals and energy. New scientific disciplines such as geology, paleontology, and prehistory all began to identify the Pyrenees as a landscape worthy of study from the late eighteenth century onward. According to the *Encyclopedia Britannica*, the first study of the Pyrenees "based on modern scientific methods" was not carried out until as late as 1933, and many of the methods and techniques that have since been used by geologists and paleontologists, such as radiocarbon dating, DNA and pollen analysis, and satellite photography, were still in their infancy even then.

As early as 1601 Henry IV commissioned an official named Jean de Malus to carry out an investigation into the mineral wealth in the Pyrenees, which resulted in the publication of *La recherche et découverte des mines des montagnes Pyrénées* (The Search for and Discovery of the Mines of the Pyrenean Mountains). Until the late eighteenth century such efforts were sporadic. In 1779 the Swiss physicist, geologist, and climber Horace Bénédict de Saussure (1746–99) published the first volume of *Voyages dans les Alps* (Travels in the Alps)—an innovative combination of alpine adventure, scientific study, and travelogue that inspired many writers and adventurers to follow in his footsteps.

In the last decade of the eighteenth century, some of the first important studies of the Pyrenees began to appear in French, many of which were inspired by de Saussure's work. In 1789, the year of the French Revolution, Louis-François Ramond Elizabeth de Carbonnières published *Observations faits dans les Pyrénées* (Observations Made in the Pyrenees), a landmark in Pyrenean literature. That same year Jean Boudon de Saint-Amans published *Bouquet des Pyrénées*. These studies were followed by Philippe-Isidore Picot de Lapeyrouse's herbarium *Figures de la flore des Pyrénées* (1795), a catalogue of Pyrenean plants illustrated with beautifully executed lithographic color prints by a Toulouse architect; Jean-Joseph Dusaulx's *Voyage a Barèges et dans les Hautes Pyrénées* (Journey to

Barèges and in the High Pyrenees, 1796); and François Pasumot's *Voyages physiques dans les Pyrénées* (Physical Journeys in the Pyrenees, 1797).

In *El Pireneo* (The Pyrenees, 1832) the Aragonese soldier, magistrate, and writer José de Viu y Moreu describes an encounter with a group of French geologists and botanists in Vignemale, during an excursion from his native Torla in Aragon. De Viu was somewhat disconcerted when one of the Frenchmen asked what led his countrymen to "disregard the great trunk of knowledge of the whole peninsular system" when more than twenty French writers had already written about the Pyrenees. His interlocutor attributed this negligence to a lack of patriotic interest in a mountain range that reflected the "honor of the Fatherland," and he also suggested that Spaniards were not particularly interested in science.

Galvanized by these criticisms, de Viu set out to write his own "homage to the natural history of our Pyrenees" for the benefit of his countrymen, but the fact that it was not published until 2015 to some extent bears out the Frenchman's observations. Spanish studies of the Pyrenees were not entirely absent in the eighteenth century. Books such as Francisco de Zamora's *Viaje por el alto Aragón* (Journey Through Upper Aragon, 1794), José Cornide y Saavedra's *Descripción física, civil y militar de los montes Pirineos* (Physical, Civil and Military Description of the Pyrenean Mountains, 1794), and the self-taught Catalan botanist Josep Peix's 1780 herbarium *Plantas usuals illuminidas* (Common Illuminated Plants) all testified to the emerging scientific interest in the mountains in Spain.

Nevertheless, such studies were rare in comparison with France's output. Even in the Spanish Pyrenees, the majority of scientists and explorers in the eighteenth and nineteenth centuries were Frenchmen and foreigners. Between 1750 and 1850, 209 articles on the Aragonese Pyrenees alone were published by French and foreign writers. In the 1820s a team of French military cartographers spent weeks lugging heavy surveying equipment through some of the most inaccessible areas of the Pyrenees to map the range for the *Carte de France*. The Swiss geologist and glaciologist Jean de Charpentier

(1786–1855) spent four years studying the most remote parts of the Pyrenees for the research that resulted in *Essai sur la constitution geognostíques des Pyrénées* (Essay on the Geognostic Constitution of the Pyrenees, 1823).

In 1829 the Russo-German naturalist Johann Jacob Friedrich Wilhelm Parrot (1791–1841) became the first person to walk the length of the Pyrenees from the Atlantic to the Mediterranean. In 1835 the Scottish traveler James Erskine Murray crossed the range for the first time from the opposite direction, through a combination of walking and riding horses and mules. In the summer of 1835 the Scottish physicist James David Forbes (1809–68), professor of natural philosophy at Edinburgh University, studied mineral streams between the Bréche de Roland and the Port de Benasque to research his paper "On the Temperatures and Geological Relations of Certain Hot Springs, Particularly Those of the Pyrenees" (1836).

Many of the early scientific studies of the Pyrenees were carried out by amateurs and autodidacts. The artist and cartographer Franz Schrader (1844–1924) devoted much of his life to the study of the Pyrenees. The son of freethinking parents who were influenced by the writings of Jean-Jacques Rousseau, Schrader never entered school in his native Bordeaux, in keeping with his parents' Rousseauian leanings, but he went on to become a gifted painter, draftsman, geographer, and cartographer who spoke five languages and became one of the great figures of nineteenth-century Pyrenean history. Among Schrader's many contributions to the study of the Pyrenees was the orographe, a device used for measuring elevations and distances. Schrader invented it in 1873 and used it to draw a 1:40,000-scale map of the area around Gavarnie and Mont Perdu / Monte Perdido, which caused a sensation when it was published by the Bordeaux Societé des Sciences et Physiques in 1875. Schrader's map contained the most detailed cartographical description of any part of the Pyrenees, and it attracted the attention of the Hachette publishing company and the French military engineering corps. Between 1882 and 1900 he produced a series of outstanding maps of the Pyrénées Centrales for Hachette and the French Alpine Club, which earned him the Légion d'Honneur and the presidency of the French Alpine Club from 1900 to 1903.

Local inhabitants of the Pyrenees also studied the mountains that they knew at firsthand. The village of Béost-Bagès in the Vallée d'Ossau has planted a botanical trail containing numerous endemic species in honor of the "shepherd-botanist" Pierrine Gaston-Sacaze (1797–1893), who was born in the village. Gaston-Sacaze worked as a shepherd, but he was also an accomplished ornithologist, geologist, minerologist, and musician, who initially turned to botany while searching for plant remedies to cure sick sheep. To further his botanical interests, Gaston-Sacaze taught himself Latin and identified and classified hundreds of plants according to the system devised by the great Swedish naturalist Carl Linnaeus, and his findings were published in the bulletin of the Société des Sciences, Lettres et Arts in Pau, in addition to various herbariums, some of which were illustrated with his own drawings.

Alphonse Meillon (1862–1933), a hotel owner from Cauterets, drew up a number of maps of the surrounding mountains, including the first 1:20,000 map of Vignemale, during his holidays, and he was one of the first cartographers to use photography in the course of his work. For Meillon, science also provided an opportunity to express his "profound love and most intense admiration" for the mountains that had first excercised their "force of seduction" during his Cauterets childhood.[4] Piérrine Gaston-Sacaze similarly regarded his work as a labor of love and insisted that the study of nature "reduces the taste for frivolous entertainments, it prevents an excess of passion and brings beneficial nourishment to the soul, filling it with the most worthy object of contemplation."[5]

Franz Schrader's beautiful maps, like his paintings, were a tribute to the mountains that he first saw during a visit to Pau as a young man. Schrader often compared cartography to art and he once wrote of "those moments of profound poetry in which one enjoys one or two hours of the full and strong flavour of life" that he experienced in the Aragonese Pyrenees.

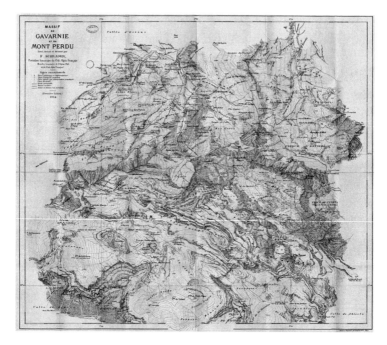

Cartography as art: Franz Schrader, *Carte du massif de Gavarnie et du mont Perdu*, 1914 (Wikimedia Commons).

The Baron in the Mountains

This passionate response to the mountains was as much a part of the "discovery" of the Pyrenees as the accumulation of scientific knowledge about the mountains. The term *pyrénéisme* was coined in 1897 by the historian, geographer, and publisher Henri Béraldi, in the first volume of his monumental history *Cent ans aux Pyrénées* (One Hundred Years in the Pyrenees, 1897). For Béraldi, "The picturesque knowledge of the Pyrenees—not to be confused with their scientific knowledge—is now complete. It has taken a century of effort, whose traces in a series of writings form the history of Pyreneism—one says Pyreneism as one says Alpinism."[6]

This emphasis on "picturesque knowledge" was very different from the physical mountain challenges and conquests of iconic peaks associated with Alpinism. In an address to the Societé de Géographie in Paris 1902, Béraldi argued that even visitors who confined themselves to Pyrenean valleys and spa towns could be *pyrénéistes*, since "the pyreneist's ideal is to know how to climb, write and feel, all wrapped-up in one. If he writes without climbing, he can do nothing. If he climbs without writing, he leaves nothing." The most influential exponent of this "picturesque knowledge" was the politician, writer, explorer, geologist, and botanist Louis-François Elizabeth Ramond de Carbonnières (1755–1827). Ramond was born in Strasbourg and studied medicine and law at the University of Strasbourg at the same time as Goethe, but he never became a doctor or a lawyer. In 1777 he traveled to the Swiss Alps, where he read the English traveler and future archdeacon of Salisbury William Coxe's *Sketches of the Natural, Civil and Political History of Switzerland*.

Ramond translated Coxe's book into French and accompanied his translation with his own commentary and observations, which often contradicted its author's. These unsolicited observations did not please Coxe himself, but the book was well received in France. In 1781 Ramond became secretary to Cardinal Louis de Rohan, archbishop of Strasbourg and a confidant of Louis XVI. In 1787 Rohan was exiled from the French court, following his involvement with a crooked scheme involving the occult fraudster Cagliostro and Marie Antoinette.

Ramond accompanied his patron into a temporary exile at the spa town of Barèges. While the disgraced archbishop took the waters, Ramond joyfully roamed the mountains. Whether climbing through ice fields above the Cirque du Gavarnie to measure glaciers, or scrambling up the Cilindro de Malboré to study rock formations, Ramond combined the meticulous research skills and eye for detail of a gifted amateur scientist with a disregard for his own safety that reflected his belief that the naturalist should "leave behind him those mountains which are vulgarly famous . . .

to abandon himself in company with the shepherd, the hunter of the izard, and the smuggler, to the dangers of their secret paths."[7]

These explorations resulted in the remarkable *Observations faites dans les Pyrénées*, which combined scientific descriptions of rock formations, glaciers, and flowers with a streak of melancholic romanticism. Jules Michelet once dismissed Ramond as a disillusioned follower of "the dreams of Cagliostro and the worship of Nature" who "took his stand on the threshold of the Revolution, hoping for the deliverance of the human race" and subsequently turned "with the same vehemency toward Nature."[8] This harsh assessment is not entirely inaccurate. Though Ramond initially welcomed the Revolution and was elected to the Legislative Assembly in 1791 as a moderate constitutionalist, in the summer of 1792 his opposition to the Jacobins obliged him to withdraw to Tarbes in order to escape the political turmoil in the capital.

In 1794 he spent ten months under house arrest, and on his release he became professor of natural history at *l'école central* in Tarbes, a position that allowed him to devote his time to his studies of the Pyrenees. In 1797 he made the first of three attempts to climb Mont Perdu / Monte Perdido, an expedition that resulted in *Voyages au Mont-Perdu et dans la partie adjacente des Hautes-Pyrénées* (Journeys to Monte Perdu and the Neighboring Parts of the High Pyrenees, 1801). Ramond was a methodical geologist, botanist, and naturalist, and he also compiled an unpublished herbarium with more than 10,000 different plants, 850 of which were Pyrenean species.

His contribution to the Pyrenees was not due simply to his scientific discoveries, however, but also to his romantic and often rapturous epiphanies, such as his description of the Campan Valley as "an apparition by which we may anticipate the future world. It exemplifies that state of calmness and peace, so well announced . . . so capable of foreseeing what may be expected from the perfectibility of the earth. Such will be, hereafter, all the vallies of the Pyrenees and of the Alps, of the Caucasus, of the Atlas and the Andes, when the powers of production shall have attained an equilibrium with those of destruction."[9]

Ramond's writings are filled with similar passages about the mountains that defined his professional and personal life. Ramond never entirely turned his back on what he called "the horizontal plane" and continued to alternate among politics, science, and the Pyrenees throughout his life, but he was always happiest in the mountains, in the company of guides, smugglers, and shepherds. In 1802 he moved back to Paris, where he became a member of the French Academy of Science and married. In 1806 he was appointed by Napoléon as prefect of Puy-de-Dôme and was subsequently made a baron of the empire for his contributions to science. In 1813 the first English translation of *Observations faites dans les Pyrénées* was published, at a time when "the banners of British soldiers are floating over the Pyrenees," as its translator put it, to provide information to Wellington's invading armies.

The following year Ramond's Paris house was ransacked by Cossacks during the Allied occupation of France, and a number of his unpublished manuscripts were destroyed. His beautifully illustrated herbarium survived and provided him with consolation in his old age. "I find myself now with my herbarium and the memories that accompany it. Outside of this everything else has become superfluous to me," he said shortly before his death in 1827.[10] He was buried in Montmartre, far from the mountains that his expeditions and writings had done so much to bring to the attention of his compatriots and the wider world.

In the summer of 2015 I drove up the Vallée d'Ossau with my wife and daughter toward the 9,461-foot (2,884-meter) Pic du Midi d'Ossau, which Ramond first climbed in 1787. "Here upon the Pic du Midi we are not beyond the sphere of the world," he wrote. "We are above it and observe it; the dwellings of man are still beneath us; their agitations fresh in the memory, and the expanding heart still trembles with a somewhat of remaining passion."[11] We had not come to climb the summit ourselves, but to do the circuit walk of the mountain that locals call "Jean-Pierre." Ramond was nevertheless very much on my mind as we left the car at the Lac de Bious-Artigues and walked up through the forest to the Bious pasturelands at the base of the mountain.

The year 2015 was a particularly bad one in the twenty-first-century "horizontal plane," with the Islamic State running amok in Iraq and Syria and thousands of refugees drowning in the Mediterranean, and it was not difficult to understand how Ramond had once found solace from the tumultuous and often brutal events of his own time. After about forty minutes we crossed the little stream and walked into the Bious pasturelands, and found ourselves in a landscape that was as perfect as anything I had ever seen. All over the meadow, hikers and picnickers were making their way past semi-wild Pyrenean ponies cavorting in the grass and herds of long-horned cattle and sheep that seemed indifferent to their presence. Directly in front of us, the forest gave way to the distinctive twin peaks of Jean-Pierre, which reached up toward the sky like a gaping mouth. It was a classic Pyrenean combination of the savage and the pastoral, and it seemed to me then like an image of peace on earth that recalled the first tryptich of Hieronymus Bosch's *Garden of Earthly Delights*.

I felt euphoric and slightly intoxicated by this spectacle, as if the weight of the world had suddenly grown lighter, as the path began to zigzag up steeply through the forest to our left. After about two hours of hard, sweaty climbing we found ourselves walking beneath the great mass of pink and rust-colored rock covered with patches of green lichen that constituted the mighty southern face of Jean-Pierre, and we continued up and around the mountain, scrambling over piles of giant boulders till we reached a high ridge looking toward the Col de Suzon. The walk was supposed to take only about five hours, but it was late afternoon before we reached the col and heard the muted voices of climbers drifting down from the summit that Ramond had once ascended more than two centuries ago.

I had no desire to join them. It was enough to contemplate the mountain from where we were, and as we made our way down marshy glens and valleys, I saw a large flock of sheep whose bells rang out across the mountains, and I felt "that charm, which I have so often known, so often tasted upon the mountains, that vague content, that lightness of body, that agility of limb, and that serenity of mind, which are all so sweet to experience, but so difficult to paint" that Ramond once described so well. I thought of him then, as a Pyrenean variant on Italo Calvino's allegory *The Baron in the Trees*—the Enlightenment aristocrat who resolves to live in trees and never touches ground for the rest of his life—and I quietly thanked him for making this unforgettable day possible and for bringing these remarkable mountains to the attention of an outside world that had previously tended to regard them as something to be avoided.

The King of Vignemale

Ramond's life and writings inspired many people to follow in his footsteps. His most famous disciple was Count Henry Patrick Marie Russell-Killough, Baron of Ulster (1834–1909), the most colorfully exotic *pyrénéiste* of the nineteenth century.[12] Born in Toulouse into a rich Irish-French family, Russell first saw the Pyrenees as a child, during a day trip from Pau, and he spent much of his adult life exploring the mountains, sometimes alone or accompanied by a guide or members of the select band of friends who called themselves "le happy few." Like Ramond, Russell rarely used ropes, ice axes, or even crampons, crossing glaciers and ice fields in a tweed jacket and waistcoat, boots and gaiters, with his alpenstock and the occasional "microscopic pocket axes" that he and his companions used to cut steps in ice.

He spurned tents and preferred to camp out in his tight-fitting sheepskin sleeping bag. Even the most life-threatening nights spent in snowstorms or torrential rain did not incline him to change his modus operandi. A thin, wiry man with piercing eyes and a goatee, Russell combined this hardiness with a taste for the waltzes, good food, wine, and classical music that he enjoyed in Pau. But like Ramond, his spiritual home was in the Pyrenees. "The worship of mountains has a profound effect on the spirit," he declared. "They offer a sublime perspective of the material world. What is gas, electric light and fireworks when one has seen the moon rise resplendent, on a beautiful summer night on the austere glaciers of the Maladetta?"[13]

In his most famous book, *Souvenirs d'un montagnard* (Souvenirs of a Mountain Man, 1878), Russell looked back on his years spent on "the bare and lonely summits where the pale northern light illuminates . . . in the brilliancy and calm of the eternal dome, in the sanctuary of that Thabor of snow, where circled by space, by frost, and by death, one meditates with as much love as sorrow on the happy hours, on the thrice blessed days, on the tranquil years which will never return." No summit moved him more than Vignemale (10,820 feet / 3,298 meters), the highest mountain in the French Pyrenees, straddling the French-Spanish border above Gavarnie, for which he developed something of an *amour fou*.

On September 14, 1861, he made the first of thirty-two ascents of the summit, and his passion for Vignemale went beyond mere contemplation. On August 26, 1880, he and his guides made a seven-hour climb to the summit, which they celebrated with hot punch and Chartreuse. Russell ordered his servants to dig a ditch and bury him in his sheepskin sleeping bag beneath a pile of earth and stones, leaving only his head exposed. For the rest of the night he remained buried on the summit, while his men descended to a more sheltered spot farther down. "There I was alone in the darkness on one of the wildest coldest peaks of the Pyrenees," he recalled. "Three hundred meters below was an immense ocean of clouds from which rose islands of snow or granite, which seemed to quiver in the subtle light of the moon. There was an unnatural deathly silence. Without being able to see the horizon, it seemed as though I had left the earth."[14]

These sensations instilled in Russell a desire to spend even more extended periods on Vignemale. Tents and huts were out of the question, since he regarded them as an indecorous civilized intrusion. Instead he decided to construct an "artificial cave" close to the

The king of Vignemale overseeing the construction of a new cave. Russell is in the foreground on the right. (Eugène Trutat, ca. 1882–1884; Bibliothèque de Toulouse, Wikimedia Commons)

summit, and he promptly obtained a lifelong lease of Vignemale from the commune of Cauterets for the purpose. In 1881, Russell's workmen blasted and dug out a cave above the Ossoue glacier, which he equipped with wine, champagne, food, and even a carpet that his long-suffering servants brought up from Pau.

Like his earlier "burial," Russell's caves were not simply an expression of aristocratic eccentricity; they were places of worship, where he and his friends could pay homage to a mountain landscape that Russell regarded as an expression of the sacred and the anteroom to the next world. On August 12, 1884, he invited two priests and a group of friends to celebrate mass in front of one of his caves at sunrise, a ceremony that he described as "more moving and eloquent than all the pomp of a basilica. Paris or Rome had never seen anything like it. One seemed closer to heaven than under the most splendid vaults of the world."[15] Russell had seven caves built, including one specifically for women, culminating in the grotto he called Le Paradis, which was built just below the summit in 1893. Visitors often came to "Paradise" in search of "the King of Vignemale" and "le Robinson des Pyrénées." In 1892 Russell's great friend Baron Bertrand de Lassus spent five nights sheltering with him from a gale in one of the lower caves. When the wind finally subsided just after midnight, Lassus suddenly announced that he wished to climb to the summit. Russell naturally approved of this suggestion, and Lassus later described how he and his porters and guides set out across the "gigantic chaos of ice, ancient as the world" and circumnavigated "a vast labyrinth of unfathomable abysses" before reaching Le Paradis in the early hours of the morning.[16]

Shortly before dawn Lassus made himself some more punch and went up to the summit with a blanket wrapped around him and immersed himself a "solitude, touched by the universal meditation of nature" as the sun came up. Finally he descended to the grottoes, where Russell greeted him with a "real banquet" and the two friends "solemnly promised, if it pleased Providence, to meet again the following year at the Paradise." By this time Russell's years of climbing were drawing to a close. In 1904, he reached the Bellevue caves for the last time at the age of seventy, and retired to his family home in Biarritz, where he took to signing Christmas cards with names like Le Solitaire du Vignemale and the Dreamer of Vignemale, before his death in 1910, far from the cave where he had once contemplated paradise.

Both Russell's writings and his romantic temperament place him firmly within the tradition of "picturesque knowledge" defined by Béraldi and have fimly enshrined him as the most influential of the "pioneers" who defined *pyrénéisme* in the second half of the nineteenth century, many of whom, such as Schrader and Béraldi himself, were members of his circle. Not all of them were cut from the same cloth. The Englishman Charles Packe (1826–96) was a friend of Russell's and a cofounder of the Société Ramond, which was established at Gavarnie in 1865 to promote the study of the Pyrenees. Educated at Eton and Oxford, Packe was another of the upper-class travelers who dominated nineteenth-century *pyrénéisme* and whose inherited wealth enabled him to dedicate his life to his love of the outdoors. Packe made numerous expeditions into the Pyrenees, sometimes accompanied by his two Pyrenean mountain dogs, and sometimes by Russell. He shared Russell's spartan toughness, describing a typical walking schedule in which he would "rise at daybreak after night on the hard ground, take a cup of tea and a nibble of bread, and thereupon walk for five, six or seven hours before breakfast; after that there was no more eating till we made our bivouac a little before sunset, and no rest, except perhaps an hour's siesta in the hottest part of the day."[17]

In other respects he was a very different character. In 1865 he and Russell spent the summer together in the Maladeta. "Whilst I indulged in eccentric, solitary ascents of untrodden and snowy peaks . . . Packe did more useful things," Russell wrote. "He mapped those peaks, he measured and named them, botanized in their valleys, and read their history in their rocks and fossils."[18] In 1867 Packe published *A Guide to the Pyrenees: Especially Intended for the Use of Mountaineers*, the first English-language guide to the Pyrenees. Packe's matter-of-fact prose avoided the rapturous passages to which Ramond and Russell were prone, on the not unreasonable grounds that "in the face of Nature itself, which speaks to its admirers in a language so far more eloquent than pen or pencil, description is worse than useless."[19]

Instead his guidebook contained detailed nuts-and-bolts information on train times, walking routes, distances, and timings, which he hoped would attract his countrymen to visit the mountains. In it Packe expressed his exasperation at the lack of such visitors and complained that "so many Englishmen and Englishwomen cross the Channel every summer for the sake of a holiday tour of a month or six weeks among the Alps of Switzerland, while so very few in proportion think it is worth their while to pay a visit to the Pyrenees, that magnificent mountain barrier that separates France and

Spain." This, Packe declared, was a "matter of astonishment" to him, because even though the Pyrenees were "inferior, indeed, to the Alps in height and expanse of barren glacier, they were "far more picturesque in form as well as colour."[20]

Such language was firmly within the *pyrénéiste* tradition. This emphasis on the picturesque did not mean that *pyrénéisme* was an exclusively aesthetic or cultural pursuit. One of Packe's clients was the British scientist and pioneer of eugenics Sir Francis Galton, who later described how he first became "bitten by the mania for mountain climbing" during a series of excursions around Luchon in 1860.[21] Galton described Packe as "an authority on the mountains and botany of the locality," and the pleasure that he took in the fauna, the vagaries of the Pyrenean climate, and the physical resilience required to explore it would certainly have appealed to his guide. Franz Schrader climbed numerous Pyrenean peaks, including a first ascent of Grand Batchimale (10,423 feet / 3,177 meters), on August 11, 1878, which was subsequently named Pic Schrader. Henri Brulle (1854–1936), a French lawyer and another member of Russell's circle, made more than two hundred ascents in the Pyrenees before World War I. Brulle was a climber more than a walker, who relished his ability to withstand hailstorms, ice, and other difficult winter conditions. On August 7, 1889, he made the first ascent of the Couloir de Gaube, a vertiginous gash in the north face of the Vignemale considered to be one of the most difficult climbs in the Pyrenees, with a team that included one of Russell's most trusted guides, Célestin Passet.

Brulle's attitude to mountaineering was summed up by the motto on his ice axe: *In utremque paratus* (Prepared for either alternative). After the death of his wife and son during World War I, he never returned to the Pyrenees. In 1936 he attempted to climb Mont Blanc at the incredible age of eighty-two; he died as a result of pneumonia contracted while descending in a heavy snowstorm. Other nineteenth-century *pyrénéistes* came from a similar social background, such as Roger de Monts, (1850–1914) another friend of Russell's, who took up mountain climbing to escape a broken heart and went on to make numerous historic ascents, such as the north face of Mont Perdu/Monte Perdido, before he finally married the object of his affections in 1896 and abandoned the mountains.[22]

If the Pyrenees did not have any mountains to match the macabre fascination of the Matterhorn, they were not without risks. In 1824 two mining engineers, Edouard Blavier and Edouard de Bully, attempted to climb the Pic de la Maladeta with their guide, a man called Barreau. While looking for a way around the snow-covered glacier that connected the mountain to the nearby Pico d'Aneto, Barreau sank into a concealed crevasse, shouting, "My God, I'm finished. I'm drowning!" His two companions were unable to come to his assistance and forced to spend the night on the mountain listening to his dying calls for help.

For the most part pyreneism was a male pursuit, but women were not absent. Though Vignemale is most famously associated with Russell, the first touristic ascent of the summit was made in 1837 by an Englishwoman known as Anne Lister (1791–1840). Lister was a Tory landowner and a lesbian, known as "Gentleman Jack" in her native Yorkshire for her masculine appearance, who once declared in her diaries, "I love and only love the fairer sex and thus beloved by them in turn, my heart revolts from any love but theirs."[23] She was also a prolific traveler and mountaineer. On August 7, 1838, she contracted with a local guide named Henri Cazaux to take her to the summit of Vignemale. Lister had already attempted an ascent two days before, but she had been forced to turn back because of bad weather. While waiting for the weather to change she heard that Napoléon Ney, Prince of Moskowa, the son of Napoléon Bonaparte's legendary marshal, intended to make an ascent on the summit that week, and she decided to make another attempt.

Wearing a cloak and petticoat with her dress taped up around her knees, Lister and her party reached the summit at one o'clock, where they wrote their names in a bottle and left it under a pile of stones. Four days later Moskowa made the same ascent with Cazaux, who neglected to tell his employer that Lister had already reached it, so that Moskowa claimed to have made the first ascent. When Lister found out she was so furious that she refused to pay Cazaux and threatened legal action until he agreed to sign a statement saying that she had reached the summit first. Though Moskowa acknowledged that Cazaux had deceived him, he subsequently wrote an account of the climb for the journal *Galigni's Messenger* that contained an account of his climb claiming that he had reached the summit first.

In September the *Messenger* published a corrective written by Lister herself, which admitted that "an English lady had, four days before, ascended with three guides to the same summit." Two years later Lister died of fever while traveling in the Caucasus mountains in Georgia. That same year *Chambers Edinburgh Journal* reported—inaccurately—that the Prince of Moscow and his brother had been the first to make the ascent in 1837, and included the prince's own account of the journey with a guide named "Cantoux." It was not until 1968 that a full account of Lister's ascent, based on her own diaries, was published in the *Alpine Journal*, which definitively recognized her place in Pyrenean history.

Pathfinders

Such climbs would not have been possible without the mountain guides, like Cazaux, most of whom behaved more honorably than he did. Many of the guides who participated in the "heroic age" of nineteenth-century pyreneism were farmers, shepherds, or smugglers, who initially worked as guides for chamois and izard hunters before turning to mountaineering. In addition to navigation, these guides often carried out the more "proletarian" tasks that climbing entailed, such as carrying food and supplies or cutting steps in ice and snow. Some became professional or semiprofessional and formed guiding dynasties, such as the Passet family from Gavarnie. Henri Passet (1845–1919) accompanied Charles Packe on some of his trips to the Pyrenees, the Alps, and the Sierra Nevada. His cousin

Célestin Passet (1845–1917)—one of Russell's favorite guides—began guiding hunters and went on to become one of the most famous guides of the nineteenth century. Elegantly dressed even in the mountains, Passet was one of the few Pyrenean guides to have a place named after him, the Punta Célestin Passet in the Vall de Boí in the Catalan Pyrenees.

In most cases, the first ascents that such men facilitated were named after their wealthier clients. By 1900, mountain guiding had become a highly competitive profession in the Pyrenees, and the demand for guides had begun to outstrip availability. In July that year guides from the town of Cauterets organized a race to Vignemale in an attempt to challenge the traditional dominance of the profession by their counterparts in Gavarnie and establish a reputation for themselves that would enable them to attract more clients. On Sunday, July 29, a large crowd of tourists and locals gathered at dawn in the main square to watch dozens of professional and amateur guides from across the Pyrenees walk the 32-mile (52-kilometer) circular route to the Vignemale summit and back again. Some contestants were barefoot, while others wore only espadrilles. As its sponsors had hoped, the race was won by three guides from Cauterets, who completed the route in six hours and seventeen minutes. Whether they succeeded in displacing the guides of Gavarnie is not known, but the race proved so popular that it began an annual competition for the "Vignemale trophy," which continues to this day.

The Second Wave

The increased popularity of the Pyrenees also meant that the aristocratic and upper-middle-class adventurers who had dominated pyreneism for most of the century no longer had the mountains to themselves. In 1874 the newly formed French Alpine Club built the first of a chain of refuges and shelters in the Pyrenees on a narrow pass overlooking the north face of Mont Perdu/Monte

Perdido. In 1902 the Centre Excursionista de Catalunya (Catalan Excursionist Centre) began to publish the first guidebooks to the Catalan Pyrenees. This was followed by the formation of the Federación Española de Deportes de Montaña y Escalada (the Spanish Alpine Club) in 1922, and the Groupe Pyrénéiste de Haute-Montagne (High Mountain Pyreneist Group), dedicated to the more challenging Pyrenean climbs known generically as "difficulty pyreneism," which was founded in Lourdes on July 11, 1933.

The climbers, hikers, and "excursionists" of the twentieth century tended to come from a humbler social background than their nineteenth-century predecessors. Unlike the nineteenth-century adventurers, they included Spaniards, such as the Aragonese climbers Alberto Rabadá and Ernesto Navarro, two friends and workmates from Zaragoza, who carried out a number of pioneering climbs in the Aragonese Pyrenees before they died attempting to climb the north face of the Eiger in 1963. For the most part, however, the most famous names in twentieth-century pyreneism were Frenchmen. They included the five sons of a French Protestant pastor named Alfred Cadier, who undertook a series of 10,000-foot (3,000-meter) climbs and explorations of the Pico d'Aneto and the Balaïtous from their home village of Osse-en-Aspe in the Aspe Valley. The British diplomat and mountaineer Sir Douglas Busk (1906–90) lived in Osse-en-Aspe in the Vallée d'Aspe while studying French as a student, and some of his first climbs were carried out with locals from the village, including the Cadier brothers themselves, whose achievements had already made them legendary.

Many years later Busk looked back fondly on these improvised expeditions in which he and his friends cycled out into the mountains on the weekends and slept under blankets in improvised bivouacs before heading up onto snow-covered slopes without crampons, ice axes, or the "hated ropes" that these "free-striding hill folk" and "magnificent natural mountaineers" spurned, for "the great Cadier brothers and their relations loved freedom as much as they loved their hills, and in such 'safe' country they need and would only rarely submit to the shackles." Other twentieth-century *pyrénéistes* also spurned these "shackles."[24] The twin brothers Jean and Pierre Ravier opened up some two hundred routes in the Pyrenees between 1950 and the mid-1970s, using the most rudimentary equipment. The Ravier brothers were born in Paris in 1933 and moved to Bordeaux with their family, where they began to climb the Pyrenees during holidays and on the weekends. By the age of seventeen, they had already climbed the fearsome Couloir de Gaube, and they went on to make numerous iconic Pyrenean ascents. Both brothers were pacifists and conscientious objectors and brought their techniques to bear in a number of political protests. During the Algerian War, Pierre Ravier was imprisoned for six months because of his opposition to the war, and in 1960 the twins climbed Bordeaux Cathedral and draped a banner opposing the war.

The Hollow Pyrenees

The English writer and Pyrenean expert Kev Reynolds has written of the "headlong search for ever-greater difficulties, leading to the exploration of novel routes on little-touched spires and long-forgotten faces" that characterized modern pyreneism, and such explorations were not limited to the surface of the mountains. In 1850 Frédéric Petit, the director of the Toulouse Academy of Science and the recently built Toulouse astronomical observatory, startled his colleagues by informing them that the Pyrenees were hollow. Petit based his conclusions on astronomical calculations made from his observatory, using pendulum oscillations and observations of the stars, which led him to conclude that "the inside of the Pyrenees was almost totally empty." This proposition was roundly rejected by Alexandre Leymerie, one of Petit's colleagues at the Toulouse Academy, and a leading exponent of the emerging science of geology.[25]

Leymerie argued that Petit had failed to take into account certain valleys "which cut the mountains throughout their length" without any obvious cavities that would have revealed hollowness, and that "an experienced geologist can follow . . . all the strata on top of one another around the granite core without the least interruption." Petit responded by accusing Leymerie of a lack of knowledge of astronomy, and the acrimonious debate spilled out into the local newspapers, until the science faculty ordered both scientists not to publish any more exchanges on the matter.

Posterity has found in Leymerie's favor, but Petit cannot be blamed entirely for thinking that the Pyrenees were "hollow" in a mountain range where the combination of limestone and running water has produced some of the largest caves in Europe. The giant Mas-d'Azil cave in the Ariège is 164 feet (50 meters) high and nearly 1,640 feet (500 meters) long, and easily incoporates the D119 road that now runs through it. The 29-mile (39-kilometer) Grotte de Lombrives cave system at the eastern edge of the Pyrénées Ariégeoises Natural Regional Park is the largest cave system in Europe and contains galleries that reach as high as 262 feet (80 meters). The caves of the Pyrenees also contain a high concentration of Paleolithic parietal (wall) paintings and portable cave art, whose discovery coincided with the emergence of prehistory as an academic discipline in the late nineteenth and early twentieth centuries.

As early as the 1860s a French scholar named Félix Garrigou had begun to explore the caves of the Pyrenees, where he found various cave pictures and carved pebbles. At this time few academic experts were willing to consider the possibility that "cave art" had Stone Age origins, and such findings were usually dismissed as the work of Roman soldiers, Celts, or children. In 1879 the Spanish nobleman Marcelino Sanz de Sautuola discovered a series of animal pictures in the Altamira cave in Cantabria, which he argued shared the same age as the Paleolithic remains he discovered on the cave floor. This thesis was initially dismissed by the academic establishment, most famously by Émile Cartailhac (1845–1921), the doyen of French prehistorians.

In 1902 Sanz de Sautuola was officially vindicated, when Cartailhac visited Altamira and issued a mea culpa. Cartailhac was one of various prehistorians attending the Montauban Congress of the French Association for the Advancement of Sciences that same year who went off to inspect various decorated caves in the Dordogne, in what was effectively the first official recognition that cave art had prehistoric origins. As a result of this breakthrough, Pyrenean caves also became an object of study for palaeontologists, archaeologists, and amateur explorers. The bison paintings in the Marsoulas cave in 1897; the animal pictures of the Mas-d'Azil in 1901; the clay animal sculptures discovered by Count Henri Begouen and his three sons during their explorations of the Tuc d'Audobert cave in 1913; the handprints at the Grottes de Gargas in 1906; the decorated galleries of the Trois-Frères caves at Montesquieu-Avantès, with their 350-odd pictures that included the anthropomorphic figure known as "the Sorcerer"—all these discoveries and explorations established the Pyrenees as a new "page" on which humanity's prehistoric origins were written.

Such explorations often demanded a similar level of physical commitment to the mountains themselves. Count Begouen and his sons explored the Tuc d'Audobert on an improvised raft, and on one occasion spent twelve hours on a ledge during a flash flood. The French clergyman and archaeologist Abbé Henri Breuil (1877–1961), the "Pope of Prehistory," explored caves in his cassock, which he was forced to take off when the shafts obliged him to crawl through them. Breuil spent hours using florist's or rice paper to trace drawings directly from cave walls, while his assistants held out candles or carbide lamps to guide his progress, or while lying on his back on sacks filled with ferns.

One of the most daring French speleologists of the twentieth century was Norbert Casteret (1897–1997), who first became enamored with caves and caving as a consequence of his boyhood reading of Jules Verne's *Journey to the Centre of the Earth*. Casteret's first Pyrenean descent took place as a boy, when he found a pamphlet in his father's attic describing the discovery of prehistoric animal bones that included hyena skeletons at the Cave of Montsaunès near his home in the Midi-Pyrénées. The next day he headed out to the cave, equipped with only a candle and a box of matches. "Lying on my stomach, candle in hand, eyes searching the gloom, I felt myself a new Argonaut on the brink of an unknown world, trying to pierce the darkness of the past," he later recalled.[26]

Casteret's physical resilience was strengthened by his experiences in the trenches in World War I. His claustrophobic memoir *Ten Years Under the Earth* (1939) is laced with military references to "forcing" and "assaulting" caves that "resisted" his efforts, such as the cave of Montespan, near Saint-Gaudens, where he made his first historic discovery. In 1923 Casteret entered the cave through a crevice using his standard modus operandi. After stripping naked he descended into the cave with a candle and matches and a rubber hat that he used to keep them dry. After he had waded through shallow water for 150 yards (137 meters), the cave began to dip. Casteret continued till he was up to his neck.

Alone in "the awful silence and loneliness," Casteret considered the various possibilities of death that awaited him, and then left a burning candle on a ledge before lowering himself into the water, swimming and using his fingertips to guide him, till he finally surfaced and found himself in total darkness. At this point he turned back, but he returned the next day till he found a bison's tooth, which convinced him that the cave had once been inhabited. The following year he came back to Montespan with his friend the swimmer Henri Godin, and the two men penetrated farther into the cave, until Casteret discovered the large clay statue of a bear with its head missing. "I was moved as I have seldom been moved before or since," he wrote. "Here I saw, unchanged by the march of aeons, a piece of sculpture which distinguished scientists of all countries have since recognized as the oldest statue in the world."[27]

In addition to the statue of the cave bear, Casteret and Godin found statues and engravings of lions, horses, hyenas, bison, and other animals, and human footprints and the claw marks of animals of Magdalenian origin. These sensational discoveries transformed

Casteret himself into a national figure and eventually earned him a gold award from the Académie des Sports. Like any pyreneist, Casteret also wrote, combining gripping descriptions of his dangerous adventures with a celebration of the beauty of the subterranean world that he explored and the sense of wonder and exhilaration that he took from his discovery of the prehistoric artifacts beneath the mountains.

The Cradle of Pyreneism

In the summer of 1881, the art critic Henry Blackburn and the artist Gustave Doré visited Gavarnie, where they found Charles Packe staying at the same inn. Packe had spent much of the summer in Gavarnie by himself, and echoed the same complaint in his guidebook that so many of his compatriots still preferred the Alps to the Pyrenees. "There is something about the life of this solitary Englishman among the mountains, that seems to us pathetically interesting," Blackburn observed, "because notwithstanding all he has done to lay down routes and lead the way through the Pyrenees, he has but few sympathizers and scarcely any followers, even amongst his confrères, the members of the Alpine Club."[28]

Within a few years this situation had already begun to change dramatically. By the end of the century so many tourists had begun to arrive in Gavarnie every summer that a new Grand Hotel was built to accomodate them. In 1900 Henri Brulle described how "a tide of progress changed Gavarnie, the tourists, the auberges, even the traditional storm of 20 August forgot to arrive." Today Packe would have little reason to complain. Gavarnie belongs to a UNESCO World Heritage Site that spans 75,711 acres (30,639 hectares) in Spain and France, and which attracts more than a million visitors every year, who pass through to picnic, take photographs, or explore the mountains on foot or on horseback. Most walkers follow well-trod paths and trails that were once known only to smugglers

"Nature's colosseum." The Cirque of Gavarnie, ca. 1890–1900 (Library of Congress).

and shepherds in Ramond's time, and stay in refuges and shelters that are often booked up for weeks in the summer months. In the mornings these shelters echo to the sound of scraping Velcro and the swishing of Gortex, as bleary-eyed hikers strap on state-of-the-art equipment and follow the routes that were once taken by men wearing tweed coats and carrying alpenstocks.

I came to Gavarnie when it was less busy, on a chilly overcast day in early September, in a taxi from Lourdes. At the entrance to the village, we passed a bronze sculpture of Russell seated in a pensive position with his chin resting on one hand, looking up toward Vignemale. On turning the corner we saw the great cirque rising out of the flat valley floor. Even after all the descriptions I had read, and the numerous paintings, drawings, and photographs that I had seen, "the Colosseum of the Pyrenees," as Victor Hugo once described it,[29] is a moving and incredible sight, with its enormous cataract tumbling 4,500 feet (1,380 meters) down the massive bowl-shaped rock with puffs of cloud hovering over it.

The village of Gavarnie is unprepossessing and purely functional, with a permanent population of 150-odd inhabitants, most of whom make their living through the chalet-style hotels, restaurants, and outdoor shops that line the streets selling postcards, walking sticks, and outdoor gear among the more stolid and grander buildings left over from another era. The creamy-white Hôtel des Voyageurs, where Russell, Packe, Brulle, and so many of the nineteenth-century *pyrénéistes* once stayed, is a burned-out wreck, still awaiting redevelopment after a fire that destroyed the interior of the building in 2000. On the outskirts of the village a little cemetery next to the twelfth-century church contains some of the most celebrated names of nineteenth-century pyreneism, from the great guides Célestin Passet and Francois-Bernat Salles, to twentieth-century climbers such as Dr. Jean Arlaud (1896–1938), mountaineer and president of the French Skiing Federation, who was buried here after his premature death in a climbing accident.

In one corner of the cemetery a mound of rock and earth contains various plaques commemorating "our dear martyrs dead in the mountains" who have died exploring, climbing, or walking in the mountains. Another plaque is dedicated to the *pyrénéistes* who died during World War I. Walk out up and beyond the village to the right, and the path climbs gently upward toward a little plateau overlooking the cirque, known as the Turon de la Courade. Here a flat tomb just out of the nearby rock face bears two plaques, for Louis and Margalide Le Bondidier, (1878–1945, 1880–1960) two of the great figures of twentieth-century pyreneism. In 1921, the Bondidiers persuaded the local authorities in nearby Lourdes to establish the first museum dedicated exclusively to the Pyrenees. Acting on the principle that "nothing Pyrenean must be foreign to us," the Le Bondidiers became curators of the Pyrenean Museum at Lourdes castle, which now contains the most comprehensive collection of books and documents relating to the history, culture, folklore, and ethnography of the Pyrenees in the world. For the Le Bondidiers, like Franz Schrader's maps and paintings, this initiative was an homage and a labor of love. Their tomb is inscribed with an observation that Schrader once made; it serves as an epitaph for Ramond, Russell, and the *pyrénéistes* who first brought the mountains to the attention of the outside world, and for those who followed them:

When the mountain has captured your heart
Everything comes from her and everything returns to her.

8

Visitors

They want me to sing *Ebben', per mia memoria* this evening. . . .
I did not come to Cauterets to go to parties and find Paris in
this countryside full of antelopes and eagles. No, I am going
off to see the snows, waterfalls, and bears, God willing.

—George Sand[1]

By the end of the nineteenth century, the Pyrenees were very different from the isolated and inaccessible mountains that Henry Swinburne had visited more than a century before. When Swinburne entered Spain through Le Perthus Pass in the company of a traveling circus in 1775, he commented on the recently built road on the French side, which "reflects great honour on the engineer who planned it. It is now very wide, the rocks are blasted, and spread out, and bridges are laid over the hollows, which formerly were most dangerous precipices."[2] At that time such roads were rare in France, and even rarer in Spain. In 1759 Antoine Mégret d'Etigny (1719–67), *intendant* of Gascony, Béarn, and Navarre, instigated a major road-building program using the corvée forced-labor system in and around the historic spa town of Bagnères-de-Luchon. In addition to a new road through the Vallée d'Aspe along the pilgrimage route to the Somport Pass, d'Etigny also commissioned a series of public works to make Bagnères-de-Luchon more accessible and attractive to outsiders, and he astutely invited members of the French court to see what he had achieved, thereby attracting a stream of eminent visitors, whose visits would subsequently transform Luchon into the "Queen of the Pyrenees."

These efforts were later expanded by Napoléon III. After an 1859 visit to nearby Luz-Saint-Sauveur, the emperor commissioned a vast public works program that eventually resulted in the construction of a new carriage road connecting the spa towns of the Pyrenees, and an extension of the railway network from Lourdes to Pierrefitte.

With the opening of the "Route Thermale" in 1864, the Pyrenees were now directly connected by road and railway to Paris and other European capitals. In Spain, once again, the communications infrastructure connecting the Pyrenees to the rest of the country lagged behind that of France. In the late 1860s the border town of Puigcerdà became a popular summer resort for the Barcelona elite. Yet until 1914 most Spanish visitors were obliged to reach the town from France, via bus or rail from Perpignan or from the "Little Yellow Train" that connected Puigcerdà to Villefranche-de-Conflent that was built in 1903.

The new proximity of the Pyrenees to the wider world was reflected in other ways. In the late nineteenth and early twentieth centuries, the first large reservoirs on both sides of the range brought hydroelectrical power to major Spanish and French cities and to the Pyrenees themselves. In 1896 Cauterets was equipped with electric lighting. Four years later an electric tramline was built to connect the town to Pierrefitte and Luz-Saint-Sauveur and transport the visitors who were now converging on Cauterets and other spa towns each summer. These infrastructural developments inevitably attracted visitors. As early as the end of the Napoleonic Wars, some of Wellington's officers were so impressed by the hunting and mild winter climate in Béarn that they settled there with their wives and families. Within a few decades a permanent English colony of affluent expatriates had established itself in Pau that increased to some four thousand in the winter, with a year-round sporting calendar that included cricket, card parties, polo, golf, Anglican churches, and a tri-weekly fox hunt.

Pau also attracted a smaller colony of rich Americans, such as James Gordon Bennett Jr., the proprietor of the *New York Herald*

The route to *la vie des eaux*: The Pont Napoléon at Luz Saint-Sauveur, one of the great feats of nineteenth-century Pyrenean engineering, ca. 1890–1906 (Library of Congress).

and sponsor of Henry Morton Stanley's expedition in search of David Livingstone, and Abraham Lincoln's widow, Mary Todd Lincoln, who spent four years there for health reasons from 1876 to 1880. In 1878, as part of a European tour, Ulysses Grant passed through Pau, where the British and American expatriate community held a lavish banquet in the former president's honour. Other English "colonies" sprung up in Pyrenean towns such as Vernet-les-Bains and Bagnères-de-Bigorre. In the last decades of the century Cauterets was receiving an average of twenty thousand visitors a year. On the one hand these visitors were a consequence of the "discovery" of the Pyrenees. At the same time they also contributed to the imaginative reinvention of the Pyrenean landscape through their travel writings, letters, paintings, and photographs, thus bringing the mountains even closer to the consciousness of the modern world—even as that world penetrated deeper into the Pyrenees themselves.

Pyrenean Sublime

The "discovery" of the Pyrenees was also a consequence of a wider aesthetic and cultural discovery of mountain landscapes that took place from the late eighteenth century onward. In 1276 King Pedro III of Aragon (1239–85) made the first recorded ascent of Mount Canigou (9,134 feet / 2,784 meters) in the present-day Pyrénées-Orientales. According to the Italian monk and chronicler Salimbene di Adamo, who visited Aragon in this period, the king set out on horseback accompanied by two well-armed knights before continuing the ascent on foot. The party had not gone far when a thunderstorm broke, which so alarmed the king and his attendants that they "fell to the ground and became as dead men for the fear and anguish that was come upon them." Even when the storm had abated the two knights were too terrified to continue, and the intrepid king went on alone. On approaching the summit, Pedro passed a lake and threw a stone into it, whereupon "a monstrous dragon of loathly aspect issued therefrom, hovering round in the air until the face of heaven was darkened with the vapour of his breath."[3]

Pedro survived this encounter, and his successful ascent no doubt added to his kingly luster, but the terror of his knights was a more accurate indication of the prevailing attitudes toward mountains in the Middle Ages than his precocious desire to climb an unconquered summit. For most medieval Europeans, mountains were *loci horridi*—fearful places, to be avoided whenever possible, whose summits were inhabited by dragons, devils, or witches.[4] Seventeenth-century English travelers in the Alps were horrified by the "high and hideous" mountains that they regarded as the "rubbish of the earth." Such attitudes were not as universal as some writers have suggested. In 55 BCE, the Roman poet and philosopher Lucretius celebrated the pleasures of walking in mountains and included mountains among the landscapes that enable the goddess Venus to "strike love into the hearts of all."[5]

In 1336, the poet Petrarch and his younger brother climbed Mont Ventoux in Provence "to see what so great a height had to offer."[6] In a letter to a friend in 1541, the Swiss botanist and humanist Conrad Gesner wrote of his "admiration of mountains" and declared his determination "as long as God grants me life to climb every year several mountains, or at least one, in the flower-seasons, partly for the sake of botanical studies, partly for honest bodily exercise, and for my own satisfaction."[7] In 1693 John Dennis described a journey across the Alps in which "we walk'd upon the very brink, in a literal sense, of Destruction; one Stumble, and both Life and Carcass had been at once destroy'd." Yet Dennis also found, "The sense of all this produc'd different emotions in me, viz., a delightful Horrour, a terrible Joy, and at the same time, that I was infinitely pleased, I trembled."[8] From the late eighteenth century onward, mountains were increasingly seen as landscapes of delight rather than dread, and even as worthy objects of adoration. The initial impetus behind this transformation came from the Romantic movement, with its quasi-religious yearning for grandiose natural spectacles. By the mid-nineteenth century, the Victorian art critic John Ruskin explicitly rejected the dread and horror that had previously been attached to mountain landscapes and hailed "these great cathedrals of the earth" as the epitome of natural beauty. The new appreciation of mountains did not dispense entirely with the negative emotions that they had once inspired. "Whatever is fitted in any sort to excite the ideas of pain, and danger, that is to say, whatever is in any sort terrible, or is conversant about terrible objects, or operates in a manner analogous to terror, is a source of the sublime," Edmund Burke declared in 1757.[9]

To connoisseurs of the sublime, mountains embodied many of these qualities. "None but these children of God know how to join so much beauty with so much horror," wrote the poet Thomas Gray of the Scottish Highlands in 1765. Many travelers sought these qualities in the Alps in the last decades of the eighteenth century, but a growing number also went in search of this combination in the Pyrenees. In 1797, the French politician and poet Charles-François Brisseau de Mirbel (1776–1854) climbed the Pic du Midi de Bigorre and celebrated the "mountains, precipices, glaciers, ancient snows, aerial lakes, the immense and silent workshops of nature and fruitful fields, watered by fertilizing streams of the mountain currents."[10] De Mirbel contrasted this landscape with his own expectations, noting how "those peaks, which once seemed to me only a useless chaos, and the result of some strange caprice of Nature, now appeared as the sublime work of a beneficent hand."

The English novelist Ann Radcliffe (1764–1823) set the first part of her eighteenth-century Gothic bestseller *The Mysteries of Udolpho* (1794) in the Pyrenees. Radcliffe had never actually visited the mountains, and the landscape she described was quite literally a landscape of the imagination, made up of barren summits, dizzying crags and precipices, lingering melancholy sunsets, gloomy forests, towers, and tumbling cataracts, inhabited by shepherds and lawless "banditti." In a long travelogue at the beginning of the novel, Radcliffe's heroine Emily St. Aubert travels with her ailing father across the Pyrenees to the Mediterranean, a journey that has little narrative purpose except to take her readers through a classic landscape of the sublime in which her heroine is able to contemplate the "higher regions of the air, where immense glaciars exhibited their frozen horrors" past crags of "stupendous height, and fantastic shape; some shooting into cones; others impending far over their base, in huge masses of granite, along whose broken ridges was often lodged a weight of snow, that trembling even to the vibration of a sound, threatened to bear destruction in its course to the vale."[11] Such descriptions are softened by descriptions of meadows, forests, and running streams to complete her picture of what she called "a perfect picture of the lovely and sublime, of 'beauty sleeping in the lap of horror.'"

Many travelers who did visit the Pyrenees came to the mountains already steeped in the vocabulary of the sublime. Ramond's writings are filled with references to "terrible cataracts," "frightful ravines," "hideous" precipices, and "desolated heights." The nineteenth-century English traveler Louisa Stuart Costello described her first sight of the "long chain of the magnificent Pyrenees" from Pau and the "everlasting awful mountains, purple and transparent and glowing with delight."[12] Adjectives like "awful" and "hideous" were intended to be complimentary. Writing to his wife of a nocturnal walk above a waterfall near Cauterets, Victor Hugo described how "a hideous, terrible roar arose out of the darkness below, from the precipice under my feet. . . . All around me was dark and as though pensive. The immense spectres of the mountains showed themselves to me through the rifts of the clouds as though across torn shrouds."[13]

Even the authors of an avowedly scientific text such as *A History of Mountains, Geographical and Mineral* (1809) described the "disorder and confusion" of Pyrenean rivers spating in springtime, and the "gloomy terrible silence which precedes this scene of horror," while still insisting that "the woods, the rocks, and the torrents, display all the characteristics of the sublime and the beautiful."[14] Like Radcliffe's, such descriptions were often accompanied by references to the gentler "picturesque" qualities of the Pyrenean landscape. In a book of essays that first defined the concept of the "picturesque," the English artist and Anglican priest William Gilpin (1724–1808) argued that the beauty of picturesque landscapes lay in their forms, colors, and "accompaniments" rather than the grandeur associated with the sublime.[15]

The Pyrenees contained many such accompaniments. In 1840 the Scottish writer Henry David Inglis compared the "Eden" of the Argelès-Gazost Valley near Cauterets to his travels through the Alps. "More sublime scenes—as picturesque scenes—may be found in many places," he wrote, "but none where the union of beauty and picturesqueness is so perfect—no spot in which the charm of mountain scenery is so mingled with the softest and loveliest features of fertility."[16] In *A Motor-Flight Through France* Edith Wharton praised "the sweetness and diversity of the Pyrenean border. Nowhere are the pastoral and the sylvan so happily mated, nowhere the villages so compact of thrift and romance, the foreground so sweet, the distances so sublime and shining."[17]

Writing the Pyrenees

For Henry Russell these contrasts in the landscape not only distinguished the Pyrenees from the Alps, but also evoked a very different response in those who visited them. Where the former inspired terror, Russell insisted, the latter "seduced. The Pyrenees were for artists and poets."[18] This was not strictly factual. Poetry and the Alps were by no means mutually exclusive, as a long line of poets from Wordsworth to Emily Dickinson can attest, but there is no doubt that the Pyrenees have often found their way into poetry, and the variations in the landscape have often inspired surprising and unpredictable literary responses. In 1831 the youthful Alfred Tennyson, then a student at Cambridge, passed through Cauterets with his close friend and fellow poet Arthur Hallam. In a letter to his brother, Tennyson lyrically evoked a classic romantic Pyrenean landscape of "precipitous defiles, jagged mountain tops, forests of solemn pine, tavelled by dewy clouds, and encircling lawns of the greenest freshness, waters in all shapes and all powers, from the clear runnels babbling down over our mountain paths at intervals, to the blue little lake whose deep, cold waters are fed eternally from neighbouring glaciers, and the impetuous cataract, fraying its way over black, beetling rocks."[19]

In 1838, however, the seventeen-year-old Charles Baudelaire spent the summer at Barèges with his stepfather and painted a very different picture of the mountains in his miserabilist poem "Incompatibilité," in which he wrote of the "mournful waste" of a mountain lake dominated by "silence, that makes you wish to escape; / that eternal silence of the mountainous bed / of motionless air, where everything waits."[20] Many years later, Baudelaire recalled the same "motionless little lake" in "Cake," one of the "little poems in prose" that make up *Paris Spleen*, as an example of "inexpressible grandeur and sublimity" in which "my thoughts fluttered about, as light as the atmosphere. Vulgar passions, like hatred and profane love, now struck me as being as far away as the clouds that processed by in the depths of the abysses that lay beneath my feet. My soul seemed to me as vast and pure as the cupola of the sky that enveloped me."[21]

This reverie does not last long. When the poet sits down to eat a piece of bread, he is interrupted by a starving urchin who mistakes it for cake. Baudelaire cuts him a "generous piece," but before the child can eat it he is set upon by "another little savage" who turns out to be his brother and who tries to take it from him. The two boys fight viciously "for possession of the previous booty, neither one willing to share it with the other," till the second boy bites off a piece of the first child's ear and the crumbs of "cake" are scattered on the ground, "indisguishable from the grains of sand with which they were mingled." Even here, in the Pyrenean paradise of his youth, Baudelaire reminds us, man is not born good after all, and "there is a superb country where bread is called *cake* and is so rare a delicacy that it is enough to start a war, literally fratricidal!"

In the spring of 1862 the English "decadent" poet Algernon Charles Swinburne (1837–1909), a great admirer of Baudelaire, came to Cauterets to stay with his family. A descendant of the traveler and writer Henry Swinburne, Swinburne was an avid wild swimmer and he also suffered from epileptic convulsions that occasionally made him pass out. His family often worried about his health, and they would not have been pleased at his willingness to swim in the freezing waters of Lake Gaube. These solitary dips nevertheless produced one of the most remarkable English-language poems of the nineteenth century, "The Lake of Gaube," and one of the greatest poems ever written about the Pyrenees.[22] Swinburne begins his poem with an evocation of a classic Pyrenean landscape that many of his readers would already have been familiar with, where "the sun is lord and god, sublime, serene / and sovereign on the mountain. . . . The lawns, the gorges, and the peaks, are one Glad glory / thrilled with sense of unison / In strong compulsive silence of the sun."

The poet then dives into the lake and presents his readers with very different sensations, where "that Heaven, the dark deep heaven of water near / Is deadly deep as hell and dark as death / The rapturous plunge that quickens blood and breath / With pause more sweet than passion." These extremes of heat and cold, light and darkness, become a process of sensual/spiritual transition that Swinburne compares to the salamanders that populate the surrounding forest: "As the bright salamander in fire of the noonshine exults and is glad of his day / The spirit that quickens my body rejoices to pass from the sunlight away / To pass from the glow of the mountainous flowerage, the high multitudinous bloom / Far down through the fathomless night of the water, the gladness of silence and gloom."

In a review of Victor Hugo's travel writings written in 1890, Swinburne recalled how he had once captured and tamed salamanders at Lake Gaube and described his fascination with "the fiery exuberance of flowers among which the salamanders glide like creeping flames radiant and vivid up to the very skirt of the tragic little pine wood, at whose heart the fathomless little lake lies silent; with dark dull gleam on it as of half-tarnished steel."[23] Many holidaymakers regularly swim in Lake Gaube, but very few will have experienced the sensations that Swinburne described when he dived into its snow-fed waters in the spring of 1862 and found "far down through the fathomless night of the water, the gladness of silence and gloom / Death-dark and delicious as death in the dream of a lover and dreamer may be."

The Pyrenees also featured in another classic nineteenth-century poem, when the German poet Heinrich Heine (1797–1856) visited Cauterets in the summer of 1841 in search of a cure to the unspecified illness—probably venereal disease—that would reduce him to a half-blind prisoner in his "mattress-vault" seven years later. Heine's Pyrenean health cure coincided with a low point in his Parisian exile, in which he was embroiled in various literary and political feuds. In a letter to a friend, he denied rumours of impending blindness and death but described himself "very slack as a consequence of the baths which I am taking here; very slack, and it costs me much to hold my pen in my hand."[24]

Heine took consolation from his treatment and also from the mountains themselves: "The springs work miraculous cures every day, and I too hope to recover. We hear little of politics. People live a quiet, peaceful life, and it is hard to believe that revolution and war, the savage sport of our time, passed even over the Pyrenees." That "savage sport" was unfolding in parts of the Pyrenees even as Heine took his cure, in the form of the first Carlist War, and Heine included both Cauterets and the war in his mock-epic poem *Atta Troll*, which he began in the autumn that year. The "final Woods-song of Romanticism," as Heine described it, describes the attempts of Atta Troll, an escaped dancing bear from Cauterets, to lead an animal revolution against human domination. From this premise, Heine launched a series of scabrous attacks on the many objects of his scorn, including God, the Swabian poetry school, egalitarianism, literary pretentiousness, and Prince Felix Lichnowski, a German prince who fought in the Carlist War, known in the poem as "Schnapphahnski."

The poem also references various known Pyrenean landmarks, including the Pont d'Espagne, Bagnères, Roncesvalles, and Lake

Gaube. Heine's attack on Romanticism did not allow him to cele-brate the mountains ("What to thee seemed blue and gold/Is, alas, but idle snow/Idle snow, which, lone and drear/Bores itself in solitude"), and the landscape he described, where "Hulking and enormous cliffs/Of deformed and twisted shapes/Look on me like petrified/Monsters of primeval times" was very different from Ten-nyson's delicate lyricism—and from the Pyrenees that he described in his correspondence.[25]

Other nineteenth-century writers expressed a more unambigu-ously positive vision of the mountains. "I am so captivated by the Pyrenees, that I will never dream, or speak, my whole life, of any-thing but mountains, torrents, grottoes and precipices," wrote the twenty-one-year-old Aurore Dupin, better known as George Sand (1804–76), to her mother during her first visit to the mountains.[26] Sand's friend Ivan Turgenev later remembered his 1845 walking tour of the Pyrenees as the "happiest period of my life"—a recollec-tion that was inextricably bound up with his love for the singer Pauline Viardot. Years later he recalled in a poem how "I walked among tall mountains / By gay rivers and through dales / And everything that met my gaze / Spoke of just one thing to me: / I was loved! I was loved!"[27]

The English-speaking world was also beginning to discover the Pyrenees through a burgeoning genre of travel writings in the nineteenth century. J. Hardy's *A Picturesque and Descriptive Tour in the Mountains of High Pyrenees* (1825); Frederick H. Johnson's *A Winter's Sketches in the South of France and the Pyrenees* (1857); James Erskine Murray's *A Summer in the Pyrenees* (1837); Thomas Clifton Paris's *Letters from the Pyrenees During Three Months' Pedestrian Wanderings* (1843); Louisa Stuart Costello's *Béarn and the Pyrenees* (1844); Ernest Bilborough's *'Twixt France and Spain; or, A Spring in the Pyrenees* (1883); Mary Boddington's *Sketches in the Pyrenees* (1837); the Princeton history graduate Edwin Asa Dix's *A Mid-summer Drive Through the Pyrenees* (1890)—the seemingly endless stream of travel books led one underwhelmed reviewer of Johnson's *A Winter's Sketches* in the *Spectator* in 1857 to observe wearily that

"Pau and the Pyrenees are not so haeknied as Italy and the common lines of travel in France and Germany, but they have been described by various writers of various pursuits."

French travel books such as the Comtesse de la Granville's *Retour des Pyrénées* (1841) and Jules de Fer's *Souvenirs pittoresques des Pyrénéees* (1843) also helped to make their authors' compatriots more familiar with the mountains. Adolphe Thiers's descriptions of his travels in the Cerdagne were translated into English, as was Hippolyte Taine's *Voyage aux Pyrénées* (1857) and Jules Michelet's *La Montagne* (1885). In 1895, Victor Hugo's *Alpes et Pyrénées*, based on letters written to his wife from two journeys to the Alps and Pyrenees in 1839 and 1843, was published in English for the first time.

Many of these books followed a very similar formula, combining appealing descriptions of the Pyrenean landscape with descriptions of towns and cities, local color, and historical background. Some have stood the test of time, such as the English priest, novelist, and polymath Sabine Baring-Gould's *A Book of the Pyrenees* (1907). The English traveler Harold Spender spent two summers walking and camping with friends in the more remote French and Spanish Pyrenees and Andorra in 1896 and 1897, and his account of these excursions "for pleasure and exercise" in *Through the High Pyrenees* (1898) remains one of the essential works of Pyrenean literature.

Hilaire Belloc's *The Pyrenees* (1909) combined a nuts-and-bolts compilation of essential travel information with an erudite overview of Pyrenean history and geography. Belloc was a mountain purist who ventured out into the Pyrenees alone with a rucksack, a map, a few essential provisions, and a pair of espadrilles rather than boots. Belloc was scornful of the "cosmopolitans, colonials, nomads, and the rest" at Cauterets and other spa towns. For Belloc, "cosmopolitan" was generally synonymous with Jewish—a category that he held in only marginally lower esteem than the vulgar rich he observed in Cauterets, who "destroy the things that they themselves desire. And the things that they desire are execrable to the rest of mankind."[28]

John Bingham Morton, the *Daily Express* columnist and travel writer known as "Beachcomber," was a friend of Belloc's who shared similar views. In *Pyrenean* (1938), his account of a solo trek across the Pyrenees from the Mediterranean to the Atlantic, Morton depicted the Pyrenees as an antidote to a modern world made up of "the herds penned in garden suburbs," "Bolshevik-barrack flats and hotels," and the "unwieldy" French tourists he observed at Gavarnie who "in the very shadow of the great solemn peaks . . . flounder and waddle along, the oaths of the perspiring men mingling with the shrill giggling and screaming of the monstrous women." Morton found solace in high mountain places, such as the "delightful little valley" he encountered near Roncesvalles, which "looked as fresh as though the world had been created that morning, and I stopped dead in my tracks, as though I had met Youth and Innocence face to face. For it was a landscape so evidently unaware of the evil ways of the world, so confident."

Artists

The reimagining of the Pyrenees was not simply due to the written word. From the eighteenth century onward, the Pyrenees attracted a stream of artists and illustrators, whose paintings, engravings, and illustrations provided the wider European public with their first visual impressions of the mountains. Such images featured regularly in French publications such as *La nature*, *Le tour du monde*, and *L'illustration*, and also in books about the Pyrenees, which were often illustrated by their authors. Ramond's books contained his own sketchings and drawings, as did James Erskine Murray's and Lady Georgiana Chatterton's. The French lithographer Louis-Julien Jacottet (1806–80) made the Pyrenees the subject of two albums, *Souvenir des Pyrénées* (1835–36) and *Souvenir des Pyrénées, nouvelle excursion* (1841–42). Albert Tissandier's account of his journeys through the Aragonese and Catalan Pyrenees in 1889 was illustrated with his own immaculately rendered drawings.

Some artists focused on the more dramatic Pyrenean landmarks, such as Gavarnie. Others were attracted by more intimate details and contrasts in the landscape and terrain. In a letter to a friend from the spa town of Eaux-Bonnes in 1845, Eugène Delacroix (1798–1863) complained that "the beauty of this nature of the Pyrenees is not something that one can hope to capture happily through painting. Regardless of the work that follows, all of it is so gigantic that one does not know where to begin amongst these masses and the multitude of details."[29] Delacroix eventually published a series of drawings and watercolors of the mountains and their inhabitants in an *Album des Pyrénées* that same year. Gustave Doré visited the Pyrenees on numerous occasions, and both his paintings and the haunting pencil-and-ink drawings of blasted tree trunks, cataracts, and stormy skies that illustrated Taine's and Blackburn's travel books contained images that could easily have accompanied Ann Radcliffe's imagined Pyrenees.

Franz Schrader's Pyrenean paintings tended to focus on the shapes and shades of rocks and mountains, in keeping with his belief that art, cartography, and the study of topography were complementary pursuits.[30] The Parisian artist and engraver Charles Jouas (1866–1942) was known largely as a painter of Parisian opera sets before presenting himself to the writer and publisher Henri Béraldi in 1896. Béraldi was so impressed with his work that he promptly dispatched him to Luchon to come up with the illustrations to accompany *100 Years of the Pyrenees*. Jouas subsequently made numerous visits to the Pyrenees, and these visits transformed the urban artist into the quintessential "illustrator of the Pyrenees," whose elegant and deftly drawn sketches and watercolors focus on people as well as landscape, from shepherds sitting in front of fires to courting couples skipping down mountain paths and teams of roped men and women walking up through the snow-covered ridges.

The differences in climate, light, and terrain from one end of the Pyrenees to the other appealed to artists across a wide spectrum of styles and sensibilities. Most artists focused on the sunnier Eastern

Pyrenean sublime: Gustave Doré, illustration from Hipployte Taine's *A Tour Through the Pyrenees*, 1875 (Flickr API).

Pyrenees and came to them through visits to the southern coast of France. In 1908 the consumptive young Welsh painter James Dickson Innes (1887–1914) followed Matisse's footsteps to the port of Collioure, near Banyuls-sur-Mer, with a fellow artist, in the first of various visits. A graduate of the Slade School of Fine Art and a close friend of Augustus John, Innes was known for his moody studies of the Arenig Fawr mountain in Snowdonia, and also for a taste for the gypsy lifestyle that led him to sleep outdoors in the open air despite its adverse impact on his fragile health. His visits to southern France produced some striking studies of Mount Canigou and the Pyrénées-Orientales, whose moody intensity was partly due to Innes's habit of painting at sunset or twilight in order to avoid the Mediterranean heat, and perhaps also to intimations of his own mortality and the tuberculosis that killed him in August 1914.

Death and ill health stalked the Scottish modernist architect and designer Charles Rennie Mackintosh (1868–1928), who came to paint in Collioure and nearby Port-Vendres with his wife, Margaret, in 1924. Mackintosh's move to France was a form of self-imposed exile from a country where he felt marginalized and ignored, and his decision to abandon architecture and concentrate on painting produced a dazzling late creative flourish, as he dedicated himself to watercolors of Port-Vendres and the surrounding coast—and also of the villages and flowers of the Eastern Pyrenees. Mackintosh's portraits of Pyrenean forts and villages are flooded with bright light, in which the physical details of walls and buildings are brought to life by sharp contrasts of light and shade. Despite his constant financial difficulties, Mackintosh set himself an objective of fifty paintings that he wanted to exhibit in London, and he had completed forty of them before he died of throat and tongue cancer in 1928. These paintings have never been exhibited as a complete body of work in the UK. It was not until 2004 that Mackintosh's marvellous artistic swan song received official recognition in France with the inauguration of the Chemin de Mackintosh—the Mackintosh Way—starting at Port-Vendres, where visitors can see the places that he painted so unforgettably.[31]

The Pyrenees also featured in the work of the French *anamalière*—animal painter—Rosa Bonheur (1822–99), the most famous female artist of the nineteenth century. A feminist, a lesbian, and the daughter of Christian-Socialist parents, Bonheur had just begun to establish a reputation as an animal painter when she visited the Pyrenees for the first time in 1850 following the death of her father the previous year. Together with her lifelong friend and fellow artist Nathalie Micas, she traveled to Eaux-Bonnes, Luz-Saint-Sauveur, and Lourdes on horseback, after receiving permission from the police to wear men's clothing—something that Bonheur always preferred. The trip was financed by Micas's mother, who was concerned about her daughter's health, and the two women rode from town to town taking the waters, while Bonheur mostly sketched and painted.

On one occasion, the two women climbed Mount Bergons, where Nathalie described to her mother the view of the Marboré and the Brèche de Roland, the sight of eagles and Rosa "sketching while I'm being lazy and writing you this letter. It's five, and the sun is casting its last rays; the cows are moving from one meadow to another with leisurely moos. The tinkle of their bells is drawing near, and the poor beasts seem to be thanking God for the evening cool. When you see them running around the mountains, you'd think that they were deer. They're not only fleet of foot, but rather small."[32]

What their guides made of the two women in men's clothing can only be imagined, but Bonheur frequently returned to the Pyrenees to paint chamois, cows, sheep, and muleteers with her distinctive naturalist precision. In Bonheur's Pyrenean paintings the mountains are always in the background, but works such as *Muleteers Crossing the Pyrenees* (1857) and *Chamois* (1888) are some of the most compelling and alluring visual representations of the High Pyrenees in nineteenth-century art. Bonheur's less famous brother, Auguste Bonheur (1824–84), was also a gifted artist and *anamalière*, who painted animals in the Pyrenees, such as the marvelously dramatic portrait of cattle fighting in the high mountains, *Le Combat* (1862).

The Mecca of Cubism

The Pyrenees also became a source of inspiration for Pablo Picasso. In 1906 Picasso spent the spring and summer with his then girl-friend Fernande Olivier at the town of Gósol, in the province of Lleida, near Andorra, where he painted and sketched the local in-habitants and the arid, ochre-colored mountains. Picasso's joyful rediscovery of his Spanish and Catalan roots was expressed in his touching portraits of peasant women in scarves or without clothes, naked swineherds, and his nonagenerian landlord Josep Fondevila, whom Olivier described as "a fierce old fellow, a former smuggler, with a strange, wild beauty." Picasso was so fascinated by Fondevila's stark, shaved appearance and smuggler past that he made a model of his shaven head, and even shaved his own as a tribute.

Picasso's fondness for the Pyrenees inadvertently gave a small town in the Pyrénées-Orientales a special place in the history of modern art. Today the French town of Céret, the capital of the *comarca* (district) of Vallespir near the French-Catalan border, is a pretty, well-heeled country town, surrounded by cherry orchards and vineyards. Only a few miles away to the northeast lies the border pass of Le Perthus, and farther east you can see Mount Canigou. Beneath the tall pastel-colored buildings and enormous plane trees, the proliferation of cafés and trendy shops and a museum of mod-ern art are a testament to Céret's unlikely place in the artistic his-tory of the twentieth century that began in 1909, when a French painter named Frank Burty Haviland and the Spanish sculptor Manolo arrived in the town from Paris intending to follow in Picasso's footsteps to Gósol.

These aspirations had to be placed on hold when war broke out between Spain and Morocco. Unwilling to risk being drafted, Manolo returned with Haviland to Paris. In February the follow-ing year they came back to Céret, at the instigation of Manolo's wife, and decided to settle there, and in the summer of 1911 Haviland invited his friend Picasso to join them. The year 1911 was a particularly momentous one in Picasso's career. In April, the term "Cubism" was used in the French press for the first time to describe two collective exhibitions in Paris and Brussels that appeared to mark a radical—and to many critics scandalous—departure from Impressionism.

Picasso's work was not exhibited at either exhibition, but he and his friend and collaborator Georges Braque were regarded as the spiritual founders of the new movement. Braque famously compared their relationship to "a pair of climbers roped together," and the two painters spent three weeks together in Céret in the summer of 1911. By the time Picasso returned to Paris in September, he had painted *Landscape at Céret* and the iconic cubist painting *L'homme à la pipe*—a startling conglomeration of triangular geometrical shapes, which ironically referenced Van Gogh's painting of the same name. Braque remained in Céret until the following January, and his iconic *Man with a Guitar* was probably painted there. The two painters spent the following summer in Céret, and in the spring of 1913 Picasso returned once again in March, accompanied by the poet Max Jacob and Olivier. Picasso had intended to spend that summer painting in the mountains, but he returned to Paris when his lover Olivier developed terminal cancer, and his beloved dog Frika also fell ill and had to be put down by a local hunter. In August that year he returned to the town once again, where a local newspaper reported, "The small town of Céret is rejoicing. The Master of Cubism has arrived, ready to enjoy a well-earned rest."

That same year Haviland and Manolo established an art school in an abandoned Capuchin monastery near the town, and this initiative soon began to attract a succession of Parisian artists, including Juan Gris, Jean Marchand, Marc Lafargue, and Joaquim Sunyer, to Céret. Though Haviland and his wife briefly left Céret during World War I, the town continued to attract a steady flow of artists looking for a cheap place to live and paint in the years that followed. They included the tormented Russian Expressionist painter Chaim Soutine, who spent two years here between 1919 and 1921, together with the Russian-French artist Pinchus Krémègne.

It is something of an understatement to say that Soutine did not settle easily into his country retreat. He was prone to violent rages in which he tore up canvases that displeased him, and left those he finished in a dank toolshed while he eked out an impoverished and disorderly existence that scandalized the locals. "He was raving mad, constantly drunk and dirty," Krémègne recalled. "People took him for the village idiot. He always hated Céret. When people would ask him how old he was, he'd say that his two years in Céret didn't count."[33] Soutine nevertheless produced more than two hundred finished paintings in those two years, including some savagely idiosyncratic studies of the surrounding landscape that revealed more about his inner state of mind than they did about the Pyrenees. Following the Nazi occupation, a number of writers and artists, including Marc Chagall, Jean Dubuffet, and Jean Cocteau, passed through Céret on their way out of France, and some of them are now represented in the Musée d'Art Moderne, established in Céret by Haviland in 1950, with the support of Picasso and Matisse, in a tribute to the town that the art critic André Salmon once called "la Mecque du cubisme"—the Mecca of Cubism.

At the Forest's Edge

In the early twenty-first century many of the world's most famous and far-flung landscapes are already engraved in our minds long before we see them and even if we never see them. A quick Internet search can pull up high-quality photographs of almost anywhere in the world, and even the most unskilled photographer with a mobile phone can now take pictures of a much higher standard than was possible even a few decades ago. New technologies have made it possible to capture even familiar landscapes from the most improbable angles and perspectives. Given these possibilities, it is easy to forget that there was once a time when images of the world's more distant places were entirely dependent on the vision and skill of individual artists, and it is also easy to ignore the very particular subjective vision that painters can bring to landscapes that we think we already know.

One of the few major contemporary artists working in the Pyrenees is the English plein air painter Ray Atkins. A graduate of Bromley College of Art in Kent and the Slade School of Fine Art, Atkins is a former pupil of Frank Auerbach's whose reputation is largely due to his giant studies of industrial landscapes such as the Reading gasworks and Millwall Docks. In 2009, at the age of seventy-three, Atkins took the radical decision to relocate to a remote farmstead near the village of Aspet in the French Pyrenees. In July 2015 I saw an exhibition of Pyrenean paintings at the Art Space gallery. The paintings were deeply impressive; vibrant semi-abstract studies of woods, fields of haricot beans, flowering pear trees painted at different times of the year that blazed with light and color. I was also struck by the absence of the Pyrenees themselves from these paintings. The mountains were inevitably relegated to the distant background, in paintings that focused primarily on the subtle variations in texture and color in the immediate foreground. The following month my wife and I went to visit Atkins in his Aspet farmhouse. To reach it, you have to drive along a narrow 2.5-mile (4-kilometer) dirt and gravel road, through hills that are covered for miles around in dense green forest that often blots out the mountains completely and feels quite claustrophobic and oppressive.

Atkins greeted us with his partner, the dancer and choreographer Hsiao-Hwa Li, at his immaculately restored farmhouse. With his ponytail, beard, and glasses, Atkins looks like an aging hippie, with a touch of a Taoist monk and tai chi master. He was in a good mood, having just finished a four-foot canvas that he had been working on for some weeks. Atkins is wary of discussing his work and prefers to let the paintings speak for themselves but he obligingly answered my questions as we sat in the kitchen and ate Hsiao-Hwa's homemade cakes.

His initial decision to come to Aspet was the result of his divorce, which obliged him to sell the Cornwall barn next to his ex-wife's house and find storage for his six hundred paintings. Having made the complicated move to the Pyrenees to save his paintings, Atkins found a new subject that was ostensibly at odds with his preference for factories, gasworks, docklands, scrapyards, and Cornish tin mines over what he calls "simplistic, idyllic landscapes." Atkins initially struggled to come to terms with an environment that he described to Frank Auerbach as "too rural." From his garden you can see the Pic de Ger protruding in the distance out of the Vallée d'Ossau, as it appears in many of his paintings. For Atkins the mountain was an unwelcome reminder of Cézanne's classic paintings of Mont Sainte-Victoire—a legacy that he felt obliged to escape from.

Atkins was not satisfied with his initially "over-romantic" work in the Pyrenees, nor was his dealer, Michael Richardson, who described his work as "chamber music without a symphony"—a reference to Atkins's love of classical music. When Richardson suggested that he focus on the forest rather than the mountains, Atkins took to the idea immediately, because "very often the real subject is so obvious you don't see it, and thinking along those lines I suddenly thought, yeah, it's the forest. Because I hate it. Sometimes I hate it. It's so dark. Very oppressive." This decision was a practical as well as an aesthetic choice. Atkins suffers from serious macular degeneration and can only see bright colors with his peripheral vision, "beyond the rim of the glasses."

Where Charles Jouas once declared that "nature dictates to me," Atkins is obliged to rely on memory and guesswork to find the colors that burst out of his paintings—a process that he describes as "working in the dark." His macular degeneration also explains to some extent his lack of interest in the mountains beyond his garden. "Now when I look at the distant landscape I can see it's there, but I don't see any detail," he says. "I really see very little, so it doesn't interest me so much. Everything's out of focus, so that affects what I choose now." Atkins was fatalistic and matter-of-fact about his predicament, but for a painter with his commitment I could not imagine anything worse, and it made the sumptuous mesh of flowers, leaves, and bushes displayed on the canvas in his garden even more astonishing.

As he showed us around his barn-warehouse and his beautiful light-filled studio, it seemed to me that he was truly a painter's painter, literally raging against the dying of the light, on the margins of the forest and of the British and French art establishments, the sole custodian and curator of the hundreds of paintings in his storeroom. For an artist who eschewed romanticism, he was a strikingly romantic figure, and as we drove back out the long dirt road, I wondered whether his paintings would find a permanent home, and whether one day visitors would come to the forest-covered hills for the same reason that travelers now followed the trail of Charles Rennie Mackintosh, because they knew that Ray Atkins had once lived here, and because they wanted to see the landscape that he had painted.

La Vie aux Eaux

Many of the poets, artists, and writers who came to the Pyrenees in the nineteenth century initially came as tourists, holidaymakers, or visitors to Pyrenean spa towns. Since Roman times, the sulfurous hot springs of Pyrenean spa towns such as Ax-les-Thermes and Luchon have been used for hydrotherapeutic purposes. For centuries, visitors have come to drink and bathe in the waters or take mud baths in order to heal sicknesses and wounds or simply to make themselves healthier. In the nineteenth century many of these towns benefited from a boom in "health tourism" that was initially due to the patronage of Napoléon III and the empress Eugénie, who began to visit Pyrenean spas during their holidays in Biarritz. Napoléon's Pyrenean public works program was partly inspired by the wretched French military veterans from the battle of Solferino whom he encountered at Bagnères-de-Bigorre in the summer of 1859, and he specifically asked for a new military hospital to be built in the town.

In the decades that followed, well-established spa towns such as Cauterets, Bagnères-de-Bigorre, Vernets-les-Bains, Luz-Saint-Sauveur, and Eaux-Bonnes experienced an exponential increase in the number of visitors, while smaller Pyrenean towns rushed to take advantage of what Graham Robb has called the "mineral water bonanza" and obtain medical and scientific confirmation of the healing properties of their waters.[34] Some towns culled the bear and wolf populations and banished pigs, sheep, and paupers from their streets in order to provide a more civilized environment for the new urban clientele. Others advertised cures for particular illnesses. Aulus-les-Bains offered a cure for "invalids of love" (syphilitics). The thermal waters at Barèges have a reputation for curing wounds and skin diseases that has attracted Roman legionnaires and veterans of the French wars in Indochina.

As these towns became popular they also attempted to widen their touristic appeal. Railway posters offered Parisians the enticing prospect of a rural arcadia only eight hours from the capital, with images of snow-covered mountains and shepherds in regional costume. The more prominent spas transformed themselves into summer resorts, replete with fairs, magic shows, donkey races, brass bands, smoking rooms and casinos, Parisian *comiques* and "singing cafés," peep shows, stalls selling tourist tat, and rides in the small two-wheeled carts known as *vinaigrettes*. Some of these towns were transformed into mountain seaside resorts. The actress Sarah Bernhardt first came to Cauterets with her family in the 1850s following her confirmation and remembered it as an "abominable but charming little hole of a place, with plenty of verdure, and a great many huts belonging to the mountain people."[35]

By the end of the century Cauterets was a very different place. In the summer of 1878 clients on the town's main thoroughfare, the Promenade des Oeufs, included Sarah Bernhardt, Randolph Churchill, Émile Zola, the mayor of Saint Petersburg, and assorted marquises, counts, and dukes. In 1888 the fifty-four-year-old Edgar Degas came here in an attempt to cure his bronchitis and returned for two more consecutive summers. Pyrenean spa towns also attracted a number of illustrious foreigners. Rudyard Kipling and his rheumatic wife, Carrie, were frequent visitors to Vernet-les-Bains, a spa town that was thoroughly anglicized by the end of the nineteenth century, with a botanical gardens, a gentlemen's club, and horse races.

Kipling was heartened by the positive impact of sulfur drinks and water massage on his wife's health, and enraptured by the nearby presence of Mount Canigou. "I came here in search of nothing more than a little sunshine," he wrote in a letter to the French Alpine Club in 1911. "But I found Canigou, whom I discovered to be a magician among mountains, and I submitted myself to his power. . . . I watch him with wonder and delight." Other visitors to the "paradise of the Pyrenees" at Vernet-les-Bains included Kipling's friend Lord Frederick Sleigh Roberts, the commander of British forces during the Boer War, and Marshal Joseph Joffre, commander in chief of French forces on the western front during the first two years of World War I.

Bagnères-de-Bigorre also attracted a significant British colony in the nineteenth century, such as the Anglo-Irish Brooke family, whose seventh child Alan was born there in 1883, and went on to become Field Marshal Lord Alanbrooke, chairman of the British chiefs of staff during World War II. In October 1933, Bagnères played host to a more unlikely visitor, when the exiled Leon Trosky and his wife Natalya spent three weeks there recuperating from a series of disastrous personal and political events that included the suicide of his daughter Zina and the nomination of Hitler as chancellor of Germany that same year. Trotsky later referred to his Pyrenean sojourn to refute allegations at the Moscow show trials that he had been conspiring against the Soviet Union in Italy at the time.

It is difficult to imagine that Trotsky would have taken to the lifestyle described by the art critic Henry Blackburn at Eaux-Bonnes, in which walks along the "Promenade Horizontale" were slotted in "between the time of taking each glass of water, the after-breakfast cascade, the noon siesta, the ride at three, another cascade and more water, or a bath, at four, promenade at five, dinner at six, 'promenade horizontale' until eight, then the Casino, balls, 'societé,' écarté, or a moonlight walk—and then, decidedly early to bed."[36]

For some visitors, the season offered the possibilities of *aventures de coeur*, which were fanned by the racy novels and magazines in spa town libraries and reading rooms with titles such as *Un chevalier d'amour*, *Les femmes d'aujourd'hui*, *Le dernier amour*, and *Nymphes des eaux*. In 1829, the sixty-one-year-old writer and diplomat François-René de Chateaubriand visited Cauterets to take the waters before leaving for Italy to take up a post as French ambassador. In *Memoirs from Beyond the Tomb* he describes how he was writing poetry in the forest when "I saw a young girl sitting on the bank of a mountain stream; she rose and came straight towards me: she knew, by a rumour at large in the hamlet, that I was in Cauterets. I found that the unknown girl was an Occitanian, who had written to me two years previously without my ever having met her; the mysterious unknown unveiled for me: *patuit Dea*: *the Goddess revealed herself*."[37] The "Occitanian" was the twenty-six-year-old Léontine de Villeneuve, Countess of Castelbajac, Chateaubriand's "last love," with whom he enjoyed a short affair before proceeding onward to Rome.

Not all visitors were impressed by such behaviour. The architect Eugène Viollet-le-Duc was appalled by the wealthy old men he observed at Cauterets in 1833 who "go to pick up girls at Pierrefitte to take them to Barèges. . . . They are masters of debauchery; they keep themselves going with good wines, sulphur baths, and pure air. Take that away from them and their legs will refuse to work, their emaciated features will turn pale, all their limbs will lose their strength and rot."[38] Eugène Delacroix despised the "disjointed life" he was obliged to lead at Eaux-Bonnes, where he was obliged to take the waters in the summer of 1845 following an outbreak of tubercular laryngitis, and expressed his horror at the "sad spectacle" of sick people seeking cures who had already been "condemned by all their faculties."[39]

Today Barèges is a popular base for walkers and skiers, with a cinema and a swimming pool as well as a spa. In 1890 Edwin Asa Dix described it as an "incubus of depressingness" and a "shuddering, shivering, banshee-haunted line of hospitals" filled with "sad-faced invalids, who have tried other baths in vain and have been ordered hither as a last resort; wounded or broken-down soldiers; cripples, who stump their crutches past us down the earthen road."[40] Hippolyte Taine described the "pitiable spectacle" of "lines of umbrellas and soaked mantles" on rainy days at Eaux-Bonnes and the "worried and dejected faces" drinking one glass of water each hour, followed by ubiquitous musicians "galloping along, above the note and below it, with admirable fearlessness, despoiling every repertory in their musical race," and reading rooms whose users "read nothing but the gloomiest dramas; they discover leanings towards suicide in themselves, and construct the theory of assassination."[41]

Octave Mirbeau (1848–1917), the writer and anarchist fellow traveler and author of *The Torture Garden* and *The Diary of a Chambermaid*, viciously satirized *la vie aux eaux* in his hilariously misanthropic novel *Twenty-One Days of a Neurasthenic*. Mirbeau's protagonist, Georges Vasseur, comes to an anonymous spa town to escape from civilization, only to find it populated with generals, politicians, and other human fauna he has been trying to escape from. "What I loathe most about the Pyrenees is that they are mountains," Vasseur writes. "Now, I have a wild, boundless and poetic appreciation for mountains, as much as the next man: nonetheless they represent for me everything the universe can possibly bear of incurable melancholia, hopeless discouragement, an unbreathable, deadly air. . . . I admire their grandiose shapes, their changing light. But their inner life terrifies me . . . I feel as though the land of the dead must be nothing but mountains upon mountains, like these which I am staring at now, as I write."[42]

Today the golden age of hydrotherapy has long since passed. Some spa towns have updated their facilities for a new clientele. The thermal buildings at Vernet-les-Bains offer aquafit, aquagym, and aquaboxing in addition to courses of thermal "séances" that hover around the $620 (€500) mark. The casino and botanical gardens where so many English tourists once whiled away their summer months are still immaculately preserved, and contemporary visitors can now visit a Kipling museum and follow a trail of "Kipling walks." Aulus-les-Bains calls itself "the Cholesterol Spa" and its location at the head of the Garbet Valley makes it popular with walkers and day-trippers looking to explore the surrounding mountains. Cauterets has reinvented itself as a base for skiers and walkers, with cable cars leading up to Lake Gaube. Some of its spa facilities have closed, but its winding streets combine an appealingly faded belle epoque elegance with the flavor of a seaside town. In the summertime the Promenade des Oeufs, where Sarah Bernhardt, George Sand, and Degas mingled with generals and politicians, is filled with families, hikers, and holidaymakers who can enjoy a range of twenty-first-century pleasures from yoga classes, classical music, and jazz concerts to more energetic pursuits such as canyoning and a *via ferrata*—protected climbing route—that are available in the surrounding mountains and forests.

Other towns have fallen on hard times. In 1830 Eaux-Bonnes played host to three hundred invalids. In 1856 it received 6,400, largely as a result of its patronage by the empress Eugénie. Looking down from his hotel balcony in 1881, Henry Blackburn observed, "The noise and bustle in the square (instruments playing more discordant music than any Italian organs), the squeaks and rattles of juvenile civilisation, the chattering of their *bonnes*, the incessant ringing of bells, the shouts and cracking of whips, the voices of different nations—all confined within a limited space, and echoed back from the surrounding rocks, can scarcely be conceived."[43]

Today Eaux Bonnes is a hollowed-out ghost town, with a population of less than five hundred, surrounded by a magnificently dramatic landcape of forest, crags, and steep gorges. Its hotels and apartments are mostly empty, its streets and parks deserted, and many buildings are visibly falling apart. The once-splendid six-storey Hôtel des Princes, with its terra-cotta walls and marble window frames, is a hollow relic of the belle epoque that shows no sign of imminent resuscitation. We stayed at a hotel that might have been an appropriate location for *The Shining*, with darkened empty corridors, faded carpets, and a stairway that was sealed off from the empty attic, and the sound of melancholy piano music drifting from the back room like music from another century.

The staff kept all this going with stoical dignity, in a town where everything exuded the same decay, from the boarded-up or empty windows to the signs with letters missing, the post office with the blocked-up mailbox, and the spooky cathedral, which protruded above the town like a rocket ship. Even the postcards had been left so long that they were bent out of shape. At the "Promenade Horizontale" we passed the dizzying pink checkerboard casino with its plaque from the YMCA thanking the town for allowing American soldiers to use its facilities "for rest and recreation" during World War I, and the rows of giant plane trees planted under the empress Eugénie's orders.

A little supermarket named after the empress provided a plaintive reminder of the glory days of the nineteenth-century spa boom. The town's inhabitants are putting their hopes for the future in the *Projet de Bulle* (Bubble Project)—the spectacular new facility in the former spa where clients can float in hot water in a giant glass ball that looms over the surrounding decay like a spaceship, and listen to music when they dip their heads in water or "cover themselves with chocolate," as our hotel receptionist described it, with a faintly incredulous irony. The "bubble" was originally scheduled to open in 2016. By January 2018 it had still not been opened, though it was very near completion, and it remains to be seen whether twenty-first-century ingenuity can prevent the Empress Eugénie's former playground from further disintegration and bring in the visitors that this still-charming spa town deserves.

Europe's Second Playground

The Pyrenees have also benefited from other forms of "health tourism"—as a reacreational landscape offering fresh air, exercise, and an escape from industrialized cities. Today this kind of tourism is a major part of the Pyrenean economy, from the walkers and hikers who swarm through the High Pyrenees each summer to Scout groups and schoolchildren who come to the mountains for weekends and summer camps. In the French and Spanish Pyrenees, holiday companies compete to offer rafting trips, canyoning expeditions, slalom and cross-country skiing, cycling, camping, hunting, snowboarding, and treewalking adventure parks. Until the late 1970s and early 1980s, canyoning—the rappeling, swimming, and scrambling in wet suits and helmets through river gorges—was barely known in the Pyrenees. Now it has become a major tourist attraction in the Sierra de Guara of Aragon and other parts of the Spanish and French Pyrenees.

All these activities are so much a part of the appeal of the Pyrenees that it is easy to forget how recent they are. In 1870 the British mountaineer Leslie Stephen famously described Switzerland as the "playground of Europe" in an account of his climbs and travels in the Swiss Alps.[44] At this time the Pyrenees were only just beginning their evolution into a different kind of mountain "playground." In 1881 *Blackwoods Edinburgh Magazine* ironically observed that "the true Pyrenees—the Pyrenees of the present French mind and of the present French traveller—are only mountains by accident. Their function is not to be high but to be pleasant, to behave as a summer district of amusement and health, and to conduct themselves properly as rivals of Vichy and Trouville: they have no other use or destination, and to persist in regarding them as mountains is nonsense."

Not all visitors followed this advice. "The grandest scenery of these vast solitudes is alone accessible to the pedestrian," declared Thomas Clifton Paris.[45] Henry David Inglis preferred to travel on foot through the Pyrenees and insisted that there were "few occupations more agreeable than sitting down with a good map, and tracing one's future route through a country that is yet untravelled by us."[46] George Sand reveled in her joyous climbs through "inaccessible mountains, which neither carriages nor even horse could ever reach," and boasted to her mother that she had rejected the offer of a sedan chair in order to walk. "Bridges of snow, over which pass processions of shepherds and flocks of sheep!" she wrote in her autobiography. "How can I describe it! You cannot see enough; you cannot take it all in with your eyes. It is astonishing. You do not even think of danger. My husband is the most intrepid of men. He goes everywhere, and I follow him."[47] "Mountains seem to crush me and stifle me," complained Sarah Bernhardt. "I must, at any cost, have the horizon stretching out as far as the eye can see and skies to dream about. I wanted to go up the mountains, so that they should lose their crushing effect. And consequently we went up always higher and higher."[48] In 1911 the local French paper at Vernet-les-Bains reported with some astonishment that a party of fourteen English ladies had ascended the summit of Mount Canigou.

By this time walking and climbing were well-established activities in the Pyrenees, and other sports began to establish themselves in the early twentieth century. In the last decades of the nineteenth century the French Alpine Club began holding its first annual skiing competitions in the Alps, the Vosges, and the Pyrenees. In his history of skiing, E. John Allen describes how the French Alpine Club saw the new sport as a "moralizer" that emphasized Gallic virtues such as suppleness, sangfroid, and courage that were considered essential to the survival of the French nation against the threat of Germany.[49] One competition at Eaux-Bonnes in 1910 was overseen by a patronage committee that included the minister and undersecretary of war and five generals. It was not until the aftermath of World War I that skiing acquired a more purely recreational purpose and became firmly established in the Pyrenees. In 1921 the first Pyrenean ski resort was built in the spa village of Barèges, thus beginning the evolution of the Grand Tourmalet into the largest ski area in the French Pyrenees.

By this time the Col du Tourmalet was already well established in the French sporting calendar as one of the toughest stretches of the Tour de France. In May 1910 Henri Desgrange, the editor of *L'Auto* newspaper and the organizer of the new competition, sent his friend Alphonse Steinès to investigate a possible route for the tour through the Pyrenees. While driving up the 9,639-foot (2,115-meter) Col du Tourmalet, Steinès's hired car was blocked by a snowdrift. Steinès's driver refused to continue to the top, and Steinès continued alone on foot. He soon got lost in the snow and fell into a ravine, before he was eventually rescued by a search party, and famously sent a telegram to his boss informing him: "No trouble crossing Tourmalet. Roads satisfactory. No problem for cyclists. Steinès."[50]

In July that same year the Pyrenees were included in stages nine and ten of the race's fifteen stages in a 202-mile (326-kilometer) route through four Pyrenean mountain passes, including the Tourmalet. On the last stage of stage ten at the Col d'Aubisque, Steinès and an assistant stationed themselves high up the pass with a crowd of spectators and waited anxiously for the first riders to appear. To their amazement the first rider was an unknown outsider who was so exhausted that he did not even answer their requests for his name. The second rider was the favorite and and the Olympic bronze medalist Octave Lapize, who exclaimed, "Vous êtes des assassins! Oui, des assassins!" (You are murderers! Yes, murderers!) at the sight of Steinès and his assistant and announced his intention to quit the race.

Lapize remained in the competition and went on to win the general classification that year, and the Col du Tourmalet became one of the four Pyrenean passes that constitute the "Circle of Death"— an astonishingly grueling ordeal that required an average of fourteen hours in the saddle on poor roads that were often little more than dirt mule tracks. The Col du Tourmalet is also associated with one of the great legends of the tour. In the village square of Sainte-Marie-de-Campan stands a curious metal sculpture of a large, thickset man, standing on a bed of flames, triumphantly holding a bicycle fork in an upraised hand. With its brawny arms and legs, the figure looks like a Stakhanovite shock worker monument from Stalinist Russia and commemorates an episode in 1913 when the "three times unlucky" French cyclist Eugène Christophe reached the top of the Col du Tourmalet after a neck-and-neck race with the Belgian cyclist Philippe Thys.

Christophe was then eighteen minutes clear and was the favorite to win the stage and the race itself. While descending to Luchon, his fork broke and he was obliged to carry his bicycle some 6 miles (10 kilometers) down to Sainte-Marie-de-Campan, weeping as he watched the riders he had previously passed streaming past him. According to the strict rules of the tour, Christophe was not allowed to replace his bike or have it repaired. He was allowed to repair it himself, however, and he eventually found a local blacksmith in Sainte-Marie-de-Campan who allowed him to use his forge. Though he was penalized ten points (later reduced to three) for allowing a seven-year-old boy to work the bellows, he completed the remaining 37 miles (60 kilometers) of the stage four hours later to finish at number twenty-nine in the stage classification.

Christophe never won the tour, but his refusal to give in made him an exemplary figure in French cycling history, "victorious in the face of bad luck" as the monument puts it. When we drove over the pass on a foggy afternoon, cyclists of all ages were grinding their way up toward the huge statue of a naked cyclist known as the *Géant du Tourmalet* that commemorates Octave Lapize's legendary 1910 ascent. With its straining muscles and agonized face, the statue is an eloquent expression of the physical torment associated with Tourmalet. As we made our way cautiously down toward the thick fog, cyclists hurtled perilously down the precipitous mountain road in bright flashes of yellow and orange Lycra, or strove toward the pass with gritted teeth, in the shadow of the naked cyclist in whose historical slipstream all of them were moving.

The Mystic Pyrenees

The Pyrenees have also attracted visitors with more otherworldly aspirations. No history of the mountains can ignore the fourteen-year-old peasant girl named Bernadette Soubirous, who claimed to have seen the Virgin Mary fourteen times in the grotto of Massabielle at the little market town of Lourdes in 1858. Though the Catholic Church was initially skeptical, the papacy eventually endorsed these visitations and transformed Lourdes into the most well-known Marian shrine in the world, attracting 4 to 6 million pilgrims each year. Some come merely to pay homage to the Virgin, while the grotto's supposedly curative waters also attract the sick, the disabled, and the dying in search of miracle cures.

The Lourdes pilgrimage has transformed this little Pyrenean market town into a garish outpost of Catholic religious kitsch, in which fast-food restaurants alternate with endless shops selling Marian souvenirs and windows filled with nothing but plaster statuettes of the Virgin. This transformation was already well advanced in 1903, when Edith Wharton visited the town and expressed her horror at "this vast sea of vulgarism—the more aggressive and intolerable because its last waves break against one of the loveliest landscapes in this lovely country."[51] Two decades later Leon Trotsky was equally contemptuous of what he called "a shop for miracles, a business office for trafficking in Grace," which combined "the paltry miracles of the Gospels side by side with the radio-telephone . . . the union of proud technology with the sorcery of the Roman chief druid."[52]

In the interwar years, the Pyrenees also began to attract devotees of a very different cult, as a result of their proximity to the former strongholds of the medieval Cathar heresy. In 1931–32 a young German scholar named Otto Rahn (1904–39) came to the former Cathar fortress of Montségur, in the Ariège *département*, where the Cathars held their last stand before their military defeat in 1244. Rahn's interest in the castle was largely due to Wolfram von Eschenbach's thirteenth-century epic poem *Parzifal*, which also inspired

Wagner's opera of the same name. A romantic and erratic literary scholar, Rahn, like Wagner, believed that the poem contained coded messages dictated by the Cathars to an Occitanian troubadour who had made his way to Germany. These messages allegedly proved that the Cathars had once possessed the mystical cup or container known as the Holy Grail, and both Rahn and Wagner believed that the "Gral Castle" Muntsalvatsche in Eschenbach's poem was located near Montségur.

Rahn first began to develop these crackpot theories in a book entitled *Kreuzzug gegen den Gral* (1933), which was translated into English as *Crusade Against the Grail: The Romantic Culture in Creation and in Death*. These efforts caught the attention of Heinrich Himmler's "ancestral-clairvoyant" guru, the runologist Karl Maria Wiligut, more commonly known by the pseudonym Weisthor, who worked for the Department for Pre- and Early History at the SS Race and Settlement Main Office in Munich. Weisthor and Himmler were both fascinated by Holy Grail mysticism and they were so thrilled by Rahn's ideas that they invited him to join the SS. This was not an invitation that could be refused lightly, and any lingering inclination Rahn may have had to refuse it was swiftly overcome by a 1,000-reichsmark advance to write a sequel. Asked by a friend at the 1936 Olympic Games why he was sporting an SS uniform and dagger, Rahn reportedly replied, "My dear Paul, one must eat."

The SS ensured that Rahn ate well. In 1936 he went to Iceland with a team of twenty SS-supplied "researchers" to look for the Grail. The same quest brought him back to Montségur and resulted in the publication of *Luzifers Hofgesind, eine Reise zu den guten Geistern Europas* (Lucifer's Court: A Heretic's Journey in Search of the Light Bringers, 1937)—a grab bag of allusions, insinuations, and improbable fantasies that requires an almost total suspension of logic and disbelief to accept even its most basic premises. Many readers might share Rahn's disgust at the Catholic Church's brutal suppression of the Cathars but struggle to accept that the Holy Grail was made from a jewel fallen from Lucifer's crown that was kept in Montségur by the Cathar "queen" Esclarmonde de Foix, or that the Cathars were descended from Hercules, Jason and the Argonauts, and the god Apollo "the lightbringer," all of whom belonged to "Lucifer's court."

Rahn believed—or allowed his readers to believe—that the Cathars had buried the Grail and other treasures in a cave somewhere near Montségur, and he spent many hours looking for it, accompanied by his Senegalese servant and bodyguard Habdu. It would be something of an understatement to observe that these investigations generally lacked empirical rigor. On the contrary, Rahn's portentous and overblown prose often hints at dark mysteries and secrets that might have pleased his SS sponsors but are likely to have little appeal to readers with a modicum of common sense or critical analysis. He was prone to exaggeration and even falsification. On one occasion he was caught in one of the Montségur caves tracing an extension of a painting that he found there. He also wrote various draft replies for a written interview in which he claimed to have found a "sculpted stone dog-figure" in the Fontanet Cave, whose dimensions he changed from 10 feet to 30 (3 meters to 9). In another episode he kills a viper in the Val de L'Incant (Enchanted Valley) near Montségur, which he suggests was protecting the Grail.[53]

Rahn's hazy quest for "the ghosts of the pagans and heretics who were my ancestors" nevertheless pleased Himmler sufficiently to earn him a promotion to the rank of SS-Obersturmführer in September 1938. Later that year "the original Indiana Jones," as some of his admirers have called him, fell from grace, possibly because of his homosexuality and/or his alcoholism. In March 1939 he was found frozen to death in the Kufstein mountains near Tyrol, in circumstances that have been disputed by "secret historians" with very similar ideas and preconceptions. Some claim he was murdered by the SS. One of his biographers insists that Rahn was himself an "Argonaut" who found the Holy Grail and heroically concealed its location so that Hitler would not be able to make use of its mystic powers.[54]

* * *

Rahn's writings may not have carried much scholarly weight, but they were instrumental in establishing the Pyrenees as a sacred landscape in the Nazi imagination, where the Holy Grail and other arcane mysteries were waiting to be discovered. In November 1938 a Dutch Nazi paleontologist named Assien Böhmers visited the mountains on behalf of the SS's esoteric research unit, the Ahnenerbe, in order to investigate Himmler's belief in the divine origins of the Aryan race. Böhmers did not believe this theory himself; he saw this mission as an opportunity to prove his own belief that the Aryan race was descended from Cro-Magnon origins and thought he had found confirmation of this hypothesis in the antlered shaman-like painting of "the Sorcerer" in the cave complex of Les Trois-Frères in Montesquieu-Avantès, in the Ariège.

These findings did not please Himmler, who informed Böhmers that the notion that Aryans were descended from primates was "insulting to humans," and the "Pyrenean Holy Grail" theory continued to haunt the Nazi imagination even during the war.[55] According to the Catalan writer Montserrat Rico Góngora, Himmler personally visited the Catalan abbey of Santa María de Montserrat during a state visit to Barcelona in October 1940 in an attempt to find out whether the monastery really was the "marvellous castle of Montsalvat in the Pyrenees."[56] Other stories speculate that Otto Skorzeny—the SS colonel who led the rescue mission to liberate Mussolini—was sent on a secret mission to the Pyrenees in 1944, where he located a number of Cathar treasures, including the Ark of the Covenant and the Holy Grail, and hid them in the Schleigeiss Glacier; and that a plane carrying the Nazi racial ideologue Alfred Rosenberg flew over Montségur during a 1944 ceremony to mark the seven hundredth anniversary of the destruction of the Cathars, and formed the shape of a giant Celtic cross in the sky as a mark of respect.

The Cathar lands of southern France have also generated more recent quasi-religious fantasies as a result of books such as Dan Brown's *The Da Vinci Code* and Michael Baigen, Richard Leigh, and Henry Lincoln's 1980s bestseller *Holy Blood, Holy Grail* (1982), which the *New York Times* once described as "one of the all-time great works of pop pseudohistory." Both books were based on the conspiracy uncovered by Bérenger Saunière, the priest at the town of Rennes-le-Château near Montségur, when he found parchments hidden inside a hollow altar pillar in the town's church in the 1890s. These documents allegedly revealed the existence of a secret centuries-old Catholic society called the Priory of Sion, supposedly established to conceal the fact that Mary Magdalene had married Jesus and escaped to France after the Crucifixion, where she founded the Merovingian dynasty of French kings, thereby transforming the *san greal* (Holy Grail) of Christ's bloodline into the *sang real* (royal blood) of the Merovingians.

In the 1990s these documents were revealed to have been planted in the Bibliothèque Nationale de France by a fraudster named Pierre Plantard in 1956 as part of an elaborate hoax to establish his own connections to the Merovingians. This debunking has not diminished the flow of visitors to Rennes-le-Château and its environs. In December 2012 hundreds of visitors and journalists converged on the nearby village of Bugarach, in the foothills of the Eastern Pyrenees, in the belief that the world was going to end on December 21 that year and that Bugarach would be the only place left standing. This prediction appears to have originated from an Internet story that claimed that the five-thousand-year-old Mayan "Long Count Calendar" had predicted this outcome.

It was never clear why the Mayans would have selected a sleepy Pyrenean village of two hundred residents to be one of the few places left standing, or whether they agreed that the Pic du Bugarach, which overlooks the village, was a UFO landing site from which aliens would emerge to take the surviving humans to another planet. But in the febrile and often evidence-free world of the twenty-first century, this combination of Cathars, Mayans, aliens, and the end of days proved irresistible, and Bugarach found itself so overwhelmed with visitors in the winter of 2012 that canny locals were selling "Apocalypse Pizza" and "End of the World" vintage, and renting rooms for $1,600 (€1,300) a night. On December 21, dozens of journalists converged on Bugarach, none of whom reported seeing any UFOs arriving or departing. The world did not end, but the Pyrenees were once again confirmed as a treasure trove of secret histories and grand conspiracies, where ancient mysteries are always hidden, but never found.

9

Lost Kingdoms

The Pyrenees are a cedar flung high;
Peoples nest, like birds, amongst its branches,
Whence no race-feeding vulture can remove them;
Each and every range where life takes hold
Is but a branch of this superb colossus,
This mighty trunk of life.
                    —Jacint Verdaguer, *Mount Canigó*, 1886[1]

The fascination with the Cathars is not limited to Nazis and connoisseurs of mystical conspiracy theories. Today the Department of Aude advertises itself as "Pays Cathare"—Cathar Country—and promotes its Cathar castles and towns as part of its identity as a "land of history and tourism, of warmth and authenticity." Each year thousands of walkers trek through the medieval castles of the "Sentier Cathare" (Cathar Way), which runs roughly parallel to the Pyrenees from Foix in the west to Port-la-Nouvelle on the coast. Numerous "Cathar holidays" in France and Catalonia follow the trails supposedly taken by the Cathar Bon Hommes (Good Men) across the Pyrenees while fleeing persecution into Spain. One company advertises a walking holiday in the Pays Cathare through "a time forgotten landscape of legend and great natural beauty." Another promises clients the opportunity to "discover the land of the heretical Cathars and solve the mystery of Rennes-le-Château— inspiration for Dan Brown's *Da Vinci Code*." Yet another offers "good local food, robust Languedoc wines and a part of the Pyrenees that has a strong Mediterranean influence," where visitors can "find secret trails and castles of the châteaux Cathars."

The unlikely transformation of one of Europe's most brutal episodes of religious persecution into a leisure destination for gastronomers, winetasters, and recreational walkers owes as much to pop culture and esoteric fantasy as it does to the more enduring romantic fascination with the Cathar tragedy itself. But the reinvention of "Cathar Country" is only one of many different ways in which history and the imagination have combined to give the Pyrenees their very particular *genius loci*. On one level this should not be surprising. For a mountain range that has so often been depicted as a savage and inhuman wilderness, the Pyrenees are saturated with history. Physical evidence of thousands of years of human settlement can be found up and down the mountains, from prehistoric dolmens, watchtowers, castles, churches, and mountain chapels to medieval walled towns and villages, statues and monuments. Yet until the eighteenth and nineteenth centuries this history received little attention from the outside world. Before their "discovery," the Pyrenean past, insofar as it was known or remembered at all, tended to be considered solely in terms of its relevance to the history of Spain or France.

With the emergence of the Pyrenees as a tourist destination in the nineteenth century this began to change, as travelers and tourists increasingly included the more notably dramatic or picturesque components of the Pyrenean past in their travelogues and itineraries. Thus the erudite polymath Sabine Baring-Gould insisted that his book on the Pyrenees was "not a guide, but an introduction to the chain, giving to the reader a sketch of the History of the Country he visits." Other nineteenth-century travelers included key places associated with Pyrenean history alongside their descriptions of the mountains and the landscape.

Such references generally served the same purpose that historical summaries do in contemporary tourist guides; they provided atmosphere, intellectual interest and stimulation, and a colorful embellishment to the landscape itself. In establishing the (romantic)

Pyrenean past as a tourist attraction, however, these potted histories also helped to shape the way the Pyrenees were imagined and perceived by those who passed through them and by those who imagined them from a distance. This interest was not only touristic. As was the case with mountain ranges elsewhere in Europe, the Pyrenees acquired a new significance in the nineteenth century in both Spain and France as a unique and grandiose landscape that was a source of national pride; as repository of national resources and national power; as a site of scientific exploration and discovery—and also as a landscape of culture and history that was both regional and national. In effect, the mountains became part of the way that both Spain and France imagined and defined themselves, in which the old image of the "savage frontier" was displaced by the recognition that the Pyrenees had a history, and this history was also part of the national stories of Spain and France. In the same period, Pyrenean history began to fire the nationalist imagination of the "states within states" whose territories also reached into the Pyrenees.

For the history of the Pyrenees is not just the history of Spain and France; it is also the history of Aragon, Catalonia, Navarre, and the Basque Country, of Languedoc and Occitania, of the ancient counties of Foix and Toulouse and the former viscounty of Béarn, of the "co-principality" of Andorra and many other lordships, counties, and viscounties associated with particular localities and Pyrenean places. Some of these states and statelets belong to what the historian Norman Davies calls "half-forgotten Europe," and some are barely remembered at all.[2] But others have provided cultural inspiration to nations-in-waiting whose territories reach across both sides of the Pyrenees, and which have never fully accepted the reality of the Pyrenean border.

States into Provinces

A complete political history of the Pyrenees before the advent of the nation-state is beyond the scope of this book. Such a history would have to go back to the Celtiberian tribes conquered by the Romans, to the Franks and the Visgothic province of Septimania. To do justice to its subject, such a history would have to trace the political histories of individual Pyrenean valleys whose rulers often had only tenuous control over them, and the convoluted evolution of dynastic houses, countships, and lordships as a result of armed conflict, territorial acquisition, dynastic changes, and strategic marriages. Some of the great Pyrenean seigneurial houses, such as Foix, Ribagorça, and Sobrarbe, established by the Franks in the Spanish March, controlled the lives of thousands of people until well into the sixteenth century, and would require entire books dedicated only to them.

Today the "*foral* (chartered) community" of Navarre in Spain is all that remains of the medieval Kingdom of Navarre, which once extended from the Basque provinces in the west to the upper Ebro Valley in the east, with its capital in Pamplona. During the high-watermark of Navarrese power under Sancho III "the Great" (994–1035), Navarre also reached northward across the Pyrenees into France and south into Spain almost as far as Burgos. By the end of the fourteenth century, a traveler crossing the Spanish Pyrenees from west to east would have passed through the Castilian Basque provinces, the remnant of the Kingdom of Navarre and its former territories in the Crown of Aragon, the co-principality of Andorra, and the principality of Catalonia.

On the French side of the mountains the same journey would have taken the traveler through a mosaic of territorial jurisdictions, beginning with the French royal territories of Guyenne and crossing the viscounties of Soule and Béarn and the countships of Bigorre, Comminges, Armagnac, Foix, and ending with Languedoc—part-annexed to France in 1229 following the suppression of the Albigensian heresy—and the countship of Roussillon, which was part of Catalonia. In 1512 Ferdinand of Aragon assumed the title of king of Navarre and invaded the seven-hundred-year-old kingdom, driving its rulers Catherine and Jean d'Albret north into the splinter kingdom of Basse-Navarre in the *ultra puertos* (beyond the passes) of the Pyrenees, thus initiating more than a decade of war, which finally came to an end when Hispanic Navarre was annexed by Castile in 1524, leaving only the viscounty of Béarn and Basse-Navarre under the control of the Albrets.

In 1589 the kingdoms of Navarre and France were united when Henry III of Navarre (1553–1610) became King Henry IV of France, and in 1620 the two kingdoms were definitively merged. By 1694 a French map of *Les Monts Pyrénées* placed all these territories within the *confins* (borders) of Spain or France. The same map also includes the former Catalan territories of Roussillon as part of the French *confins* in recognition of the acquisitions obtained as a result of the Treaty of the Pyrenees. Other countships and viscounties of the French Pyrenees were subsequently absorbed into new administrative departments created as a result of the French Revolution. These new boundaries were confirmed in the marvelous maps designed by the nineteenth-century French cartographer Victor Levasseur (1800–70), which combined cartographic detail about the regions of France with evocative illustrations of historic places and personalities associated with them.

A similar process unfolded in the Spanish Pyrenees. In 1479 the Crowns of Castile and Aragon were formally merged in an arrangement that laid the basis for the creation of the Spanish state and the end of Aragonese autonomy. Even after the union of the two crowns, the Aragonese and the Catalans continued to hold on tenaciously to their medieval autonomy. In 1716 the Catalans lost their language and their medieval liberties as a result of the Nueva Planta decrees, promulgated in the aftermath of the War of the Spanish Succession by the Bourbon monarch Philip V. On paper, the only independent remnants of the medieval past in the Spanish Pyrenees in the eighteenth century were the Val d'Aran and Andorra. Until 1834, the former continued to enjoy

the autonomy granted by James II of Aragon in 1313, which exempted its inhabitants from feudal duties in exchange for annual
tributes of wheat.

The co-principality of Andorra was first granted a charter by
Charlemagne in the eighth century as reward for its assistance in
fighting the Saracens, and it still retains the status of a semi-
independent state under the co-administration of France and the
bishopric of Urgell. By the end of the nineteenth century a journey
across the Spanish Pyrenees was administratively, if not culturally,
a journey through Spain and France, with the exception of Andorra, and it was in this period that travelers first began to discover the lost Pyrenean past as a point of attraction and an object
of fascination.

The Lord of Foix

As is often the case, such interest inevitably tended to focus on the
more colorful and romantic aspects of Pyrenean history that reflected contemporary assumptions and expectations about mountains and their inhabitants. Victor Hugo noted the republican spirit
of the Basque provinces and the "deep secret bond, which nothing
has been made to break, [that] ties, in spite of treaties, those diplo-
matic borders, and in spite of the Pyrenees, those natural borders,
all the members of the mysterious Basque family." During a visit to
Lourdes, James Erskine Murray reminded his English-speaking
readers of the days when Edward the Black Prince had ruled the
Western Pyrenees as prince of Aquitaine during the fourteenth
century and invited future visitors to consider "while they admire
the fine situation of the castle of Lourdes, and the gorgeous scenery
which surrounds it, that there was once a time when the banner of
England floated from its towers, when the elite of France could not
pluck it from its resting-place."[3]

In *Castles and Chateaux of Old Navarre and the Basque Provinces*
(1907), the American writer Francis Miltoun informed his readers

of his intention to go beyond the "geographical and topographical limits" of the old French provinces and generate an "imaginary hub" that would "radiate lines of historic and romantic interest."[4] Many travelers followed these conventions, and certain names and places tend to recur repeatedly in their writings. Few visitors to Cauterets resisted the temptation to describe the picnics where Marguerite of Angoulême, the queen of Navarre (1492–1549), allegedly composed the story cycle the *Heptaméron*—the French variant of Boccaccio's *Decamaron*—with her courtiers.

Visitors to the towns of Orthez and Foix invariably recounted the life and character of its most famous lord, Gaston III, Count of Foix and Viscount of Béarn (1331–91), more commonly known as Gaston Phoebus, and easily the most celebrated "romantic" figure in Pyrenean history. Phoebus was born in Béarn, which had only recently become part of the Comté de Foix at the end of the thirteenth century, and he was steeped in the independent traditions of the Pyrenean valleys and the Bearnese mountain clans, whose motto, *Toquey si gauses* (Touch me if you dare), he adopted as his own. Phoebus often demonstrated this prickly defiance in his dealings with outsiders. Though he pledged the allegiance of Foix to Philip VI during the Hundred Years' War, he refused to do the same on behalf of Béarn, on the grounds that "my lord Count is now in his own land of Béarn, which he holds from God and from no man in this world, and for which he is not required to aught but what pleases him." Phoebus maintained an equally lofty distance from the victorious Plantagenets and the Kingdom of Aragon.[5]

A courageous warrior and prolific hunter, he fought in various wars against an array of opponents that included the English, his archrivals the Counts of Armagnac, and Prussian pagans. Phoebus was not short of confidence or self-esteem; he gave himself the name Gaston Phoebus because of his blond hair and good looks, and he combined a taste for war and killing with a cultured and refined sensibility. He spoke three languages and various local dialects and wrote poetry and books, including the illustrated hunting manual known as *Le livre de chasse*, which contains a marvelous image of

Phoebus himself wearing a splendid purple gown embossed with gold griffons. His well-stocked library at the Foix château included translations of Arabic works on philosophy, math, and medicine, and his courts were renowned for their opulent entertainments and for the poets, musicians, and troubadours who gravitated to them.

Phoebus was also prone to violent rages and paranoia. He once stabbed a cousin to death. He also imprisoned his only son and heir, who he believed had tried to poison him, and killed him shortly afterward. In 1388 the chronicler Jean Froissart visited Phoebus in Orthez and was immediately smitten. "I have, in my time, seen many kings, princes, and knights," Froissart wrote, "but I have never met such a good-looking and well-formed man, with such a fine figure and such a pleasing and attractive face."[6] Froissart attended the nocturnal feasts that began at midnight, when guests were summoned to Phoebus's castle by trumpet to be entertained by an "indoor circus," confections served in the shape of castles, mythical beasts, and allegorical figures, and an array of jugglers, dancing bears, wrestling matches, strongmen, and minstrels, who included Phoebus himself.

Froissart's writings did much to create the reputation of the "lord of the Pyrenees," which continues to attract visitors to the imposing castle that looms over the medieval town of Foix, where Phoebus held one of his courts. Phoebus's place in French history is primarily due to his ability to maintain his independence on the contested French/Aragonese borderlands, and his unsuccessful attempt to create what the French historian Pierre Tucoo-Chala once called "a grand homogeneous Pyrenean state from Foix to Orthez."[7] But his colorful character and his associations with medieval chivalry and troubadour culture made him an obligatory reference in nineteenth-century Pyrenean travelogues. Louisa Stuart Costello paid tribute to the "magnificent Count of Foix" and James Erskine Murray lamented the transformation of his former castle in Foix from an "abode of royal power and lordly pomp" into a debtors' prison.[8]

* * *

Another indispensable historical figure in nineteenth-century travelogues was Henry IV of France (1553–1610), one of the most popular of all French kings. Like Phoebus, Henry was a product of the
independent Bearnese/Navarrese tradition. The son of the dour
Huguenot bigot Jeanne d'Albret (1528–72), the queen regnant of
Navarre, he was born in Pau but grew up with the children of peasants and servants, where he learned the rough-and-ready manners
that later earned him the mockery of the French court. As a child
and a young man, his mother subjected him to a harsh parental
regime that included regular beatings, poor food, and visits to the
high mountains in all weathers to toughen him up. On one occasion Albret sent the young Henry into the mountains in the middle
of a storm to prevent a duel that she had invented.

Like Phoebus, Henry was a passionate hunter and was fond of
hunting bears. Though he fought bravely and ruthlessly for the
Huguenot cause during the Wars of Religion as king of Navarre, he
was a considerably more tolerant and amenable character than his
mother, with a fondness for food, women, and tennis. Though he
converted to Catholicism in 1589 in order to gain the French throne,
his experience of the Wars of Religion and as an independent ruler
of a peripheral Pyrenean state gave him sufficient independence of
mind to sign the Edict of Nantes in 1598, which legalized freedom
of conscience for the first time in France. Regarded by the decadent
French court as an uncouth ruffian, he never lost touch with his
Pyrenean roots. He regularly asked for grapes, figs, and even geese
to be sent to his court from his native Béarn, and he famously
promised that every peasant would have a "chicken in his pot" on
Sundays—a gesture that undoubtedly owed much to his familiarity
with the peasants he had known as a child.

Many nineteenth-century visitors traveled through the Pyrenees
carrying a copy of Froissart's medieval chronicles or *The Song of
Roland*, which they often quoted or referred to in describing what
they saw. On visiting Roncesvalles Lady Georgiana Chatterton

A landscape steeped in history: Pau with a view of Henry IV's chateau in the background, ca. 1890–1900. (Library of Congress)

imagined Roland's "brilliant cortège winding through those romantic defiles, and thought of the various songs and legends which describe the battle" before quoting from the poem.[9] "The shades of Henry and Sully [Maximilien de Béthune, Duke of Sully and Henry's informal chief minister] are said sometimes *to walk* along the ramparts even now," wrote Louisa Stuart Costello of a visit to Henry IV's château at Pau in 1844, "and it is firmly believed that near the great reservoir into which was said, Queen Jeanne used to have her Catholic prisoners thrown, numerous ghosts of injured men might be seen flitting to and fro."[10]

The historical fascination for men like Phoebus and Henry IV and women like Marguerite of Angoulême was not due simply to their personalities or their achievements. Such rulers also demonstrated a streak of independence and defiance to central authority that many outsiders regarded as characteristic of the peoples of the Pyrenees in general, and which they found attractive and even inspiring. "Each valley is still a little world which differs from the neighbouring world as Mercury does from Uranus," wrote the French economist Michel Chevalier in 1837 during a visit to the Eastern Pyrenees and Andorra. "Each village is a clan, a kind of state with its own form of patriotism. There are different types and characters at every step, different opinions, prejudices and customs."[11] Henry Swinburne commented on "the violent spirit of the Catalans, and their enthusiastic passion for liberty, [which] have often rendered the country the seat of civil war and bloodshed."[12] Michelet celebrated the "two impetuous spirits—the Basque and the Catalan"— as "warders" at the two extremities of the Pyrenees, "who introduce the stranger with marked appropriateness into the strange country of Don Quixote."[13] There were also those who saw the Pyrenees as a kind of living premodern museum, in which the appealing spirit of independence that many of them admired in the individual rulers of Pyrenean mountain-kingdoms had been miraculously preserved in whole communities.

Pyrenean Utopias

Such notions often converged on the Pyrenean "micro-republic" of Andorra. A stream of books and articles such the *The Republic of the Pyrenees* (1869), *Andorra, the Hidden Republic* (1912), and "Andorra: The Republic of the Pyrenees" (1895) give an indication of the curious fascination for the autonomous Pyrenean co-principality in the second half of the nineteenth and early twentieth centuries. Andorra's curious status dates back to Charlemagne's eighth-century expedition against the Moors—an event that is still celebrated in the Andorran national anthem, "El gran Carlemany" (The Great Charlemagne), which praises "The great Charlemagne, my father / from the Saracens liberated me." In 1287 a constitutional arrangement known as the Pariatges (Sharing) signed between the Count of Foix, Roger-Bernard III, and the bishop of Urgell exempted Andorrans from their feudal obligations in exchange for a biennial tribute to the Counts of Foix and the bishopric of Urgell.

Though Foix—later France—and the bishops of Urgell ruled the co-principality through their deputies, or *viguiers*, Andorra effectively governed itself through a general council elected by members of its six communes, or parishes. It had no police force and no army, except for a standing militia of six hundred men drawn from individual households, each of which was obliged to keep a musket, one pound of gunpowder, twenty-four balls, and caps, in the event of a call-up. Such events were rare. Until the completion of a road connecting it to the town of La Seu d'Urgell in 1914, Andorra could be reached from France or Spain only by bridle paths and mule trails. The territory is only 150 square miles (388 square kilometers), and at the end of the nineteenth century it had little more than three thousand inhabitants.

The existence of this remote mountain republic nevertheless intrigued many outsiders. When one of the male protagonists in Charlotte Gillman Perkins's feminist utopian novel *Herland* (1915) suggests that his companions' search for an uncharted female enclave might be fruitless, Vandyck "Van" Jennings responds, "What's that old republic up in the Pyrenees somewhere—Andorra? Precious few people know anything about it, and it's been minding its own business for a thousand years."

In the nineteenth century a number of travelers visited the co-principality and depicted it as a lost mountain utopia of a different kind. For James Erskine Murray, Andorra was "the oldest free republic in existence," whose inhabitants enjoyed "more real and substantial liberty, than was ever enjoyed under the purest of the Italian republics."[14] More than half a century later Harold Spender and his compantions met the former president of Andorra Francesco Duran at the Andorran capital, Andorra la Vella, and spent hours quizzing him about the organization of the republic and its constitution. Spender left these conversations "well content that there should be still one country in Europe where the power of wealth plays so small a part and the health of simple living is as yet so little marred by the 'sick disease of modern life.'"[15]

Spender was pleased that a recent attempt to transform the spa at Les Escaldes into a "combined bathing and gaming centre—a sort of second Monaco"—had been blocked by France, even though it was supported by the bishop of Urgell, because "there is no need to thrust a gambling hell into the centre of this quiet pastoral country." Other travelers echoed the image of Andorra as a republican Shangri-La that had remained miraculously untouched by the modern world. American travelers were particularly impressed by Andorra's republican virtues. In *The Republic of the Pyrenees* (1869) the American poet and diplomat Bayard Taylor described the co-principality as "an ark of safety to strangers, as well as an inviolable home of freedom to its own inhabitants." Taylor wrote of his first sight of this long-sought-after mountain republic, in which "the day was exquisitely clear and sunny; the breezes of the Pyrenees blew away every speck of vapour from the mountains, but I saw everything softly through that veil which the imagination weaves for us."[16]

Other travelers viewed the co-principality through a similar veil. In *Andorra, the Hidden Republic* (1912), another American, Lewis Gaston Leary, a Presbyterian minister and teacher at the American College in Beirut, described his first sight of the co-principality he had spent years thinking about: "Yonder, in the golden glory that broke between the black storm clouds which shrouded her mountain ramparts, lay sheltered the strangest, least-known country in Europe—the hidden Republic of Andorra." For Leary, the inhabitants of Andorra were "the freest persons in the world," despite their grinding poverty and the domination of their government by a landowning aristocracy. Even the "invincibile taciturnity" that so many travelers noted in Andorrans was a product of their proud tradition of independence, Leary believed, since "you feel that they are so undemonstrative, not because they are churlish, but because, for all their poverty and illiteracy, they have the instincts of gentlemen."[17]

Not all travelers were so enamored of Andorra's anachronistic rustic charms. For the English traveler Victor Scott O'Connor, the Andorrans were "redeemed by their spirit of independence, by their love for this, their own fraction of the earth; otherwise there is little about them that is attractive. . . . They have accomplished nothing, they have no history, no great memories; unpicturesque to look at, they have moved forward but little in ten centuries. What profit is there in such independence? This is no idyllic peasantry, children of Hellas and of light, but just the rude Catalan in his primitive state."[18]

Some seekers of Pyrenean mountain utopias found an even more improbable object of desire and wish fulfillment in the tiny hamlet of Goust in the French commune of Laruns. Situated 3,264 feet (995 meters) up on a mountain plateau less than a square mile (2.5 square kilometers) wide at the southern end of the Vallée d'Ossau, Goust consists of eight or ten houses and its population has rarely reached more than a hundred or so inhabitants. Many of them have lived for a long time. Centenarians have been common on the Goust plateau, and one man who was born in 1442 was allegedly given a pension by Henry IV before he finally died in 1605. Goust's claims to republican status have always been nebulous, and it is not clear whether it has ever officially been a republic. Nevertheless, an 1848 article in *Chambers's Edinburgh Journal* described the "unknown Republic" as a "little fairy oasis, belonging more to the air than the earth," ruled by a twelve-member government of wise patriarchs whose absence of pretension, ostentation, and hypocrisy was in stark contrast to the world below.[19]

In a year in which Europe was wracked by revolutions, the author found in Goust "an almost absolute equilibrium, individual, social and territorial" and "an expression of the democratic state in its simplest and purest form," whose only defect as a model for the rest of the continent was the narrow conformity of its social organization, which meant that "in it individuals are nothing, and the mass everything." Other visitors similarly portrayed Goust as a repository of ancient republican virtue. In 1890 Edwin Asa Dix visited what he called "this unique settlement, solitary, indifferent to time, and its new ways, Nature's 'children lost in the clouds.'" On climbing the steep path to the plateau and finding a handful of peasant women outside "eight hoary, grey-stone hovels," Dix and his companions doffed their hats while he explained that "we have come from America to see this settlement, and that any courtesy they may extend will be considered as official by the nation we represent."[20]

Dix's tongue may have been firmly in cheek, but he was genuinely impressed by the egalitarian nature of the Goust republic and its inhabitants, whom he described as "those who fill, and fill faithfully, their single niches, living moveless as the trees." In an 1894 feature on "pinhead republics," a reporter from the U.S. *Democratic Standard* visited Goust and observed that "since the seventeenth century the population has varied but little . . . the inhabitants are long lived and robust, are shepherds and weavers of cloth and seem entirely contented with their lot, having little ambition either for riches or power." The reporter was struck by the absence of churches and cemeteries, which obliged "the inhabitants of this tiny mountain republic" to build a chute "down which they slide heavy articles and the bodies of their dead to the cemetery far below." In fact Goust was never quite as hermetically sealed as it seemed. Its inhabitants regularly descended to the surrounding valleys to sell their wool, seek wives and husbands, attend mass, and marry and baptize their children. Nevertheless, the idea of such Pyrenean "mini-republics," whose ancient virtues had remained preserved through their isolation, was often more alluring for some of those who visited them than the reality—and perhaps also for more distant readers who never would.

Nations-in-Waiting

In his celebrated history of cultural attitudes to mountains, the historian Walther Kirchner noted the emergence of a "new national spirit" in Europe in the aftermath of the Napoleonic Wars, marked by a "more aggressive and exclusive character" that permeated "music, literature, art, and most of all politics" and which also reached into "the world of mountains, which soon begin to offer a field of special attraction for competitive nationalism."[21] In Kirchner's view, such competition was expressed primarily through the conquests of mountain summits that were seen to embody the courage, daring, and physical prowess of individual climbers and the nations they represented.

The Pyrenees offered few such tests of national endeavor in comparison with the Alps or the Himalayas, but Pyrenean history did provide a different kind of inspiration to the nationalist imagination in the nineteenth century. The emergence of Navarre as a Carlist stronghold during the Carlist Wars was partly due to the fear that medieval liberties, or *fueros*, which now define Navarre as a "chartered community," were under threat from the Spanish government, and such freedoms were often taken particularly seriously in the Pyrenean valleys that had governed their own affairs for centuries. Navarre's medieval past has also served as a reference point in modern Basque nationalism.

For most students of military history, the Maya Pass in Navarre is most famous for Marshal Soult's assault on Wellington's army in 1813. To many Basques however, the pass is associated with the battle that took place in 1522, when two hundred Navarrese knights fought off seven thousand Castilian soldiers in a castle just above the village of Maya (Amaiur in Basque), for the best part of a month, before they finally surrendered. The fall of the Maya castle ended the attempts of the Albret dynasty and its French allies to recover Navarre's lost territories from Castile, and paved the way for the temporary military occupation of much of Basse-Navarre by Castilian troops, who destroyed the castle to prevent its ever being used again.

Today the castle is undergoing restoration. At the center of the ruined battlements and ramparts, an obelisk of more recent construction pays homage in Spanish to "the men at the Castle of Maya who fought for the independence of Navarre: Everlasting Light." For Basque nationalists, the eleventh-century Kingdom of Navarre was the first and only time in their history in which the seven Basque territories were united in a single kingdom. This history inspired the monument that was built in 1922, which was blown up by Spanish nationalists in 1931, at a time when Navarre and the Basque provinces were debating a statute of regional autonomy under the Spanish Republic. It was not until 1982 that the monument was reconstructed, and it remains a landmark in Basque and Navarrese politics, to the point where a Basque leftist-nationalist electoral coalition gave itself the name Amaiur in 2011.

Other would-be nations have their own Pyrenean sites of remembrance. In front of the town hall at the Catalan town of Sort in La Seu d'Urgell, a bronze bust of the long-haired General Josep Moragues, the defender of Castelciutat in the War of the Spanish Succession, pays homage to the "forgotten hero" and defender of Catalan national identity, who was drawn and quartered by Bourbon troops in Barcelona in 1715. Every year on September 11 locals gather here to mark the National Day of Catalonia. To many Occitan nationalists, the Cathar fortress of Montségur remains a symbol of resistance to the French "foreign invaders" led by Simon de Montfort, whose victories paved the way for the annexation of Languedoc by France. The anticlerical poet and historian Napoléon Peyrat (1809–81) once described Montségur as "an Essenian Zion, a Platonist Delphi of the Pyrenees, a Johannite Rome, condemned and untamed in Aquitaine."[22]

The role of the Pyrenees in the nationalist imagination of these nations-in-waiting is not confined to memorializing and commemorative sites. From the music of Grieg to the Rocky Mountain painters, mountain landscapes often featured in the cultural nationalist imagination in the nineteenth century, and a similar process accompanied the development of a new national consciousness among Basques, Catalans, and Occitanians in the nineteenth century. Occitanian nationalists and linguistic revivalists have sometimes cited Gaston Phoebus as an inspiration. In his monumental dictionary compiling the dialects of southern France, the Occitan poet Frédéric Mistral compared himself to a "thoughtful shepherd" who "high up on the mountain slope . . . places a pile of stones in honor of his country, and marks the pastures where he has passed the summer."[23]

The Basque composer José María Usandizaga entitled his Basque-language 1910 opera *Mendi mendiyan* (High in the Mountains). In the Catalan composer Felip Pedrell Sabaté's opera *Els Pirineus* (1893), the "bard of the mountains" invites the audience "to see the Pyrenees . . . as I see them, cathedral of glory, fortress and palace, tribune and temple, reliquary of all that is great and refuge of all that is splendid, the splendours, haven for every thinker and every proscribed thing, protection for every liberty and every school."[24] The contemporary resonances of Balaguer's references to the persecution of the Cathars would not have been missed by nineteenth-century Catalan audiences who saw Catalonia as a prisoner of the Spanish state.

The Pyrenees were a key focus of the Catalan "excursionist" movement of the late nineteenth century. In 1890 the Associació Catalanista d'Excursions Científiques (Catalan Association of Scientific Excursions) was reestablished as the Centre Excursionista de Catalunya (Catalan Excursionist Centre, CEC). For the CEC, "excursionism" was never simply about hiking and the outdoors: it was combined intellectual and aesthetic discovery with a strongly nationalist and patriotic orientation. Its members were encouraged to explore the Catalan countryside and also to "get to know synthetically and analytically the ethnic personality and philosophy of Catalonia," as one of its members put it.

For the excursionists who contributed to the CEC's journal the *Butlletí del Centre Excursionista de Catalunya*, hiking was a process of discovering—or rediscovering—*nostra terra* (our land), in which history, literature, folklore, and Romanesque churches were as significant as the study of rocks and plants. As Robert Hughes has written, "The reward for one's efforts was not only knowledge but a kind of historicist rapture, an ecstatic dreaming of the lost cultural past,"[25] which the artist Santiago Rusinyoll expressed during a hike through the Ter Valley in 1880 to the monastery of Santa María del Ripoll: "Ripoll!! What sweet inspirations and great memories crowd on the mind when we hear the echo of your glorious name among the mountains!! How the hearts of true Catalans beat when we hear it uttered! Ah! At last we are near you, jewel of the Middle Ages! Soon we will be in your humble monastery! We come to breathe the same air that hundreds upon hundreds of Benedictines have breathed here . . . we are entering an unknown land, dreamed of a thousand times."[26]

In 1908 the CEC established a Mountain Sports Section partly in order to avert the possibility, as one of its members anxiously put it, "of converting our excursionism into a mere pastime and giving it an essentially sportive character."[27] Though the new section promoted mountain sports such as skiing and sledging, these activities were always less significant than the physical, emotional, and intellectual journeys into the Catalan past. These aspirations inevitably focused on the Pyrenees, and on one mountain more than others.

The Sacred Mountain

No single individual was more responsible for bringing the Pyrenees to the attention of the nationalist imagination than the Catalan "poet laureate" Mossèn Jacint Verdaguer (1845–1902). A Catholic priest whose troubled relationship with the church almost resulted in his excommunication, Verdaguer was a prose writer as well as a poet, and a towering figure in the nineteenth-century Catalan cultural renaissance known as the Renaixença who almost single-handedly revived and revitalized the Catalan language after centuries of neglect. Verdaguer was also a fervent excursionist and pyreneist, whose reputation is largely due to his two epic poems, *L'Atlàntida* (1877) and *Canigó* (1886), both of which featured the Pyrenees as a background and even as a protagonist.

In 1879 he walked in the Pyrenees for the first time while undergoing medical treatment at the spa in Prats-de-Mollo, and between 1887 and 1894 he undertook numerous solitary walks in the Vall Fosca, the Val d'Aran, the Conflent Valley, and other parts of the Pyrenees, carrying a notebook in his rucksack in which he wrote meticulous descriptions of landscapes, rivers, compass bearings, and folktales that he collected in his journeys. Verdaguer's poetry and travel writings were often infused with a mournful and painful sense of Catalonia's lost medieval grandeur, and he found cause for inspiration and demoralization in his Pyrenean journeys.

He climbed various summits, including Aneto, the Pica d'Estats, and La Maladeta, but he is most famously associated with Mount Canigou (Canigó in Catalan), the most celebrated mountain in the Catalan Pyrenees, which became the subject of his epic poem *Canigó: llegenda pirenaica del temps de la reconquista* (Canigou: Pyrenean Legend from the Time of the Reconquest). Of all Pyrenean mountains, Canigou was particularly suited to become the subject of what the literary scholar Ricard Torrents has called "the foundational poem of the Catalan people." Standing at 9,134 feet (2,785 meters), just inside the present-day French province of Roussillon, Canigou has long been known as the "sacred mountain" of the Catalan people and a symbol of Catalonia itself. Every summer on June 23, hundreds of people carry burning torches down from a fire on top of the mountain to light bonfires across Catalonia for the festival of Saint John.

The mystique of Canigou is due partly to its location. It occupies a dominant position overlooking the historic Catalan territories of Roussillon, looming out of the flat plain in a curving fanlike shape that seems to be always visible wherever you are, and which offers views as far as Barcelona on clear days. Verdaguer climbed Canigou various times, and these hikes were reflected in the detailed descriptions of the landscape that permeate *Canigó*. The poem's 4,378 lines recount the tragic events that ensue when Gentil, a noble in eleventh-century Catalonia, falls in love with the fairy queen Flordeneu, who places him under a spell on the slopes of Canigou, so that he fails to answer the call to fight against the invading Saracens. Around this narrative, Verdaguer merges real places, people, and events from Catalan history with legends, myths, folktales, and a poetic celebration of the Pyrenean mountains and Canigou in particular: "Mount Canigó is an immense magnolia / That blooms on a spray of the Pyrenees / For bees it has its faeries hovering round / For butterflies, its eagles and its swans / And for its calyx rise its rugged cliffs / Silver in winter and golden in summer / Great goblet where the stars come drink their fragrance."

I first climbed the sacred mountain in the autumn of 2015, with my old friend Andreu from Barcelona. Andreu is a large, bear-like man who had not walked in serious mountains for some time, and he had never climbed Canigou. He also has asthma, and neither he nor I was entirely confident about his ability to reach the summit. But Andreu is also an ardent Catalanista who has been at the heart of the latest phase of Catalonia's struggle for independence over the last five years, and his determination was intensified by Catalonia's imminent regional elections, in which he hoped to see a new radical-nationalist coalition that would defy Madrid's refusal to allow a referendum on Catalan independence.

We met at Vernet-les-Bains two days before the elections. The next morning we made our way up the mostly boarded-up streets of the out-of-season spa town that Kipling once made famous. From Vernet, Canigou is less impressive than it appears from a greater distance. The summit is difficult to make out along the extended ridge that curves upward above a bare, hollowed-out cliff strewn with rocks and stones, and the mountain's fanlike shape is enhanced by the numerous smaller ridges, which converge on the summit like natural buttresses. Within half an hour this view had disappeared, as we were walking up a zigzag through a thick forest of pine and fir trees.

It was not until we had been walking for about two hours that Canigou reappeared again, and we saw the specks of Vernet-les-Bains and other towns and villages gleaming in the bright sunshine below. For the rest of the morning we walked mostly in shade, as the dirt path gave way to rocks and stones and curved its way briefly out onto ridges, promontories, and cliff edges before dipping back into the trees. There was no wind, running water, or birdsong, and only the sound of our own voices and footsteps disturbed the silence and stillness. Andreu walked slowly, stopping frequently to rest or take photographs, so that I sometimes walked on ahead. Whenever I was on the point of going back to look for him, he reappeared in his straw hat and red shirt bearing the slogan *Ara es l'hora* (Now is the time), walking at the same slow, steady pace. By midday we had begun to leave the forest behind us and were panting upward in the sunshine beneath an immaculate blue sky, or picking our way along narrow traverse paths and open trails with the most amazing views of the Conflent Valley and the Mediterranean to our left and the high peaks of the Pyrenees to our right.

In the late afternoon we reached the fork that led up to the summit and down toward the Portalet refuge. We had already decided to leave the summit to the next day, and we trudged down past the marshy remnants of the lake where King Peter III once claimed to have seen a dragon. We shared our table with Joan, a vigorous seventy-five-year-old Catalan from Barcelona, who had come to Canigou with his twenty-six-year-old daughter, Ana, he explained, to bring Catalonia good fortune in Sunday's elections. We went to bed early, after a dinner table conversation dominated by passionate discussion of politics, referendums, and independence, and the next day we woke up at dawn, just as the sky was turning red far below along the coast toward Perpignan.

After breakfast we headed back up to the fork and along the craggy ridge that led toward the summit, past hikers speaking a babel of languages: French, English, Spanish, and Catalan. Along the way I found Joan conversing with two "Catalans from the North," from Perpignan. "We want to escape from this shit that is Spain," he said. "I don't mean the Spanish—I mean Spain." The two Frenchmen nodded politely, but I sensed they were not entirely on board with this. When I commented on the range of nationalities present on Canigou that morning, one of them beamed and said plaintively, "But we are all brothers!" In the mountains that morning at least, we were. We had been walking for about an hour when we reached the narrow pile of sharp rocks that led up from the ridge to the summit, and I scrambled up to the little obelisk bearing a quote from the Catalan singer Lluís Llach and an extract from Verdaguer's poem.

Even though the sun was well up above the horizon, it was so cold that I could hardly feel my hands, and the wind and the narrowness of the summit unnerved me, as I sat down to look at the view. Far below me to the east a luminous plain of beige, brown, and sand dotted with the white patches of towns and cities gave way to the shimmering ocean. To the west the Pyrenees stretched out in all their jagged splendor beyond the metal cross with a Catalan flag attached to it, where Joan and his daughter and some of the other Catalans were draping themselves in flags and taking photographs.

A few minutes later Andreu came lumbering over the rocks at his sloth-like pace and whipped out the unofficial Catalan separatist flag known as the Estelada that he had brought along for the occasion. I sat and shivered while he posed for a photograph to send back to his local *asamblea*, and I was relieved when we descended from the summit and I was able to feel the sun's heat again. Andreu, Joan, and Ana were exhilarated by their political pilgrimage to what Joan called "the mythical mountain of Catalonia" and optimistic about the emergence of a pro-independence bloc in the next day's elections. Their pilgrimage had no obvious religious implications, but Canigou's "mythical" significance is at least in part due to the melancholy priest who had climbed it so many times. Nations have to be imagined before they can acquire a political form, through language, history, territory, landscape, and tradition, and Verdaguer reminded the Catalan people of what they had been, and could be, as he invited his countrymen to imagine a mountain that he described as "a giant of Spain / Of Spain—and Catalan."

PART IV

A Home Above the World

Mountains of the Pyrenees
you are my beloved,
Fortunate cabins,
You always please me.
Nothing is more beautiful than my homeland,
nothing is sweeter than my friends.
O mountain men
sing all together
the peace and the fortune of my country.
Halt, halt, halt there
The mountain men are there.
—Alfred Roland, *Tyrolienne des Pyrénées*

10

Mountain People

We were soon accosted by two young mountaineers, handsome and well made; they were walking barefooted, but with
that grace and agility which so particularly distinguish the
natives of the Pyrenees. Their bonnets were tastily orna-
mented with mountain flowers; and an air of adventure about
them interested me exceedingly.
—Ramond de Carbonnières, *Travels in the Pyrenees*, 1813[1]

In the course of history Pyreneans have often been subject to the
shifting perceptions of the outside world, which have changed in
accordance with the perceptions of the mountains themselves.
Strabo wrote disparagingly of the "rough and savage manners" of
the barbarian tribes of Asturias, Cantabria, and the Pyrenees who
slept on the ground, fed on goats, and wore their hair long "after
the fashion of women." These Iberian mountain men were fond of
athletics, boxing, running, and martial games; they drank beer
instead of wine and danced to the sound of flutes and trumpets,
"springing up and sinking upon the knees."[2] Strabo wrote at a time
when mountains were generally associated in the Greek and
Roman imagination with primitiveness and barbarism. Long after the
Christianization of the Pyrenees, and the integration of the Pyrenees
into the Santiago de Compostela pilgrimage, however, their inhabitants were still regarded as a breed apart.

The *Codex Calixtinus* described Basques as "ferocious people;
and the land in which they dwell is savage, wooded and barbarous."[3]

The *Codex* reserved even harsher language for the Navarrese, who were comprehensively denounced as "debauched, perverse, perfidious, disloyal and corrupt, libidinous, drunkard, given to all kind of violence, ferocious and savage, impudent and false, impious and uncouth, cruel and quarrelsome, incapable of anything virtuous, well-informed of all vices and iniquities."[4] These vices supposedly included "incestuous fornication" with animals, which allegedly led the Navarrese to attach locks to the behinds of their mules or horses in order to reserve exclusive rights to them—a ludicrously impractical precaution that undoubtedly existed only in the author's imagination.

From the eighteenth century onward, Pyreneans tended to be depicted more positively. Clarence Willoughby, the English hero of Anna Maria Porter's romantic novel *Roche-Blanche; or, The Hunters of the Pyrenees* (1822), grows up in Béarn and develops his agility, strength, and manly virtues through his interactions with the "inhabitants of the Pyrenees, to whom activity of body, and joyousness of spirit, were particularly dear." "The besetting sin of the Swiss—greed—I have never found in the Pyrenees," wrote the Scottish traveler and journalist Henry David Inglis in 1840. "The intercourse of the mountaineer with strangers has hitherto been too limited to dull his natural feelings of justice, kindness and generosity. . . . Crime of every description is rare in the Pyrenees; theft is very infrequent, and murder altogether unknown."[5]

The French cartographer Aymar d'Arlot de Saint-Saud (1853–1951) made numerous mapping expeditions of the Spanish Pyrenees, and often praised the mountaineers who assisted him for their sharpness and intellectual curiosity. In *Contribution a la Carte Des Pyrénées Espagnols* (Contribution to the Map of the Spanish Pyrenees, 1892), he listed "Goodness, amiability, generosity, candour, honesty, native pride" (my translation) as the principal characteristics of the Spanish inhabitants of the Aragonese and Catalan Pyrenees—virtues that he contrasted favorably with the mountaineers of his own country, who he found "less lively of body and spirit."[6] Nineteenth-century travel writings, paintings, postcards, and tourist posters often echoed these depictions in a more general celebration of

Pyrenean virtue, as the incorporation of the Pyrenees into the modern world was accompanied by the "discovery" of the people who lived in them. As was often the case in other "discovered" places in the same period, this fascination often focused on the more exotic and picturesque Pyrenean types, who were often depicted through the same romantic prism as the landscape itself.

Shepherds

Few occupations are more quintessentially Pyrenean than stock-breeding and animal husbandry, and few have been more romanticized and idealized by the outside world. Archaeological evidence suggests that shepherds were already grazing sheep, goats, and cattle and storing winter fodder in the Pyrenees in the Neolithic era, and some scholars contend that the abundance of prehistoric dolmens in some parts of the mountains mark ancient grazing trails to the high pastures. In his study of medieval transhumance in the Eastern Pyrenees, David Blanks described a pastoral economy whose essential hallmarks remained unchanged for centuries, in which peasant families depended on the sheep, goats, and cattle that provided them with milk, cheese, wool, soap, meat, and fertilizer, and bones to make containers, cards, knives, and flutes.[7]

Within this local village economy each member of the household played his or her part: the men who did the shearing; the women who spun the wool; the young boys who took the sheep to pasture; and the girls who carried them food or brought churns of milk and butter down from the mountains. Where possible, these herds were taken by adolescent boys to the nearest pastures and then brought back home the same day to share the house with their owners. If the pastures were farther away, these boy-shepherds would spend the night, and sometimes the whole summer, in the high mountains, where they were attended and supplied with messages and freshly baked bread by a team of messengers—usually girls—from the village. From November to mid-May their animals would feed on fodder.

At the other end of the spectrum were the big landowners, monasteries, or more distant entrepreneurs who hired professional shepherds to take large herds to and from the high pasturelands. These wage-earning shepherds were paid in coin and also in food to take sheep into the high pasturelands for the summer and then down to Catalonia and even as far as Valencia during the winter months. Some worked for multiple employers during their working lives and went on to become herders themselves. All these shepherds had to take into account the local *traités* agreed between the valleys and villages whose lands they passed through, and the tithes and other demands imposed by the secular and ecclesiastical authorities, for cheese, milk, and wool.

Once in the high mountains, the shepherds more or less governed themselves. From the Inquisitorial interrogations carried out by Jacques Fournier, the bishop of Pamiers, into the Cathar heresy in Montaillou in the Comté de Foix from 1318 to 1325, we know that the more well-established professional shepherds, or *bergers*, lived communally in groups of up to ten shepherds in shared huts, or *cabanes*, with flocks of one hundred animals or more. They spent the summer months watching over their animals and making cheese and milk, which they kept cool in specially dug pits or in little "reservoirs" in streams. The *cabanes* were organized into a rigid hierarchy that descended from the *chef de cabane* (head shepherd) all the way down to the lowly migrant shepherds, who were obliged to live in separate fenced-off sheep holds, or *cortals*, with their animals. Strict rules governed these medieval shepherd societies. Lower-ranking shepherds were not allowed to eat or drink before the head shepherd, and those who breached this etiquette could expect to be beaten or deprived of their supper.[8]

Pyrenean Arcadias

These medieval shepherd societies were regarded with suspicion by the Inquisition, as a result of their independence and their mobility, but they were often seen very differently in more recent times. Shepherds were a romantic staple of early modern and ancien regime literature, and in 1778 the popular French writer Stéphanie-Félicité de Genlis (1746–1830), better known under her nom de plume Madame de Genlis, described the real-life Pyrenean shepherds she encountered in the Campan Valley in terms that were fully in keeping with the conventions of Marie Antoinette's court. De Genlis's depictions of these shepherds were firmly rooted in the Arcadian tradition, whether she was describing the "rustic sounds of the flageolet and bagpipe; and the rural airs which the shepherds sung, seated on the brinks of rocks" or the "daughters of the Pyrenees, every one of them remarkable for their beauty and handsome shapes," taking baskets of fruit and cheese to their retired shepherd grandfathers.[9] On witnessing a shepherd throw a bouquet of roses to his betrothed, de Genlis concluded that "if happiness exists on earth, these are the manners, and these the sentiments, which should insure its possession."

These reflections were accompanied by a detailed description of the organization of these shepherd societies, in which shepherds as young as eight or nine guarded sheep on the hills immediately above the valley, while older shepherds went up into the high pastures. While the younger shepherds were able to "exercise themselves in clambering up the rocks; and leaping the rapid brooks they accustom themselves to look without horror on the amazing height of our precipices," retired shepherds worked in the valley below them as laborers, plowmen, or farmers. At the age of fifteen these boy-shepherds were handed the shepherd's crook by their fathers, who were given a spade to symbolize their new role as laborers, until finally they retired from all work and spent their days "supinely extended in the grass . . . plunged in deep and profound reveries."

Other visitors echoed de Genlis's celebration of the shepherds of the Pyrenees. The "true inhabitant of the Pyrenees, the native shepherd of these mountains, however uncultivated or poor is lively, generous, and noble, proud even in a state of degradation, and under every reverse of fortune," wrote Ramond of the men who often gave him shelter during his Pyrenean journeys.[10] For Ramond, these shepherds embodied a "true nobility" that was descended from "race not climate." Jules Michelet described "the roving life of these shepherds" as "one of the most picturesque elements in the south. These nomads, companions of the stars in their eternal solitude, half astronomers, half sorcerers, carry their goods with them."[11]

The life of a Pyrenean shepherd was not always as appealing as it seemed to outsiders. Shepherds on the transhumance routes in the high pastures, or *estives*, spent months away from home with little or no contact with their families or with any other people except their fellow shepherds. In some cases they had no shelter from inclement weather except for the coffin-like wooden boxes that they carried into the mountains with them or the dome-like dry-stone shelters known as *orris*, which can be found in the Ariège and other parts of the Pyrenees. The material rewards for so much time and effort were often meager—for the shepherds if not for the owners of their flocks and herds. "For notwithstanding the luxuriance of these valleys, little of their luxury, even to-day, goes to the tillers of their soil," Asa Dix observed in 1890. "The Pyrenean farmer or mountaineer has to support his family now, as in past ages, in poverty. Little beyond the most meagre of diet can he commonly provide them, and it is the joint anxiety of ensuring even this, that wears and disfeatures him and them, as much doubtless as its meagreness."[12] Shepherds on the transhumance routes were often absent for most of the year, spending the summers in the high mountains and the winters in the lowlands, visiting their wives and children only briefly. Not surprisingly their wives were often as lonely as their husbands, as the high rates of alcoholism and early pregnancies in the Aragonese Pyrenees attested.

The harsher realities of shepherding tended to be obscured in the beaming barefoot shepherds in Rosa Bonheur's Pyrenean paintings, or the Pyrenean shepherds standing with their crooks, their flocks, and their dogs against a pristine mountain backdrop in nineteenth-century French postcards and railway posters advertising

Traditional Pyrenean mountain life in the nineteenth century. Note the splendid modern bridge through the doorway. Thomas Allom, *A Cabaret in the Pyrenees: Rainy Day, ca. 1840* (Bibliothèque municipale de Toulouse, via Wikimedia Commons).

the *route thermale*. Spanish shepherds often featured in these French postcards, as wilder manifestations of the more "savage" Spanish Pyrenees, in their wide-brimmed hats and ponchos. In the early twentieth century, the Spanish photographer and pharmacist Ricardo Compairé Escartín (1883–1965) included some striking photographs of Spanish shepherds in the high mountains in his pioneering ethnographic studies of upper Aragon. Compairé was an avid pyreneist, and his lovingly posed images of shepherds and peasants in traditional costume were consciously intended to record customs, costumes, and traditions that had already begun to vanish from the mountains. Not for the first or last time, the idealization of Pyrenean heritage and tradition in nineteenth- and early twentieth-century iconography was infused with an element of nostalgia for societies that were already being radically transformed by modernity.

The Dark Valley

Something of the magnitude of this transformation can be gleaned from a visit to the Vall Fosca (Dark Valley), just south of the Aigüestortes National Park, in the Catalan Pyrenees. The valley takes its name from the steep, narrow slopes that limit the light it receives during the winter months, and most visitors reach it from the main road that leads up toward the Vall d'Aran and France. Shortly after leaving the town of Pont de Suert you turn off to the right along a road that roughly follows the line of the Flamisell River, and then drive up a curving mountain road between steep slopes still thick with oaks and holm oaks, rising past a succession of stepped meadows dotted with the nondescript ski villages that abound in the Catalan Pyrenees.

Until the early twentieth century the Vall Fosca was almost completely isolated from the outside world. Its fourteen hundred inhabitants lived in nineteen villages and hamlets in a semifeudal agrarian society dominated by three families, without schools, electricity, or roads other than paths and cart tracks. Most of them wore wooden clogs or went barefoot. They shared their houses with their animals, as they had done for centuries, and they eked out a living from cattle and sheep grazing, breeding horses and mules, or plowmaking, saddlemaking, and other agricultural trades. In 1912 this isolation was abruptly shattered, when Energía Eléctric de Catalunya (Catalan Electric Energy, EEC) began an ambitious scheme to generate hydroelectric power from the thirty-seven glacial tarns in the present-day national park of Aigüestortes in order to power the textile factories of Barcelona, some 155 miles (250 kilometers) away.

This project was the brainchild of Emili Riu i Periquet (1841–1900), a journalist, politician, and entrepreneur from the nearby town of Sort, who established the EEC in 1911, with capital from Catalan and foreign investors. In the summer of 1912 some four thousand Catalan, Spanish, Portuguese, Italian, and Turkish workers descended on the Vall Fosca. Working at altitudes of more than 6,562 feet (2,000 meters) in all weathers, these workers built a 19-mile (30-kilometer) road from the nearest town of Pobla de Segur right up into the upper valley, in addition to a telephone line, a power station, a barracks-like encampment, and a 9.5-mile (15-kilometer) network of tunnels among a dozen lakes, which channeled water down an enormous water chute from the high mountains to the power station at the hamlet of Capdella 1.9 miles (3 kilometers) below.

All this was achieved in an incredible twenty-three months. Today the power station is still operational, but it is not until you reach the top of the valley, where the plantation forest gives way to the gaunt rocky peaks beyond the Sallent reservoir, that you realize the prodigious feat of engineering that built this system. From the reservoir you take the cable car up to the Estany Gento (Gento Lake), where the *cambra de l'aigua* (water chute) forces water 2,790 feet (850 meters) down the mountainside. The former narrow-gauge track once used by mule-drawn wagons has become a walking route that leads around the Montseny mountain past mostly abandoned old pump stations and other industrial buildings, through a succession of narrow tunnels.

A photograph shows a group of Riu's workers in waistcoats and rope-soled sandals on a pulley-drawn metal beam dangling above one of the lakes. They exude the same sense of pride in an epic task that one finds in photographs of workers on New York skyscrapers, and the physical resilience that enabled them to endure eleven-hour working days, seven days a week, in weather conditions that sometimes obliged them to use crampons, snowshoes, and ice axes. Despite the primitive working conditions at the outset, some four thousand workers eventually settled at Capdella with their families, in a colony with its own cinema, library, tennis courts, and canteen and the EEC's own hotel, the appropriately named Hotel Energía. These developments had immediate and long-term implications for the valley's indigenous inhabitants. Though some locals claimed that "their" electricity had been taken from the valley, landowners won permanent concessions from the EEC, which

Workers at Estany Gento, above Capdella, date unknown (with kind permission from Museu Hidroelèctric de Capdella).

guaranted them free electricity in perpetuity. Mass-produced goods overwhelmed the local economy, and peasants abandoned their old trades to take up the higher wages on offer at the EEC and began to send their children to the company school. Within a few years a way of life that had remained much the same for centuries had been changed beyond recognition. A similar process unfolded at different speeds across the Pyrenees.

Pyrenean society was never exclusively pastoral. As early as the first century BCE, gold, silver, copper, and other metals were being mined in the Roman provinces in the central French Pyrenees, and there were marble quarries around the town of Lugdunum, now the town of Saint-Bertrand-de-Comminges. In 1778 more than 2,400 women in the border town of Puigcerdà were occupied in spinning and weaving woolen stockings. In 1837 James Erskine

Murray observed the inhabitants of the Carol Valley making wool stockings, some thirty thousand of which were exported annually to Bordeaux, Toulouse, and other parts of France. In 1890 *Blackwoods* magazine could report that "pastoral occupations form only a small part of the business of the Pyrenees. . . . As water power is to be found everywhere, there are flour-mills and saw-mills in many of the villages. In certain valleys . . . almost every peasant has rough little grinding stones and converts his own barley, buckwheat and maize into flour. Handlooms are numerous, and coarse woollen stuffs for the peasants' clothes are largely made."[13]

As was the case in the Vall Fosca, the industrialization of the Pyrenees undermined the local village economy, and it also offered better-paid alternatives to agricultural work, as peasants, farmers, and shepherds abandoned the land to work in the cities, or sought new employment opportunities in recreational tourism or in the mines, factories, and worshops that sprung up across the Pyrenees in the nineteenth century. In the Biros Valley in the Ariège, many locals abandoned sheepherding to work in the silver- and zinc-bearing lead mines at Bentaillou and Bulard. In the French Pyrenean commune of Vicdessos, the number of farms declined exponentially following the opening of a metallurgical factory in the area in 1910.

The rise of industrialized animal farming; restrictions on communal land use and grazing routes; population decline; the reluctance of the young to take up a profession that was regarded as arduous and badly paid—all these factors contributed to a long-term decline in the numbers of shepherds and herders. The old pastoral world of the Pyrenees never disappeared completely. In his engaging account of his emigrant journey from the Bearnese Pyrenees to the United States, the restaurateur Jean Louis Matocq describes a mid-twentieth-century Pyrenean childhood that many of his medieval predecessors would not have found entirely unfamiliar, on a three-hundred-year-old farm with no water, toilet, or electricity in which he was already plowing, milking cows, tending sheep, and pitching hay for the winter at the age of eleven.[14] In

1837 James Erskine Murray wrote of the "celerity with which the shepherds of the Pyreneés [sic] draw their flocks around them" with dogs and whistles. "There is no such sight to be witnessed in these mountains such as 'sheep driving';" he wrote, "no 'knowing little collies' used in collecting the flocks, or keeping them from wandering; the Pyrenean shepherd, his dogs, and his flock, seem to understand each other's duties; mutual security and affection are the bonds which unite them."[15]

Today there are an estimated 1 million sheep in the Pyrenees, and the sight of sheep being effortlessly rounded up by mountain dogs, or *patous*, in a high mountain pasture at the end of the day remains one of the most beautiful spectacles in the mountains. In the Marcadau Valley and the Vallée d'Ossau, you can still encounter beige and cream Pyrenean cows, with their great bells around their necks, or buy freshly made cheeses from a shepherd's *cabane*, or pass men and women leading mules or donkeys laden with cheese or milk down from the high pastures. Shepherds still take their flocks into the high mountains each summer for the annual transhumance, though many now use trucks and vans to transport them, and visit their animals on motorbikes or quad bikes. But it is still possible to find shepherds living alone in the high mountains, or whistling and calling out to their animals, and to see them as the descendants of the fourteenth-century shepherd of the Ariège or Cerdagne whom Emmanuel Le Roy Ladurie called "as free as the mountain air he breathed."[16]

Night Work

The same cannot be said of another iconic Pyrenean occupation that was frequently celebrated by nineteenth-century travelers. The origins of smuggling, or "night work" (*gaulana*) as it is known in Basque, can be traced back to the sixteenth century, when Philip II first attempted to transform the Pyrenees into a "frontier of heresy" and added the control of illegal contraband to the duties of the Inquisition. Neither the Holy Office nor the secular justices were ever able to impose their authority over a mountain range that offered endless opportunities for escape and evasion. Much of the Pyrenees in the sixteenth century remained a lawless no-man's-land, where bandits, deserters, counterfeiters, and fugitives from justice lived alongside charcoal burners, woodcutters, and iron foundries.

Many of these bandits and smugglers came from noble families, such as Felipe de Bardaxí, the lord of San Juan de Plan in the Gistaín Valley of Huesca Province, whose band combined robbery with murder and horse smuggling across the frontier. Bardaxí also spied for the Spanish Crown during the French Wars of Religion and even fought with Catholic armies against the Huguenots. As a result he continued to enjoy royal protection, until some of his many enemies managed to kill him with axes while he was taking Holy Communion in his home village. Such was his reputation that the people of San Juan celebrated his murder with an Our Father and a Hail Mary—a custom that continued until 1888.[17]

During the eighteenth and nineteenth centuries the French and Spanish governments made occasional joint attempts to stem the smuggling of untaxed goods. In 1722 the Paris and Madrid courts agreed to return "thieves, assassins, and deserters" to their respective kingdoms, and these efforts were also extended to smugglers. In May 1773, 140 smugglers took temporary control of the border town of Puigcerdà and emptied its prisons of convicted brethren. In reponse, the two governments signed a series of accords allowing troops to cross the state boundary in pursuit of smugglers.

In 1830 the Spanish government enacted a harsh anti-smuggling law whose punishments included deportation to the Antilles and the garrotte, and in 1842 the paramilitary corps of carabineers established by the treasury earlier in the century to enforce customs restrictions on the country's frontiers was placed under the jurisdiction of the Ministry of War in a renewed attempt to establish control over the Pyrenean border. These efforts had no more impact than their predecessors. Many Pyrenean villages and valleys depended on these *paqueteros* (packet carriers) for their prosperity and survival. In one episode in the Aragonese village of Aísa in Huesca Province in the nineteenth century, the local priest asked Queen Isabel II to pardon twelve men from the village who had been arrested for robbing a consignment of goods from a government store and various others who had fled to France to avoid arrest, on the grounds that there were no longer any men left in the village to look after the animals and the harvest.

In Aragon and Navarre, smuggling was a professional or semi-professional activity, to the point where columns of a hundred or more armed men escorted mule trains laden with household utensils, tools, olive oil, tobacco, ham, and guns through the mountains. In the Hecho and Ansó Valleys of Aragon, smugglers routinely fought nocturnal gun battles with the carabineers. In Andorra, Spanish smugglers took advantage of the co-principality's geographical location inside France to avoid customs duties and taxes, while French businesses looking to take advantage of Andorra's exemption from Spanish taxes smuggled French products through Andorra into Spain. In the nineteenth century, Andorra became one of the main routes for contraband tobacco from Spain into France, and many Andorran households began cultivating tobacco specifically for French markets.

As is often the case, repression was never able to eliminate an industry that was driven by price differentials and shifting patterns of supply and demand. In the eighteenth century the Cerdagne became a major point of entry for the illegal transfer of Spanish gold and silver to France. In 1818 a French customs director complained that industrial looms and skilled workers were being smuggled into Catalonia through the Cerdagne to fuel the Catalan textile industry. During the first Carlist War the Spanish government frequently complained that Carlist troops were being supplied with gunpowder by French smugglers, and the French authorities issued a ban on the possession of gunpowder near the frontier in an attempt to stop this traffic.

These prohibitions failed to prevent such activities and may even have intensified them, as border restrictions often do. The Carlist

Wars also generated a demand in Spain for smuggled uniforms, grain, and weapons—and for soldiers. Crossing the French-Spanish border from Saint-Jean-de-Luz in the middle of the first Carlist War in 1840, Théophile Gautier observed how "the war has given rise to a frontier trade in two commodities: firstly, in bullets found on the battle-field, and secondly in human contraband. They export Carlists like bales of goods; there is even a tariff: so much for a colonel, so much for an officer; the bargain is made, the smuggler arrives, carries off his man, takes him over the frontier and delivers him at his destination like a dozen handkerchiefs or a hundred cigars."[18] The British Carlist volunteer Charles Frederick Henningsen later recalled the smugglers who took him "through mountain paths so steep and dangerous, that in ordinary time the inexperienced traveller would have done nothing but think on the natural horrors of the road."[19]

Given the economic importance of smuggling to the Pyrenean valleys, it is not surprising that the more prolific and daring smugglers were often regarded as local heroes. The "monarch of Hecho," Pedro Brun, fought so many gunfights with the carabineers in the first decades of the nineteenth century that Isabel II put a price on his head. In response, Brun personally traveled to Madrid from his home in Aragon to present himself at court—an act that so endeared him to the queen that she promptly pardoned him. Pyrenean smugglers were also regarded as attractive figures by the outside world. French posters and postcards often depicted Spanish smugglers in colorful costumes with muskets and loads on their backs making their way up solitary mountain paths. Gustave Doré drew a grippingly dramatic portrait of armed smugglers clinging to a mountainside. The popular French illustrator Paul Gavarni (1804–66) also drew some fabulously exotic and romantic images of smugglers he met during a visit to the Pyrenees, from which he took his own nom de plume.

Such images often referenced Ramond's description of the Aragonese smuggler he encountered descending from the Brèche de Roland: "In the countenance of this man I could perceive a mixture

"A mixture of boldness and confidence." Paul Gavarni, Pyrenean smuggler, 1829 (Bibliothèque Municipale de Toulouse).

of boldness and confidence; his thick and frizzled beard was continued up into his black and curling hair; his broad breast was open, his strong and nervous legs naked; all his clothing consisted of a simple vest; the covering of his feet, after the manner of the Romans and Goths, of a piece of cow's skin applied to the sole of the foot, and bound round it like a purse, by means of two straps, which were afterwards crossed and fastened above the ancles."[20]

In 1873 the French poet Frédéric Soutras (1814–74), a founder-member of the Ramond Society, published a 350-verse poem entitled *Les échos de la montagne* celebrating the exploits of Brice d'Estensan, a smuggler from the village of Estensan in the Vallée d'Aure who shot and killed two customs men. For Soutras, Brice was an authentic rebel, a "hunter above the peaks / On the flank of glaciers / On seeing Isards / he thought of customs men," outwitting and fighting oppressive treasury officials on behalf of the people in his valley, while wooing countless Pyrenean women as he roamed the mountains. Smugglers were not always described so fondly. Henry Russell once told the French Alpine Club how he and his companions were set upon by "four hideous Spaniards . . . with glittering daggers round their waists, an axe and a knife," in a shepherd's *cabane* high above Gavarnie. Though two of his friends were detained at axe point, Russell and his other companions managed to escape and spent the night hiding in the forest before the smugglers returned to where they came from without having harmed their two prisoners.[21]

Most smugglers were not bandits, but ordinary Pyreneans from either side of the border. In the 1830s a French army officer in the Cerdagne complained that the contraband trade had "caused the abandonment of work. There is not a single inhabitant of these frontier districts who would accept for honest and easy work the salary that he so hastily accepts for a contraband enterprise. From the one, he sees only drudgery; from the other, merit and pleasure."[22] In the early twentieth century Spanish seasonal workers often used their earnings to buy watches and other items that they brought back to their villages without paying tax. Ordinary Frenchmen and women living close to the border routinely took part in the *pacotille* (household smuggling) and crossed the border to bring back a bag of groceries from Spanish stores, and French customs officers often turned a blind eye to these activities. Some Spaniards even set up stores close to the border, selling meat, fresh vegetables and fruits, wines, spirits, and cigarettes.

For much of the twentieth century, the flow of smuggled goods across the Pyrenees followed the same general pattern: manufactured products from France into Spain and agricultural products from Spain into France. During World War II this pattern was briefly reversed as Pyrenean smugglers brought what had become luxury goods into occupied France, such as penicillin, lace, thread, sugar, and olive oil, and returned with payment in the form of money, jewels, and gold. Many Pyrenean smugglers also took to smuggling people across the frontier into Spain, from escaped Jews to Allied airmen and Free French. After the war, smuggling reverted to its prewar patterns, as smugglers transported ball bearings, copper, precision instruments, and other manufactured goods from France into Spain and alcohol, sheep, mules, cattle, and horses in the other direction. By the 1960s smuggling had begun to diminish as the price differentials on either side of the frontier decreased and the cost of smuggling itself went up. By the 1970s it had become only a marginal activity, and by the time Spain formally joined the Schengen Area in 1995, smuggling had become a historical anachronism, like the border itself.

Today this history of smuggling has become a "colorful" tourist attraction. In Andorra the Tobacco Museum of Sant Julià de Lòria celebrates what the *Lonely Planet* guide calls "the decadent pleasures of smoking and smuggling." Guidebooks still invite travelers to visit the French-Basque village of Salé which was once known as the "Republic of Salé" because of its long history of smuggling. Other Pyrenean professions have been similarly appropriated by the heritage industry. At the Museum of the Pyrenees in Lourdes, visitors can contemplate lovingly assembled displays of plows, hoes, milk churns, furniture, and models of shepherds in immaculately restored Bearnese huts.

Other Pyrenean museums are dedicated to the cork industry, local folk costumes, farming implements, mining, the salt industry, ethnography, and folklore. In the Aragonese Pyrenees, competitions and races are held each spring to remember the *navateros* (rafters) who once brought timber down from the mountains by roping tree trunks together. Local associations build these *navatas* using traditional methods and steer them down spating rivers. In the French and Spanish Pyrenees walkers and visitors can take part in the annual parties and *fêtes des bergers* (shepherds' festivals) and accompany shepherds into the high mountains, and some Pyrenean villages still celebrate customs and traditions that reach deep into the premodern history of myth and superstition that was also part of the Pyrenean past.

11

Wild Things

Prefect Brun of the Ariège described the "savage and vindic-
tive spirit" of the mountain peasant, who "shares three-
quarters of his time with the bears and wolves with whom he
engages [in] daily battles, and from whom he slowly catches
the ferocious and disturbing character of these carnivorous
animals."

—Peter Sahlins, *Forest Rites*, 1994[1]

In 2007, the French Comité Régional de la Randonnée Pédestre
(Regional Committee of Walking) added a new route through the
Port de Plan and the Vallée d'Aure to the seemingly endless array of
themed hiking trails in the Pyrenees to commemorate "the traces of
Robinson Crusoe." Crusoe is more often associated with the tropics
than the Pyrenees, and the new trail recalls a significant episode at
the end of Defoe's novel, when Crusoe returns from a visit to Lisbon in 1687 to claim a legacy relating to his Brazilian slave plantation. Accompanied by Friday and another servant, Crusoe returns
overland to England via Pamplona in October to avoid the sea, only
to discover that the Pyrenees have their own terrors. When Crusoe
arrives in Pamplona, he discovers that the Pyrenean passes are blocked
by snow. Eventually he manages to recruit a guide to take him to
"the head of Languedoc" and sets out on horseback with his servants
and four French travelers into the mountains.

Before leaving, their guide warns the party to be "armed sufficiently to protect ourselves from wild beasts," and this warning

proves to be prescient. Shortly before dark on their second night in the mountains, the guide is attacked by "three monstrous wolves, and after them a bear . . . and had he been before us, he would have been devoured before we could have helped him." Friday saves the guide's life by shooting one of the wolves, and then goes on to kill the bear. In doing so he sets off "the most dismal howling of wolves; and the noise, redoubled by the echo of the mountains, appeared to us as if there had been a prodigious number of them."

Descending through a narrow defile, Crusoe and his companions are followed by starving wolves that have "done a great deal of mischief in the villages, where they surprised the country people, killed a great many of their sheep and horses, and some people too." The wolf pack continues to grow until "we saw about a hundred coming on directly towards us, all in a body, and most of them in a line, as regularly as an army drawn up by experienced officers." After keeping the animals at bay with shots and cries, Crusoe's party retreats to a nearby wood, where they encounter the carcasses of animals and "two men, devoured by the ravenous creatures." For the rest of the night the travelers fight off successive assaults from "troops of wolves" that "came on like devils, those behind pushing on those before." After killing "about threescore of them," the party finally finds safety in a nearby village, whose inhabitants are "in a terrible fright and all in arms; for it seems, the night before the wolves and some bears had broken into the village."

Defoe may have crossed the Pyrenees himself during a business trip to Spain, though his improbable and somewhat ludicrous descriptions of this vengeful wolf army owed more to his novelistic imagination than they did to firsthand observation. His portrait of fearful Pyrenean villagers was more plausible. Wolves and bears may never have had the capacity or desire to attack passing travelers in quasi-military formations, but even in the early eighteenth century these animals were regarded by the inhabitants of the Pyrenees as a threat to their livestock and on occasion to their own lives. Yet if Pyreneans have feared and even loathed certain wild animals, they have also respected and even revered them, and depicted them in prehistoric cave paintings and in the animal carvings on the capitals of Romanesque pillars in monasteries and churches.

A number of Pyrenean villages still hold spring festivals in which locals dress up as bears and act out myths and superstitions that reach deep into the preindustrial Pyrenean past. Some of these animals have disappeared completely from the mountains yet remained part of the culture and folk memory of the Pyrenees. Other "wild" creatures, like Defoe's wolves, have sprung entirely from the human imagination and testify to the strange, disturbing, and often touching ways in which the inhabitants of the Pyrenees have variously interpreted and explained their mountain world to themselves.

La Chasse

Ever since human beings first began to settle the Pyrenees, they have hunted animals for survival or pleasure, from the bison, rhinoceroses, lions, and mammoths shown in prehistoric cave paintings to the wolves, bears, foxes, boars, badgers, and otters depicted in Gaston Phoebus's celebrated fourteenth-century hunting manual known as *Le livre de chasse* (The Book of Hunting).[2] Phoebus wrote the book himself as a loving homage to "the forest paths, the heather of the countryside and the hills" that he loved, and its lavish illustrations of hunters, servants, dog trainers, and animals celebrate a pastime that he regarded as a pleasure and an obligation. For Phoebus, all lords had a duty to hunt in order to protect their tenants' livestock from wolves, foxes, and other predators. Hunting also honed combat skills for war and promoted physical health and moral virtue, since prolonged idleness and inactivity led too easily to the "imagination of the pleasure of the flesh" and the seven deadly sins.

Phoebus's distilled wisdom on hunting methods and techniques is infused with a deep admiration and respect for the animals that he regarded as the worthy prey for noblemen. Though he included illustrations of net and hedge traps set by poachers, Phoebus regarded such devices as essentially ignoble and reserved for "villains, peasants and other commoners in dire need of fresh meat." Despite the persistent efforts of the French nobility to reserve hunting for themselves over the centuries, more humble members of Pyrenean society have always hunted in their own way. In the late eighteenth century, peasants burned forests to flush out bears, while entire villages participated in noisy battues—communal bear hunts—which were intended sometimes to kill bears, and sometimes simply to chase them away.

In the sixteenth century, Pyrenean hunters began using nets, sheets, and wooden paddles to catch wild wood pigeons, or *palombes*, during their annual migrations southward across the Pyrenees. The English historian Charles Richard Weld observed a *palombière* (fowling station) near Bagnères in 1859, where well-heeled spectators gathered to watch as pigeons were lured by a lookout stationed at the top of a mast into nets that were "so cunningly set, that, when the pigeons strike against them, they fall, being liberated by the pulling of a trigger, and enclose the poor birds in the meshes. Death rapidly follows, the work of old women who mercilessly kill the pigeons by biting their necks."[3]

Less gory variations of *la chasse au filet* (net hunting) are still practiced in the Central and Western Pyrenees, in nine designated locations that are reserved for the exclusive use of locals. Each October French Basque farmers withdraw into mountain valleys and gorges, where pulley-drawn nets are set up at one end and lookouts equipped with sheets and horns at the other. For days and sometimes weeks, these hunters wait with their paddles in the high *chasse* cabins erected above the gorges. At the sight of the pigeons, the lookouts flap their sheets to lure the birds down, while others blow their horns to alert the paddle bearers in their cabins. As the birds fly low into the gorge, the paddle bearers blow whistles and hurl their paddles at them to alter their flight pattern, driving them into the waiting nets farther down the valley, where their necks are broken.

Despite these annual rituals, there is no shortage of wood pigeons each year. The same cannot be said of the other animals in the Pyrenees that have been hunted to extinction or had their numbers drastically reduced. When Defoe wrote *Robinson Crusoe* in 1719, the animal population included wolves, bears, boars, lynx, wild goats, izards, Iberian ibex, and wild sheep. In the last three hundred years many of these species have disappeared or declined dramatically. One French scholar has claimed that three thousand Pyrenean bears were killed in the three centuries leading up to 1950. In 1837, James Erskine Murray observed that "the bear is now become scarce in the Pyrenees; but what of that?—there is more honour in killing him."[4]

This attitude was not uncommon in the nineteenth century, where "bagging" rare animals was often more important than conserving them. Between 1878 and 1887, the English sportsman Sir Victor Brooke obtained an annual hunting concession in what would later become the Ordesa National Park, which enabled Brooke and his successors to all but wipe out the *bouquetin* (Alpine ibex) population. In his breezy account of hunting expeditions across the world, *Short Stalks* (1893), the British hunter Edward North Buxton described his attempt to "bag" ibex and *bouquetin* in the Aragonese Pyrenees. For Buxton the allure of these animals was due partly to their elusiveness and inaccessibility and partly to the fact that "their aim seems to be to pass along some tiny shelf where no man can follow."[5] Four visits were required before he finally succeeded in shooting one of these animals, after enduring "tortures" sitting for hours on high rocks and hallucinating voices in the silence and solitude.

Twenty-first-century readers are unlikely to feel much sympathy for a man who boasted of shooting a three-legged izard above Gavarnie known as "the Old Soldier" because of its ability to evade the hunters and their beaters. It was partly in an attempt to halt such depredations that the Spanish government established the Ordesa National Park in 1918 as a protected area where hunting was prohibited. Similar conservation efforts have been made in other parts of the Pyrenees at various times. Despite these efforts, some species could not be saved. In the late nineteenth century the inoffensive *bouquetin* had already been reduced to a small redoubt around Ordesa. The *bouquetin* limped on until 2000, when Celia, the last surviving *Capra pyrenaica*, was hit by a falling branch. By the early twentieth century the wild sheep, or mouflon, had been all but eradicated from the Pyrenees. In Spain, by the late sixties wolves had been driven out of the Pyrenees following successive extermination campaigns conducted under the Franco dictatorship. By 1950 the Pyrenean bear population had been reduced to little more than two dozen. Even the various breeds of indigenous Pyrenean horse, such as the Pottok, the Mérens, and the Castillonais were hunted to near extinction before successive campaigns managed to designate them as protected species in the latter half of the twentieth century.

Hunting was not the only reason for this decline. Deforestation, road construction, the spread of towns, villages, and ski resorts, and the establishment of hundreds of walking trails all reduced the spaces where animals had once roamed freely. Conservationists may lament this decline, but Pyreneans themselves have often felt very differently. The disappearance of the mouflon was due partly to the fact that it depleted pasturelands that shepherds needed for their own sheep. As early as the fourteenth century Pyrenean hunters were rewarded with gold or gifts of food from grateful peasants when they killed wolves or bears. When Edward North Buxton shot a bear, there was "much rejoicing among the peasants over the death of this their enemy, than over a dozen ibex." Peasants did not always rely on visiting hunters to carry out what they regarded as a form of pest control. Shepherds and farmers shot bears and wolves on their own account and beat drums, pots, and spades during the collective battues. Yet once again, the fear and loathing directed at certain animals did not necessarily preclude fascination, respect, and even admiration for them.

Ursus arctos

Of all the wild animals of the Pyrenees, the bear has always occupied a particularly ambivalent place in the Pyrenean cultural imagination.

On the one hand the French depiction of bears as *l'ennemi* evokes the traditional shepherd's hostility toward the animals who killed or frightened their sheep to death, yet more affectionate nicknames such as "Mâitre Martin," "Monsieur Martin," or simply "Lou Monsieur" have given bears quasi-human qualities. In 1848 an obituary in a Pau newspaper mourned the death of a bear from the Vallée d'Ossau known as Dominique that was believed to have reached the age of thirty when it was shot by a local hunter. In 1906 the inhabitants of Cominac, a hamlet in the Garbet Valley, used three trained bears to chase away tax collectors attempting to enact the hated 1905 Law of Separation of Church and State transferring church property to the secular authorities—an event that was subsequently celebrated in numerous postcards at the expense of the state officials.

Pyrenean bears have also been imagined as supernatural beings. Froissart tells the story of Gaston Phoebus's bastard brother, Peter of Béarn, who killed "a wonderfully large bear in the woods near Biscay" after it had killed four of his dogs. Peter subsequently began to walk in his sleep, wearing full armor and striking out with his sword, "as if he were on the field of battle," at the bear, which now haunted his dreams. The nineteenth-century English folklorist T.H. Hollingsworth interviewed two Basque bear trainers, who described their bear as "God's dog, the dog of Saint Peter." According to Hollingsworth, the bear lived with the couple in their mountain hut when they were not traveling and "they were always careful to treat him kindly and feed him well. For example, if they had not enough of fish (which they looked upon as a luxury) for themselves and the bear, the latter must be fed and satisfied first."[6] Hollingsworth's interviewees were convinced that "the animal understands all that is said about him, and observes and comprehends any household work, trade or occupation which may be going on; and that is the reason that a bear who has lived with men should never be allowed to return to the forest and mountains, for he will tell the other bears of what he has seen and learnt, and they, being very cunning, will come down into the valleys, and by means of their great strength, added to the knowledge they have thus gained, will be able to rule men *as they did* [italics in the original] before!"

These itinerant bear trainers were already an occasional presence in Spain and southern France in the eighteenth century. From the early nineteenth century on, however, their numbers increased as peasants in the impoverished Ariège Pyrenees took up the profession of *montreur d'ours* (bear displayer) in order to make a living. After obtaining the coveted certificates identifying them as a *conducteur d'animaux féroces* (conductor of ferocious animals), these bear displayers traveled with their animals to circuses, fairs, and village festivals. It was in the nature of this profession that the *montreur* often traveled with his animal by remote paths and trails, since the smell of bears terrified local horses and livestock, and generally slept out with his animals in the open air.

The typical *montreur d'ours* traveled with a trumpet, a bear stick, rope chains, and a muzzle, dressed in velvet or wool trousers, and wore a beret. At Cauterets, Henry Blackburn observed a "haughty Frenchman in a waistcoat and long coat" holding a dancing bear by a chain, whose paws were attached to a stick above its shoulders, and a little monkey wearing a red beret and sash that collected the money. Blackburn was not impressed by the "mournful memory . . . of this dancing bear," nor of his "fellow in misfortune, the monkey that took the money."[7] The training of these bears required a great deal of time, patience, and cruelty. Cubs were first taken from their mothers, who were usually killed first. At six months old they were fitted with metal muzzles that were screwed into their jawbones or metal rings put though their noses. They were then taught how to stand upright, hold a baton, perform dance steps, and do other tricks such as juggling and playing dead.

Some of these bears provided their owners with a surprisingly good living. Bear displayers from the Ariège were found across France and Europe, and even in the United States, South America, Australia, and New Zealand, where some of them found fame and fortune. Some *ariégeois* bear trainers, or *oussaillès* as they were known in the local slang, made their way through America equipped with maps

Civilization and "Monsieur Martin": bear, Luchon, September 1900 (Eugène Trutat, Bibliothèque Municipale de Toulouse).

of American railway lines, neck rings, and "le 48 de Liverpool"— a .48 revolver. In 1889 a *montreur d'ours* named Jean Souquet and another Ariegeois named Jean Icart Moumat took a bear to England and then to Glasgow, where they boarded a Siberian ship to Canada. From there Souquet and his companion continued their journey to the United States, where they performed up and down the country as "the Souquet Brothers" before reaching Honolulu, where they continued their travels to New Zealand and Australia, before Souquet returned to France.

Even before World War I, such journeys had become difficult if not impossible, as various countries passed laws against bear displaying. By that time the bear population in the Ariège was already so depleted that bear displayers were obliged to have their animals delivered from Central Europe to Marseilles. In 1950 Pierre de Listou, the last *montreur d'ours* in the Vallée d'Aspe, was killed by his own bear. In the early 1960s there were an estimated twenty-four bears left in the entire Pyrenees, and in 1996 the French government attempted to halt this decline with a reintroduction program that brought to the surface all the old ambivalance toward Monsieur Martin.

Rewilding the Pyrenees

Species depletion in the Pyrenees has not always been an irreversible process. In 1957, long before the concept of *ensauvagement* ("wildification") was invented, the wild mountain sheep was brought back to the French Pyrenees. In the 1990s wolves began to return to the Pyrenees of their own accord. In 1948 the French surgeon, hunter, and mountaineer Dr. Marcel Couturier (1897–1973) introduced six marmots from the Alps into the vale of Barrada, in the Luz-Gavarnie Valley—the first time these animals had been seen in the Pyrenees since the end of the last Ice Age. Today these groundhog-like mammals can be found all around the slopes above Gavarnie and across the Pyrenees. In 2009 a joint project carried out by the Centre of Food Technology and Research in Zaragoza and the National Research Institute of Agriculture and Food extracted DNA from the last Iberian ibex, Celia, and succeeded in bringing a kid to life for seven minutes.

The reintroduction of bears was always going to be more controversial. In 1996–97, the Mitterand government successfully reintroduced three Slovenian brown bears into the mountains near the village of Melles in the Central Pyrenees. A further reintroduction program followed the shooting of Cannelle, the last indigenous female member of *Ursus arctos pyrenaicus*—the Pyrenean brown bear—in 2004. Two years later five more bears were introduced into the Central Pyrenees, and today there are more than twenty-two bears in the Central and Western Pyrenees.[8] The French wildlife expert Jean-Jacques Camarra is a member of L'Equipe Ours (the Bear Team), managing their reintroduction. I met him at the offices of the National Office of Hunting and Wildlife (ONCFS) in Pau, in the same building where Count Henry Russell once had an apartment. A robust, athletic-looking man in his early sixties, Camarra originally trained as a metallurgist before his enthusiasm for mountains and mountain sports brought him to the Pyrenees, where he retrained as a biologist.

Camarra is a fervent supporter of what he regards as a successful experiment in wildlife conservation, which demonstrates that "big animals, big carnivores like this, can survive close to people, without problems." His passion for bears is obvious. When I ask why the bear has had such a special place in the Pyrenean imagination, his eyes are shining as he explains, "Because the bear has a footprint like a human. He has five toes. He can stand up like humans. He can be free with his hands, to scratch trees. Second, he's very intelligent. And thirdly, he's very big. And fourth, because of his fur; he's like a teddy bear."

Camarra also recognizes that bears are "very dangerous for humans. They can be the best or the worst," and he knows that his enthusiasm for his government's conservation efforts is not universally shared. Opposition was relatively muted before the first reintroduction in 1996, but it was a very different matter ten years later, when the government reintroduced three Slovenian bears near the village of Arbas, some 31 miles (50 kilometers) to the east of Lourdes, followed by two more bears in nearby villages. Even before the reintroductions, anti-bear protesters stole bear-tracking equipment, threatened the French minister of ecology, and staged a series of angry and even violent demonstrations. In April 2006, anti-bear demonstrators in the Ariège vandalized the town hall at Arbas. In 2013 five teddy bears were hanged near the tourist office in the Ariège valley of Biros, and the road outside the office was painted with the slogans *Mort aux ours* (Death to bears) and *Mort aux touristes* (Death to tourists).

Such opposition is founded on the very real prospect of "Martin's tithe"—the regular killing of sheep by bears. Such deaths are sometimes the result of direct attacks, but even the proximity of bears has caused sheep to die of fright or spontaneously abort. In

2013, bears killed 174 sheep in the French Pyrenees and another 35 in Spain. Given that the total number of sheep in the French Pyrenees generally exceeds 600,000, these losses may seem negligible to outsiders, but shepherds and sheep breeders are angered by them, and they also resent having to pay for the Pyrenean mountain dogs, or *patous*, and fences to protect their animals. In theory this protection is subsidized by the state, which also pays $370 (€300) in compensation for any animal losses.

Such measures have not dissipated the resentment felt by some pastoralists toward the conservationists and the "garbage bears" they have imported from Slovenia into the Pyrenees in the name of an abstract principle that has no relevance to the pastoral economy. Conservation has more appeal for villages like Arbas, whose economy is more dependent on tourism than sheep farming. In Camarra's opinion, bears provide an invisible or semi-visible "ghostly presence," which can be sensed but not seen. In some parts of the French Pyrenees, local authorities promote their areas as "bear country," even producing place mats in restaurants that give the whole history of the bear conservation project.

Camarra believes that opposition to the French government's reintroduction program is gradually disappearing and that shepherds can be persuaded to accept it. In his view, the bear is as much a part of Pyrenean and French heritage as sheep farming, and he also regards the reintroduction of bears as an indirect instrument of landscape conservation, since "if you don't have bears, it's more difficult to be against the roads, ski resorts and other things." There is no doubt that the reintroduction of bears has benefited the Pyrenean tourist economy. In Aragon I led a walking group for five days through the Senda de Camille (Camille's Path)—a circular walking route that had been specially created in honor of a male bear that is believed to have died in the region in 2010. There was no sign of Camille or any bears along the route, nor did we expect to find any, but a bear's claw provides the motif for the local company that developed the circular trek, in another indication of the enduring attraction of Camarra's "ghostly" ursine presence.

Bears also constitute an indirect tourist attraction in the bear festivals of the Eastern Pyrenees. Every second Sunday in February, the local youths of Prats-de-Mollo-la-Preste cover themselves in oil and soot and wrestle spectators to the ground before they are subdued by *hommes en blanc* (men in white) or "barbers" who pretend to "shave" them before another group dressed as "hunters" comes and "kills" the bears. This annual ritual re-creates a legend in which a bear is believed to have kidnapped a shepherdess and taken her into the forest to ravish her before she was rescued by a hunter. In other variants a single "human bear" dies, then stands up without his bear mask, and then picks out a woman from the spectators to dance with.

These Pyrenean bear festivals are featured in Charles Fréger's striking photo-essay on the ancient "wild men" festivals that still persist in many European countries.[9] For Fréger, these festivals constituted an "image of the savage" that hearkened back to the pre-Christian "tribal Europe." One photograph taken in the French Pyrenees shows a man in a bear mask with monstrous teeth against a backdrop of forests and distant snow-covered mountains, an anthropomorphic image that simultaneously humanizes the "bear" and evokes the blurred boundaries between the wild and the human, in which the direction is by no means certain.

Shapeshifters

The Pyrenees have often constituted a stage on which this convergence has been acted out and imagined. One of the most famous "freak" attractions in early seventeenth-century London was a man called Don Sanchio Fernando, known as "the Bold Grimace Spaniard" for his ability to make unusual facial expressions, which he had allegedly learned from living with wild beasts in the Pyrenees for fifteen years. These experiences, according to a contemporary handbill, had given the Spaniard the peculiar ability to change the shape of his face at will: "He lolls out his Tongue a foot long; turns his Eyes in and out at the same time; contracts his face as small as an Apple; extends his mouth six inches and turns it into the shape of a Bird's beak, and his eyes like to an Owl."[10]

In *Systema naturae* (1758) the Swedish botanist and zoologist Carl Linnaeus added a new species, which he called *Homo ferens* (wild man), to his taxonomy of primates. Linnaeus characterized this species as *mutus, tetrapus*, and *hirsutus* (dumb, quadruped, and covered with hair), and he cited a number of episodes of feral children brought up by animals, who included the "two Pyrenees boys" cited in Jean-Jacques Rousseau's *Discourse on the Origin of Human Inequality* (1754). In a note rejecting Aristotle's theory that humans were descended from quadrupeds, Rousseau referred to a 1719 newspaper report on two "savages . . . found in the Pyrenees, who ran through the mountains in the manner of quadrupeds."

Rousseau mocked the idea that the Greek philosopher's descendants might once have been "as hairy as a bear, and if moving on four feet with his gaze directed at the earth," and insisted that these "Pyrenees boys" had reverted to all fours as a form of atavism, thereby demonstrating that *Homo sapiens* had always been as "structured at all times as I see him today, walking on two feet, using his hands as we use ours." To a world that still saw the Pyrenees as a savage mountain wilderness where civilization had only a tenuous foothold, these atavistic feral children seemed as credible as Defoe's wolf armies. The peoples of the Pyrenees have also projected their own anthropomorphic fantasies onto the surrounding landscape. The enigmatic figure of "the Sorcerer" at Les Trois-Frères cave depicts a deerlike figure with antlers that appears to be walking on two legs. Generations of Basque children have grown up with the legend of the *basajaun*—the wild man who inhabits the mountain forests. Sometimes described as a merciless ogre who feeds on human flesh and attacks lone travelers, the *basajaun* also appears as the benign guardian of the mountains and forests who warns shepherds of impending storms and approaching predators with a whistle that can carry more than a mile.

Such assistance, when it comes, must be rewarded, with donations of milk, cheese, bread, or nuts. The Basque philosopher and poet Joseph Augustin Chaho (1811–58) once described the *basajaun* as "tall and of prodigious strength: his whole body is covered with a long smooth coat resembling hair: he walks upright like a man, surpassing the stag in agility." The *basajaun* also appears in the Spanish writer Dolores Redondo Meira's bestselling Baztan trilogy, a crime series set in the Baztan Valley of Navarre, both as a threat and also as a source of solace to her tormented police inspector protagonist, Amaia Salazar.

In the first of the series, *The Invisible Guardian* (2013), one of Salazar's colleagues is accidentally shot in the forest and wakes to find "a creature squatting down at my side, his face was almost totally covered in hair, but not like an animal's, more like a man whose beard starts right below his eyes, intelligent, sympathetic eyes, almost human, except the iris covered almost the whole eye; there was barely any white, like a dog's eyes."

Basque mythology abounds with similar half-human, half-animal figures. There is the female version of the *basajaun*, the *basandere*, or "wild woman"; the one-eyed and sometimes cannibalistic giant known as the *tartalo* and his monstrous doglike companion the *olano*; the beautiful forest-dwelling fairies known as *lamias*, with female upper bodies and the legs of goats or cats, or fishtails, who spend all night combing their long blond hair and washing their white robes on golden washboards. Other regions of the Pyrenees have their own local variants—from the fairies known as *hadas* or *encantadas* that populate the mountains of Aragon and Catalonia, to the *demoiselles* or *dames blanches*—white ladies—of the French Pyrenees.

In 1859 Charles Richard Weld was surprised by the "curious superstitions" that still lingered among the peasants of Luz-Saint-Sauveur. These included "the Loup-Garou, a species of malevolent fiend corresponding to the Banshee of Ireland"; a "strange wicked demon called Yona Gorri, who though generally seen of a fiery red colour, has the power of appearing to the terrified peasants in a

The monster of the Pyrenees: Blaise Ferrage, cannibal (Alamy stock image).

variety of hues"; and "L'Homme Noir"—the Black Man—who hurled ice showers down from the mountaintops.[11]

Such myths and fantasies were often associated with caves. According to Weld, the Yona Gorri was believed to inhabit a cave on the Pic d'Anie, where it "desecrated the country with thunderstorms" on the arrival of unexpected strangers, and the *dames blanches* were also imagined as cave dwellers. The Grottes de Gargas, south of Montréjau in the Hautes-Pyrénées, are famous for their stenciled wall prints of mutilated hands, which date back to the Upper Paleolithic era. According to legend, the caves were once inhabited by a giant named Gargas, and they are also associated with a series of brutal crimes carried out by the Pyrenean "serial killer," Blaise Ferrage, in 1779–90, whom the Marquis de Sade used as the model for the cannibalistic giant Minski, the "Hermit of the Apennines," in *Juliette*.

Little is known about Ferrage, except that he was born in 1757 and worked as a stonemason until he was twenty-two years old, when he abruptly left home and went to live in one of the Gargas caves that was so small it could be entered only by crawling into it. From this refuge, Ferrage embarked on a spree of rape, necrophilia, and cannibalism that terrorized the surrounding valley. In little more than three years he shot, strangled, and sometimes ate more than two dozen men, women, and children, most of whom were shepherds and shepherdesses out with their flocks. His crimes were still well-known more than a century later when Sabine Baring-Gould visited the region.

Baring-Gould described Ferrage as "a small man, broad-shouldered, with unusually long arms, and . . . possessed of extraordinary strength," who sometimes carried his victims alive to his cave, so that "the shrieks could be heard from afar, paralysing the timorous peasantry with fear." Ferrage was the incarnation of some of the darkest Pyrenean myths and fears: the lupine cave dweller who, as Baring-Gould puts it, "had converted into a wild beast, who had renounced the society of his fellows to live among the rocks and tread the snow-fields, hearing naught save the howl of the wind, the cry of the birds of prey, and the baying of the wolves."[12] Such was the terror that Ferrage exercised over the local population that on one occasion he entered the village of Montagu in broad daylight, causing the villagers to abandon their market stalls and lock themselves in their homes. Even when he was arrested later that day he managed to escape and went on to commit more crimes.

Despite a reward on his head, no one dared to approach his hiding place for fear of being shot. Ferrage was eventually captured, when the police managed to persuade an informant to befriend him, share his cave, and eventually lead him into an ambush. In 1780 the Parliament of Languedoc put him on trial, and on Friday, December 13, 1783, the "anthropage of the Pyrenees" was broken on the wheel and his corpse exposed on the gibbet in the Place Saint-Georges, Toulouse.

The Ladies' War

Pyrenean peasants were not always fearful of the wilderness and its real and imagined inhabitants. In the spring of 1829, forest guards, charcoal burners, iron manufacturers, and royal officials in the Castillonais district of the Couserans were attacked and threatened by groups of peasants brandishing firearms and other weapons, who sometimes pillaged and burned their houses. State officials reported that many of them referred to themselves as *demoiselles* (ladies) and dressed as women, wearing long shirts hanging down below their knees like skirts. Some of these "ladies" painted their faces red and black or wore cardboard carnival masks or white masks with holes punched into them. Others wore military headgear and sported pigs' bristles on their faces or covered their heads with sheep or fox hides. One *demoiselle* "officer" arrested in the Ustou forest in July 1829 was found wearing "a French [soldier's] hat, a wolf's tail serving as panache for this hat, a net for masking his face, a rifle, two sacks of powder, and a pair of blue pants."[13]

The "War of the Demoiselles" or Ladies' War, was a direct response to the French government's 1827 Forest Code, which imposed or reimposed restrictions on rights of access to Pyrenean forests that had previously been held in common. These restrictions were partly justified on the grounds of efficiency, but they were also designed to favor the interests of iron manufacturers and charcoal burners at the expense of local peasants, who used the forests for fuel, grazing, or small-scale agricultural production. It has never been entirely clear why the peasants chose to protest by dressing up as women and animals. Some historians have traced these "disguises" to carnival and the charivari tradition of playful rebellion against authority. Others have seen the *demoiselles* as a product of *ariégeois* folk traditions: they transformed themselves into forest "spirits," fairies, and wild men in order to defend "their" forests against encroaching officialdom.

Whatever its causes, this metamorphosis was clearly intended to strike terror into their enemies, particularly the hated forest guards, known as *salamagnos* (salamanders) because of their green uniforms, who were charged with implementing the government's new legislation, and it often succeeded. French officials frequently expressed their disgust at how readily forest guards took flight when confronted with groups of "women" brandishing guns, hatchets, and hoes and threatening to tear their eyes out. These protests received so much support that the French authorities deployed some six hundred soldiers in the affected districts in an attempt to restore order.

These troops initially had little impact, as the *demoiselles* moved more or less at will through forests that they knew better than any outsiders. In October 1830 a government commission was appointed to investigate the disturbances; it recommended a more lenient application of the Forest Code and granted an amnesty for previous "crimes and transgressions." This policy achieved its objective. The *demoiselles* never again recovered the momentum they had shown the previous year, but their memory continued to live on. In 2006, demonstrators protesting the reintroduction of brown bears at the village of Arbas tossed bottles filled with lambs' blood at the town hall, burned a bust of a brown bear, and chanted "*Les demoiselles marchent devant vous, les demoiselles sont de retour*" (The ladies are marching before you, the ladies are returning)—a slogan that may have mystified many outsiders, but which would have needed little explanation to many Ariegeois.

The Witches of Navarre

This slippage among the animal, the human, and the supernatural has not always been so playful. The village of Zugarramurdi is located in northern Navarre in the Xareta region adjoining the French border. To reach it from Spain requires a difficult drive up a twisting Pyrenean mountain road in sore need of repair, through a series of narrow valleys, forests, and deep gorges. Human settlements are rare, and there is little sign of any life at all except for the occasional eagles or buzzards. It comes as a relief to reach the sharp ridge overlooking the French province of Labourd and to descend toward Zugarramurdi's stolid white houses, with their wooden eaves and exposed stone edges.

Just outside the village there is an enormous limestone cavern, with a white limestone roof some 50 feet (15 meters) high stained with wraith-like smoke trails left from disused limestone kilns, and numerous subchambers branching off the sides. It is a stunningly dramatic natural wonder, whose strange beauty is enhanced by the surrounding forests and fields and the stream that runs down from the narrow gorge at the upper entrance. Only the souvenir models of witches on broomsticks on sale at the entrance pay homage to the tragic events that unfolded in 1608, when a young woman named María de Ximildegui returned to Zugarramurdi and accused one of her neighbors of witchcraft.

Ximildegui claimed to be a repentant witch herself and said she had once attended a sabbath in the cave in which one of her neighbors had also participated. In the investigations that followed, ten women confessed to a series of horrendous crimes that included infanticide, vampirism, and the destruction of crops. The judicial process was initially confined to the village, and the accused were treated with surprising leniency. In 1609, however, Henry IV of France dispatched a state counsellor from the Parlement of Bordeaux named Pierre de Lancre (1553–1631) to investigate disturbing reports of witchcraft in the surrounding province. De Lancre arrived in Labourd at a time when many local Basques were absent on the Saint-Jean-de-Luz cod-fishing fleet in Newfoundland. Using torture to obtain testimony from children as young as six, he quickly concluded that this remote frontier province was infested with witches and devils who had taken refuge in Labourd after fleeing the efforts of Christian missionaries in America and Asia.[14]

The location of the Pyrenees on the periphery of France and Spain—and the presence of a large population of expelled Spanish Gypsies—undoubtedly reinforced de Lancre's genuine conviction that Labourd was sick with witchcraft. De Lancre also had a visceral loathing of the Basques. In a subsequent account of his experiences, *Tableau de l'inconstance des mauvais anges et démons* (On the Inconstancy of Wicked Angels and Demons, 1612), he argued that Basques were naturally inclined toward witchcraft because "the women eat nothing but apples, they drink nothing but apple juice, and that is what leads them to so often offer a bite of the forbidden apple."[15] From his base in Saint-Jean-de-Luz, de Lancre unleashed a storm of virtuous terror in which hundreds of men, women, and children were arrested, tortured, and executed.

These investigations produced the usual semi-pornographic testimonies that tended to accompany such episodes, in which women confessed to having flown to sabbaths on broomsticks in Zugarramurdi and other places, where they pledged allegiance to the devil by kissing his behind and participating in orgies and obscene dances. Others claimed to have eaten children, dug up the bodies of the dead, and concocted poisons and spells to harm people or cause crops to fail. As was often the case, the confessions of these *sorginak* (witches) frequently involved animals. Sabbaths usually took place in a field known as the *akelarre* (a Basque word meaning "field of the he-goat") such as the field alongside the Zugarramurdi cave, and their participants often described seeing the devil in the shape of a large goat "with a tail, and beneath it a black human face."

Many witches confessed to having taken on the shape of animals to disguise themselves. The local population initially supported de Lancre's campaign, but soon hundreds of people began streaming across the Spanish border pretending to be going on pilgrimages to Montserrat or Santiago de Compostela, as it became clear that no one in Labourd was safe from prosecution. De Lancre regarded these "refugees" as proof of his success and redoubled his efforts. By the end of the year, news of his campaign had reached the cod fleet in Newfoundland, and the fishermen returned home early to protect their womenfolk. Complaints about de Lancre's excesses reached the ears of the French Crown, and he was recalled to Bordeaux.

De Lancre's investigation also had an impact on neighboring Navarre, where the powerful Inquisition of Logroño returned to Zugarramurdi in 1610 to carry out a new investigation into the initial reports of witchcraft there. The inquisitor Don Juan Valle Alvarado spent several months in Zugarramurdi and the surrounding villages gathering testimony on some three hundred suspected witches in the area. In addition to the usual orgies outside the Zugarramurdi cave, Alvarado also reported that these witches "enjoy changing into different shapes so as not to be recognised and going out to frighten and hurt travellers. For the Devil, it seems, changes them into swine, goats and sheep, mares and other animals, whatever best suits his purpose."[16]

Eventually, nine men and women from the village confessed, and the witches of Zugarramurdi were among the eleven witches burned in the great auto-da-fé at Logroño in November 1610. Meanwhile, the trials sparked a witch scare in northern Navarre and Guipúzcoa, in which thousands of people came under suspicion, and the Logroño inquisitors informed King Philip III that an ancient witches' sect in the Pyrenees had spread its power throughout the region. By March 1611, inquisitors had concluded that 158 people in Zugarramurdi out of a total of 390 were witches and another 124 were suspected of witchcraft. These findings were disputed by the lawyer Alonso de Salazar y Frías, one of the more skeptical inquisitors at the Logroño trial. Ordered by the Inquisition to carry out a further investigation into the witchcraft epidemic in Navarre, Salazar carried out hundreds of interviews and discovered numerous inconsistencies in the testimonies presented to him. He eventually concluded that the majority had little or no credibility and told his surprised superiors that "I have not found even indications from which to infer that a single act of witchcraft has really occurred."[17]

The Inquisition accepted Salazar's report and never again persecuted witches with the intensity it had shown at Zugarramurdi. Today these bleak events are remembered in a permanent exhibition at the Witchcraft Museum in Zugarramurdi, which contains the names of the innocent men and women from the village who were executed for nothing, more than four centuries ago. The museum places the Navarre witch hunt within a continuum of persecution and intolerance that includes the Ku Klux Klan, the Nazis, and McCarthyism. Borrowing from the great Basque ethnologist Julio Caro Baroja and other modern students of witchcraft, the museum presents the concept of *akelarre* as a positive affirmation of the body, sexuality, and the natural world. Whether these witches really were the remnants of some Dionysian pre-Christian cult, as some have contended, or whether they were simply random victims of what the historian Henry Charles Lea has called "a disease of the imagination, created and stimulated by the persecution of witchcraft," can never be known, but today the memory of Pyrenean witchcraft still lives on, in the museum at Zugarramurdi, in the crones on broomsticks, and in the *chimeneas expantabrujas*—witch-scaring chimneys—that can still be found in many villages in Upper Aragon and other parts of the Pyrenees.

The Accursed Race

The seventeenth-century witchcraft panic was a brutal but passing episode in the history of Pyrenean persecutions, and it pales in significance in comparison with the centuries-long persecution of the people known as Cagots who once populated the Pyrenees, the Landes, and parts of western France up to Brittany. Very little is known about how the Cagots came to be in the Pyrenees, or indeed about their ethnicity in general. It is not even known whether the Cagots were in fact members of the same ethnic group, although they were often depicted as such. The origins of the word "Cagot," or "Agotes," "Gahets," or "Capets," as they have also been known, have been variously attributed to a fusion of *chien Gots* or *cani Gothi* (Dog Goths)—which may be a reference to the Arian Goths defeated by the Frankish king Clovis in the sixth century. Others have claimed that the Cagots are descended from Saracens, persecuted Cathars, or medieval lepers.

Whatever their origins, there is little disagreement about the discrimination directed against them. For hundreds of years Cagots were not allowed to live near non-Cagots or do anything more than the most menial tasks. They could not walk in the middle of the street, drink water from common fountains, or sell food to non-Cagots. They could not enter churches, except through specially constructed low doorways that obliged them to bow. They were not allowed to receive Communion, though some Pyrenean villages allowed the priest to hand them pieces of bread on a long wooden fork. In some parts of the Pyrenees they were forbidden from owning more than twenty sheep, though Basque Cagots were not allowed to own any sheep at all. In 1672 the Estates of Navarre banned them from marrying non-Cagots. The Cagots of Navarre and Bordeaux were also ordered to wear a red cloth in the shape of a goose or duck foot on their shoulders.

In 1695 the Spanish government ordered the expulsion of the Cagots from northern Spain and offered a reward to any of their neighbors who carried it out. Hundreds of Cagots fled or were driven into France, where they were turned back and died in the mountains. The reasons for this persecution were never clear, even to those who inflicted it. Some historians contend the Cagots were descended from lepers. Others believe that the Cagots were associated with cretinism or goiter—a despised affliction that was supposedly common among the Cagots. To some extent the hatred directed at the Cagots was itself the product of centuries of persecution that defined them as a *race maudit*—an accursed race—and which found its own justifications.

Cagots, it was believed, were not fully human and were born with tails, which their parents cut off at birth to hide their origins. The imagined "wildness" of the Cagots was also captured by an old Basque folk song that proclaimed:

> *This is how you may recognize the cagot:*
> *You must look first at his ears:*
> *One is bigger, and the other*
> *Is round and covered with*
> *Long hair on every side.*[18]

The Cagots were also alleged to exude a particular stench. In 1600, surgeons in Navarre bled twenty-two Cagots in search of "some new kind of salt in their blood" and found nothing. Other popular myths accused them of cannibalism and the power to make fruit shrivel merely by holding it in their hands. In the seventeenth and eighteenth centuries, local French authorities in the Pyrenees made occasional attempts to legislate against such discrimination, and the Cagots themselves did not always accept it passively. In 1789 French Cagots took advantage of the Revolution to destroy archives containing records that identified them. Many Cagots eventually succeeded in assimilating into their local communities or emigrated to places where their status would not be recognized, but others continued to be identified by local tradition, if not by law, and were shunned as a consequence.

The Cagots exercised a morbid fascination over many eighteenth- and nineteenth-century visitors to the Pyrenees, and also over many more distant observers such as the English novelist Mrs. Gaskell, who wrote a powerful essay that depicted their persecution as a universal warning on the evils of irrational prejudice.[19] Ramond often encountered Cagots during his Pyrenean rambles. On the one hand he claimed to see in them "a degradation, a dullness, and stupidity . . . which deprives them of the last remains of the intelligence of man, together with the last traces of his figure."[20] Yet Ramond also described the Cagots as "creatures whom society has not been able to render so vile as it has attempted to make them. I have met with brothers who loved each other with that tenderness which is the most pressing want of isolated men."[21]

Writing in 1859, Charles Richard Weld predicted that "the time is still distant when the word Cagot will cease to be a term of reproach in the Pyrenees, and that the wretched peasant afflicted with goitre will long be regarded as belonging to the 'races maudites.'"[22] Traces of these "Pyrenean untouchables" can still be found on both sides of the Pyrenees in the sixty-odd churches containing bricked-up "Cagot doorways" or Cagot holy water fonts, but the reasons for their persecution remain as mysterious as they were to many of the nineteenth-century visitors to the Pyrenees who first brought their plight to the attention of the outside world. And like the shape-shifters, feral children, and other wild things that once populated the Pyrenean imagination, they, too, belong to a world that has largely ceased to exist.

12

Ghost Towns

We are men who wish to live on our land, which we love deeply, like yourselves. We are men who have created a living community with our families, neighbours and friends, labour and means, traditions and customs, festivals and games, ways of speaking, memories and loyalties to our forebears, and to lose all of these would kill our souls . . . we are men who fear exile . . . we are men of Aragon . . . we are the same as you.
  —Open letter from the Municipal Council of Campo, Huesca Province, protesting the construction of a reservoir, 1976[1]

In the Spanish novelist Julio Llamazares's magnificent novella *La lluvia amarilla* (*The Yellow Rain*, 1998), the last remaining inhabitant of the village of Ainielle, in the Sobrepuerto district of Huesca Province in Aragon, tells the story of his life and the life of his village. Alone with the memories that have driven him to the brink of madness, with only his dog to relieve his solitude, Llamazares's hermit-like narrator lives out his last days among Ainielle's collapsed houses and overgrown streets, haunted by his wife's suicide and the memories of the family members and neighbors who have long since died or abandoned the village. With a bleakly poetic lyricism, Llamazares describes the slow collapse of a rural Aragonese community in which "the process of destruction in each house was always the same and always equally unstoppable. First the mold and the damp would silently gnaw away at the walls, before moving on to the roof and then, like a form of creeping leprosy, to the bare skeletons of the roof beams. Then would come the wild lichens, the dead, black claws of the moss and the woodworm, and, finally, when the whole house was rotten to the core, the wind or a heavy snow-fall would bring it tumbling down."

There is a real village called Ainielle in Huesca Province. In 1920 the village had a population of eighty-three inhabitants. It was partly abandoned during the civil war and then gradually drained of its population into the 1950s and 1960s through death and emigration, until its definitive abandonment in 1971. Ainielle is one of hundreds of *pueblos abandonados*—abandoned villages—in the Aragonese highlands. Some, like Ainielle, are in an advanced state of disintegration. Others are structurally intact but devoid of inhabitants. In some parts of Aragon these villages have become part of the landscape, a melancholy spectacle of ruin and decay that has become a minor tourist attraction in its own right. Whole books and blogs are dedicated to these villages, containing haunting photographs of roofless churches, collapsed buildings, and overgrown village squares, or maps outlining itineraries of ruin. More recently, amateur filmmakers have used drones to photograph these ruins. In Sobrepuerto district, some enterprising holiday companies now offer walking tours of abandoned "villages that remain off the map."

To some extent the fascination with Pyrenean ruin echoes the phenomenon of "ruin porn" that has been variously applied to Chernobyl, Detroit, or the crumbling cities and abandoned factories of the American rust belt. These spectacles of ruin have acquired very particular metaphorical qualities, whether as symbols of Soviet nuclear hubris and our common nuclear future, cycles of capitalist boom and bust and the withdrawal of the state, or the precariousness of every community and the inevitability of ruin that awaits the human project. The ghost towns of Aragon have their own melancholy symbolism. On one hand these ruined or abandoned villages are a testament to rural communities that were too poor to sustain themselves, or which were unable to survive their encounter with modernity. But these ruins also provide physical evidence of the dramatic social and economic transformation that has taken place throughout the Pyrenees in the last two hundred years, which has drained the mountains of their population on both sides of the frontier and accelerated the disintegration that Llamazares described so powerfully.

Mountains Without People

Depopulation is not a specifically modern phenomenon in the Aragonese Pyrenees. In his history of the political economy of Aragon, Ignacio de Asso describes how the Christians who once fled the eighth-century Moorish invasions "moved with the conquest to the flat plain" in the twelfth century and abandoned their villages "as a result of the harsh conditions, including the inability to feed themselves."[2] Following the expulsion of the Moriscos in 1609–14, many Aragonese villages were abandoned or partially depopulated, though most of them were eventually resettled by Christians. But the most significant movements of people in Pyrenean history have taken place within the last century and a half. From the sixteenth to the mid-nineteenth centuries the population of the Western Pyrenees actually increased, according to some scholars, to the point when some 56 percent of the mountains were under pasture and even steep terraces were under cultivation.

Beginning roughly in the second half of the nineteenth century, the population of the Pyrenees began to decline on both sides of the frontier. Between 1856 and 1956 the population of the French Pyrenees fell by 56 percent, and some towns and villages lost more than half their populations as a result of emigration. In the mid-nineteenth century the former province of the Couserans, which now forms part of the Ariège *département*, had ten thousand inhabitants; today the population is less than fifteen hundred. In the Aragonese Pyrenees, emigration reached a peak in the 1950s and 1960s, and it was in this period when so many villages were drained of their populations. On both sides of the frontier this rural exodus was caused by a combination of push and pull factors: rural poverty and the inability of the traditional pastoral economy to cope with industrially produced goods; and improved transportation and communications links between the Pyrenees and the world below, which brought new opportunities in the form of jobs, higher wages, and access to schools and services in the cities.

In 1953 Pedro Cantero, the bishop of Barbastro, in Huesca Province, complained in a Madrid newspaper that the population of his diocese was less than it had been in the 1850 census—a decline that he attributed to "the asphyxiating lack of communication channels" between towns and villages. Some historians have cited the collapse of the Pyrenean "house system" as another push factor in driving Pyrenean emigration. According to this system, which was prevalent in many parts of the Pyrenees, generations of the same family assumed collective responsibility for the survival of the family unit. Though each individual member of the house was equally beholden to the larger family unit, the family property was generally inherited by the eldest son, who acted as the effective master of the house as a consequence. "Noninheriting" children, by contrast, often lacked any possibility of advancement and sometimes lived as virtual slaves of their own households, or servants of other families.

Marriage sometimes offered an escape from such servitude. In small mountain communities where the choice of wives and husbands was limited, however, noninheriting children, or *tiones* as they were known in Aragon, were sometimes obliged to marry below their status or leave the village in search of partners. The oppressive and claustrophobic nature of the house system is powerfully described in the novelist Lorenzo Mediano's *La escarcha sobre los hombros* (*The Frost on His Shoulders*, 2012), which describes the disastrous events that ensue in an Aragonese Pyrenean village in the 1930s when the shepherd Ramón's thwarted love for the daughter of the local patriarch leads him to challenge the authority of the *casa* (house).

In addition to his lowly occupation, Ramón is also a disinherited sibling, or *tion*, whose prospects are summed up by the guilt-ridden teacher who becomes his mentor:

> When I think of the *tiones* it breaks my heart, for they're like a tree's barren branches. They sit at the same table as their more fortunate brothers, but that's where all privilege ends. They work sunup to sundown for nothing but basic sustenance, clothing when absolutely necessary and, if it's been a good year, a little tobacco. And so it goes, day after day, serving first their fathers, then their brothers, then their nephews . . . until they grow old. Then they'll be given lighter chores, like making honeycomb cells from straw and dung, or caring for children, or collecting firewood kindling . . . And finally, one day, with a sigh of relief, they get to rest forever.[3]

Such a man cannot marry above his station, and Ramón's refusal to accept his rejection leads to rebellion and violence. Many Pyrenean *tiones* chose to improve their prospects through emigration. In France, the introduction of the French Civil Code in 1804 provided an additional incentive to emigration. In recognizing individual property rights and the right of individual inheritance, the new legislation made it possible to divide the "house" into smaller units and threatened to undermine the whole system of primogeniture on which the Pyrenean house system depended. As a result, many families actively pressured "noninheriting" sons and daughters to emigrate and even financed their journeys so that they would not seek to divide the family property.

The Pyrenean Diaspora

Emigration is rarely due to internal push factors alone. It also requires an awareness of better possibilities. In the nineteenth century, young men and women left the Pyrenees to work in Bordeaux, Paris,

Zaragoza, or Barcelona, for the same reasons that people will always emigrate: because it was increasingly easier to reach these places and because there was more information available about the opportunities they contained. Jean Louis Matocq left his Bearnese village after World War II at the age of sixteen to work in a restaurant in Paris, and subsequently emigrated to San Francisco in 1958, where he worked in the legendary Trader Vic's restaurant and went on to become a restaurateur and hotelier in his own right.

Many of the men and women who abandoned the rural villages of Huesca Province went to work in Barcelona. In 1998 more than 15 percent of the population of Huesca Province was living in Barcelona, and the figure was higher than 50 percent from some Pyrenean districts. Others went farther afield, to Canada, Uruguay, Argentina, or the Americas. Following the 1860 gold rush, many Basque shepherds emigrated to the United States to become miners, only to take up sheepherding in Nevada, California, Idaho, and eastern Oregon when these dreams of wealth turned sour. These Basque shepherds were highly regarded by American ranchers and farmers for their ability to find new pastures, preserve their flocks from predators, and ensure that their ewes had the most offspring.

As a result, Basque sheepherders became part of the landscape of the American West. As in the Pyrenees, they spent months alone in the mountains with their dogs, writing arboglyphs—carved inscriptions and drawings on tree bark—to pass the time or leaving the cairns known as "stoneboys," or *arrimutilak*, as navigational markers. For much of the twentieth century the sheep industry in Southern California and Nevada was heavily dependent on Basque labor, and it was not until Basque emigration declined in the 1970s that ranchers began to turn to South America in search of shepherds.

Some Basque shepherds arrived penniless and eventually went on to own their own herds. Dominique Laxalt, the father of the Nevadan author Robert Laxalt (1923–2001), arrived in Nevada around 1906 from the French province of Soule to work in the Sierra Nevada and went on to become a sheep and cattle rancher. In his classic memoir, *Sweet Promised Land* (1957), Laxalt describes the return of his Basque father Dominique to his native village near Tarbes after an absence of forty-seven years. Laxalt's tender tribute to his sheepherder father is also a celebration of his father's origins in the Pyrenees, where "the soft, dew-drenched hills of the lowlands had given way to mountains made even more austere by longing shadows, and the villages now were of homes not gaily trimmed in red and green, but of stone, bleak and cold and formidable as fortresses."[4] Laxalt's description of his father's return to his village and his reunion with his family after a forty-seven-year absence is one of the most beautiful and moving passages in American writing. It also touches on the bittersweet and often painful experience of abandonment, separation, nostalgia, and loss that is common to emigrants everywhere and which often brings them back to the places they were once obliged to leave.

The Valley of the Americans

Situated in the Couserans region of the Ariège *département*, the Garbet Valley is not a place that conjures up poverty, emigration, and rural hardship. On a summer's day the valley is a picture of rustic serenity, as the Garbet River rolls gently down from the mountains above Aulus-les-Bains through a succession of gentle stepped meadows and pastureland flanked by steep, forested hills that are scattered with holiday homes. After a few minutes you reach the village of Ercé, the capital of the Garbet, whose two parallel streets with their beige buildings and pastel-colored shutters add to the valley's sleepy charm. Only the prevalence of old people and the absence of children give a clue to the history of emigration that has drained the Garbet of its population.

In 1850, 10,000 people lived in the Garbet and neighboring Alet Valleys. Today the population of the two valleys is less than 1,500, of whom 560 live in Ercé itself. In the nineteenth century Ercé was famous for its bear displayers, some of whom traveled far beyond the Garbet with their animals. In 1890 Jean and Joseph Barat, two brothers from Ercé, took three bears to England, where they performed an impromptu dance for Queen Victoria on the "long walk" leading to Windsor Castle on May 5. The queen was so pleased with this performance that she summoned the Barats and their animals to the castle to dance before a royal audience of princes and princesses—an event that made them instantly famous.

Today the only remnant of that past is the "bear museum" in the former village school. The Garbet is known locally as the "Valley of the Americans," not only because so many emigrants went to live and work in the United States, but because many of them have since returned to live in the valley. The Garbet first began to acquire this reputation during the third great wave of emigration from the Ariège that took place in the postwar years, when a number of residents of the valley went to work in the hotel and restaurant industry in Toulouse, Paris, and the United States. Within a few minutes of walking around the village I met Jean-Pierre Icart, a former chef who worked for forty years in New York on the Upper West Side in clubs owned by the late millionaire hotel owner Leona Helmsley. At one time Icart's customers included politicians like Daniel Patrick Moynihan, the Kennedys, and other members of the New York glitteratti.

Now, like many returned "Americans," Icart has a summerhouse in Ercé with an allotment and a house in Toulouse. Many of the emigrants who went to work in the United States have followed a similar trajectory. María Perrier is a widow who spent sixty-two years in the States, living in Manhattan, elsewhere in New York State, and Florida, and recently moved back to Ercé following the death of her husband. I spoke to her at the modest house in the village that she shares with her younger sister Madeleine and her brother-in-law Roger, a Breton chef who also worked in New York. A bubbly woman in her eighties, María arrived in New York at the age of twenty-four in 1952, without any English, and quickly got a job as an au pair before working in a restaurant on the Upper West

Side. She went on to work in a series of restaurants, including one owned by her French husband, and lived in Westchester County, New York, and Florida. Her sister Madeleine followed her five years later.

Both sisters came from a close-knit, traditional family of five children, with a devoted and loving father who worked as a shepherd and supplemented the family income by making coffins and working as a gravedigger in the local cemetery. Monsieur Perrier tried to keep his family together, but María was insistent, and he eventually agreed to let her leave the village when she reached twenty-one. For the Perrier sisters, emigration provided new opportunities and an escape from the backbreaking labor expected of both women and men in the mountains. At the age of sixteen Madeleine was already spending the summers carrying food up to her brother and uncles in the high pasturelands, bringing back twenty kilos of butter from the stone igloos, or *orris*, which shepherds once used as refrigeration in the mountains, and spending six to eight hours a day looking after horses. "It was too much," she recalls. "I was too tired. I was working like a man."

Like many emigrants, the Perrier children never forgot their homeland or their past throughout their decades away. María first returned to Ercé with her brother five years after leaving for New York, in a black funeral Chevrolet that attracted a great deal of attention in an area where roads were still too small for cars. "When the young people see us with the car, they say 'Oh my God! Grace Kelly and the Prince of Monaco are here!'" she exclaims. "When my brother gets out of the car the kids are all looking at him, shouting 'He's there! It's the prince from Monaco!' We had so much fun!"

As I listened to these vivacious women talking with such deep affection about their beloved shepherd father, their childhoods, and the lives they had forged in the United States, I was struck by the courage, optimism, and hope that had led them to make a difficult and painful break with their past and also by the pull of memory that so often leads emigrants to return, transformed, to the world they left behind them. If poverty had forced them to leave their Pyrenean home, they also remembered it fondly, so much so that they had exchanged the relative comforts of New York and Florida for the harsh winters of the Couserans and the safety and security of the small rural community that they had once escaped from.

The Fall and Rise of Jánovas

This strong emotional attachment to a rural past is not unique to the French Pyrenees. Every second week in September, former inhabitants of Ainielle return to picnic and take Holy Communion in the ruins of the Church of Saint John the Baptist—the last remaining intact building in the village. Drive out some forty minutes west of Sabiñánigo along the spanking-new N-260 road known as the Eje Pirenaico (Pyrenean Axis) and you will see a cluster of high roofless stone buildings rising out of the greenery along the banks of the Ara River to your left. Shortly afterward a crudely painted sign announces the drive that leads to the village of Jánovas. Most visitors park their cars at the top of the dirt road and walk across the suspension bridge before turning right down the narrow dirt track that leads into the cluster of stone buildings that rise out of the surrounding greenery.

It's not until you cross the narrow bridge beyond the old village *lavadero* (washing place) that you really become aware of the devastation that has made Jánovas one of the most notorious of all Aragon's abandoned villages. The narrow streets are mostly overgrown, and grass, trees, and bushes burst out through the hollow shells of windowless and roofless homes that once housed animals and people. Beyond the overgrown village square, a dirt road leads to a gutted church containing some faint Romanesque frescos and more recent Orthodox paintings that were painted above the altar when the church was used as a set for the 2002 Spanish film *Guerreros* (Warriors), about the war in Kosovo.

Jánovas itself looks like a village destroyed by war, and in a way it was. Until the 1950s, it was one of a cluster of villages in La Solana Valley, whose population of some two hundred people made their living mostly from agriculture. In 1951 the Spanish government approved a project to build a dam in the valley. Ten years later, in 1961, the electricity company Iberduero began a series of expropriations and evictions in Jánovas and the sixteen other villages in La Solana Valley, in which some 150 families lost their homes. At that time the company had yet to carry out feasibility tests on the dam, and some villagers from Jánovas refused to leave or accept the meager compensation offered by the company. As a result they were forcibly evicted, and Iberduero then blew up their empty houses to ensure they did not return. Undisturbed by democratic or legal niceties, the company proceeded to chop down orchards and olive trees, block irrigation channels, and cut off the supply of water and electricity to the village. Even then a handful of families refused to leave and the local administration was obliged to keep the school open because children were still living there. On February 4, 1966, an Iberduero employee knocked down the door of the local school, dragged the teacher out by her hair, and threw the last children out onto the street.

Still some inhabitants refused to leave. It was not until 1984—well into the democratic era—that Emilio and Francisca Garcés, the last two inhabitants of Jánovas, left the village. In 2001 a legal report on the dam's feasibility was finally produced, which found that the project fell short of European environmental standards, though the dam was not rejected officially until 2005. In June 2008 the Spanish Ministry of Environment announced the end of the project, and a protracted bureaucratic process began with Iberduero's successor, the energy company Indesa, regarding compensation and return of property. When Indesa and Ebro Hydrographic Confederation offered only limited compensation for Iberduero's expropriations, the former inhabitants began to reconstruct the village by raising funds themselves—a painstaking and difficult enterprise that is likely to last decades and may never be completed.

So far these efforts have brought about the restoration of the village's former community center, and various diggers and dump trucks are poised to carry out ongoing building work and bring the village back to life even though there is no obvious reason to do so. These works are not financed by the Aragonese regional government. The partial resurrection of Jánovas is exclusively due to the former inhabitants of the village and their descendants, who have continued to honor the resistance of the men and women whose community was destroyed by a dictatorship for the sake of a dam that was never built.

Reconstruction

Jánovas is an unusual example of forced depopulation. Most abandoned Aragonese villages have been reduced to a very similar state of disintegration by the ravages of time and nature, and some of them are also being reconstructed, by new arrivals who have come to the Pyrenees with very different expectations from their original inhabitants. The village of Ibort is situated some forty minutes away from Jánovas, on an isolated dirt road in the Pyrenean foothills off the road from Huesca to Sabiñánigo. To reach it, you have to drive along a mostly dirt road through rows of pine forest with fine views of the Pyrenees to the north and the flat plain that leads to Zaragoza and the Ebro down below. Ibort, like Jánovas, was partly abandoned during the civil war because of its proximity to the front line.

After the war, most of the population returned, but the village was subsequently drained of its inhabitants once again during the great emigratory wave of the 1950s and 1960s. By the early 1970s Ibort had become another crumbling ghost village. In 1986 three people came to live in the ruins and began to reconstruct the village with the assistance of the Aragonese government, which helped organize international summer work camps here. By 2001 there were seventeen full-time residents in the village, who obtained a twenty-year-permit from the local administration to rebuild it. Today Ibort has been almost entirely rebuilt. After the desolation of Jánovas it was a refreshing pleasure to see gardens, orchards, and allotments bursting with fruit, flowers, and vegetables and to hear the sound of dogs and children in its pretty cobbled streets.

Approximately eighty people—some twenty families altogether— live in the village all year round, and Ibort belongs to a network of repopulated villages in Huesca supported by the government of Aragon. All of them are new or recent residents. Ricardo, a bearded, sunburned Spaniard in his late fifties, came here in 1994 after living briefly in a semi-abandoned village in the nearby Sierra de Guara. Originally from Pamplona, he had been looking for a place to settle permanently in the Pyrenees, because "for me the countryside, the mountains, were liberation."

Ibort has no dominant ideology or lifestyle beyond a general preference for the rural life that its original inhabitants once fled from. Some of its inhabitants, such as Ricardo's Dutch wife Bernadette, would like to be self-sufficient, but this objective has proven difficult to achieve in practice. Most residents commute to nearby Sabiñánigo and combine their gardens and allotments with part-time or temporary jobs elsewhere. According to Ricardo, none of the former residents of Ibort have shown any desire to live there, though some of them are invited each year on the feast of San Ramón in November, to visit the village and share their memories with the current population. In theory none of these houses can be sold— though some have been—but the legal status of the village remains ambiguous. Ibort has guaranteed private property rights in the village, but only a general contract issued by the administration. As a result the population lives in what Ricardo himself describes as "a very imprecise zone. At a legal level there's a vacuum, a limbo."

Repopulated "hippie villages" like Ibort are part of the slow repopulation of the Pyrenees that began in the last decades of the twentieth century. This phenomenon includes "neo-rural" ecologists going back to the land, at least in part, and more well-heeled residents who have bought and restored houses or monasteries in abandoned or semi-abandoned villages. The hills above the Gardet Valley are dotted with the characteristic *granges* (barns) of the Couserans, with their pyramid-shaped facades laid out in descending steps, each one with its own protruding roof slate, where small farmers who lacked the space for larger herds once kept their animals. Some of them are ruined and abandoned, while others have been refurbished as second homes by French holidaymakers.

In other parts of the Pyrenees, abandoned houses have become holiday homes and investment opportunities for Dutch and British tourists, and hotels, pensions, and bed-and-breakfasts for hoteliers and restaurateurs seeking to revitalize local cooking traditions or take advantage of the relatively recent phenomenon of *turismo verde* (green tourism) in the Spanish Pyrenees. For some Pyrenean villages, this new influx is the only way they can maintain their population and prevent their communities from disintegration. The population of Senegüé, an ancient village on the main road from Sabiñánigo to Biescas in the Valle de Tena, is inhabited mostly by the few remaining elderly members of the original population, and a sprinkling of incomers who have bought or rented holiday homes. Its inhabitants have worked hard to prevent the village from further disintegration. Largely through their own efforts they have restored the old church and built a fine hanging bridge across the Gallego River, which flows just behind the village. So far this combination of local initiative and second homes has staved off the depopulation that accompanied the entry of the Pyrenees into the modern world, and which has reduced so many Aragonese villages to empty or half-abandoned shells.

Today some 1.5 million people live permanently on both sides of the Pyrenees: a small proportion of the estimated 750 million people who live in mountains worldwide. Like those who came before them, these residents have learned to inhabit a mountain world that can be difficult and demanding as well as pleasurable, and which has never been quite as idyllic as it has seemed to so many visitors. In his collection of stories *Pirineos: tristes montes* (Pyrenees: Sad Mountains, 2011), the Spanish writer and Pyrenean expert

Severino Pallaruelo powerfully evokes the darker and harsher side of the old Pyrenees: a closed and claustrophobic rural world of unwanted pregnancies, isolation, loneliness, madness, and searing village hatreds. In one story two truffle hunters, the last remaining inhabitants of an abandoned village, plot to undermine and kill each other as their village crumbles around them. That world has now gone, and few of those who have come to the Pyrenees in search of second homes or property investments in recent years are likely to remember the reasons why so many of their former inhabitants once abandoned them.

Canfranc

This history of abandonment and disintegration is not entirely due to the encounter between the Pyrenees and modernity. One of the strangest and most haunting Pyrenean ruins can be found at the former International Railway Station of the village of Canfranc, at the Aragonese side of the Somport tunnel between Spain and France. Built in the art nouveau / classical style in the first two decades of the twentieth century, this grandiose building, 790 feet (241 meters) long, is more appropriate for a major European capital than a frontier village whose population has never risen above six hundred inhabitants. With its large central dome and two smaller cupolas at either end, its 300 windows and 156 doors, its obvious abandonment only enhances its magnificent incongruousness against the mountain backdrop. The origins of the station date back to 1853, when a group of Aragonese businessmen and politicians first proposed the construction of a tunnel under the Pyrenees at Somport. Decades of lobbying were required to convince the French and Spanish governments of the commercial advantages of a railway line linking Madrid and Paris, by way of Zaragoza and Pau, that would also act an instrument for the economic regeneration of the Aragonese highlands.

In 1882 the influential Spanish politician Joaquín Costa issued a manifesto in support of the project in which he declared, "Through the railway at Canfranc Spain enters modern life." By 1893 the railroad had reached Jaca on the Spanish side, and the arrival of the "civilizing machine," as the local press called it, intensified the demand to extend it farther northward. These demands were a reflection of the new spirit of cooperation between Spain and France, and delegations of Spanish and French engineers visited Canfranc to consider the viability of what was clearly a Herculean engineering project. Annual snowfall was so heavy at Canfranc that until 1876 the local population was charged with clearing the single road between Spain and the Aspe Valley to keep it open. The extension of a railway line into the Pyrenees also required a civil engineering effort on a massive scale and an enormous financial investment from both countries.

In 1908 work finally began at both sides of the tunnel. As a result, a village previously known for smuggling and the sale of skins and wool was invaded by an army of workers who began to blast and dig the tunnel and also to construct the infrastructure required to support it. The construction was delayed by World War I, and the station was not formally opened until 1928. For both countries, this was an astonishing feat. In addition to the tunnel itself, and an unusually large station building designed to allow passengers to transfer to the narrower-gauge railway lines on the Spanish side, thousands of workers toiled for two decades constructing dozens of bridges, viaducts, dykes, and smaller tunnels on both sides of the mountains. These infrastructural works also extended to the landscape itself. As early as the fifteenth and sixteenth centuries, extant contemporary documents in Aragon and Béarn described the devastation wrought in both regions by floods, avalanches, and snowfalls. In the winter of 1915 some 35,315 cubic feet (1,000 cubic meters) of snow fell across the Aragon River and the main road running through Canfranc, covering the area where the station was being built. To eliminate these risks, engineers on both sides of the frontier rerouted various rivers, excavated canals, built walls and dykes, and planted forests to act as natural barriers against avalanches. In Aragon alone, Spanish engineers planted more than 8 million trees.

In 1928 the *Voz de Aragón* hailed the transformation of the "savage well" of the Aragon River into a sedate canal. On July 18 that year the new station was inaugurated in the presence of King Alfonso XIII of Spain, the Spanish dictator Miguel Primo de Rivera, the French president Gaston Doumergue, and the Bearnese politician Louis Barthou, who had been instrumental in driving the project forward. The ceremonies were also attended by thousands of soldiers, Civil Guards, and carabineers, anxious at the possibility of an anarchist uprising. Security precautions were so strict that the meals available at the station hotel were mostly uneaten, because only people known to the authorities were actually allowed into Canfranc that day.

The latest "disappearance of the Pyrenees" was hailed in the Spanish and French press, which predicted the regular transport of freight and passengers under the Pyrenees that would make the railway profitable and bring prosperity to both countries. These expectations never materialized. Most freight transport across the Pyrenees continued to move back and forth across the easier road crossings at either end of the range, or via the easier railway crossing at Irun, and the beginning of the Great Depression dealt another blow to Canfranc's economic viability. Within a few years, the trains passing through Canfranc were mostly empty. Following the outbreak of the Spanish Civil War in 1936, Canfranc was seized by the Nationalists and the tunnel was shut down.

At the end of the war it was reopened once again and became one of the escape routes for refugees trying to reach Lisbon from Nazi-occupied France. Following the extension of the occupation to southern France in 1942, Canfranc was used by the Nazis to transport wolfram, aluminum, and other materials for the German war machine provided by the Franco regime northward, in exchange for gold, stolen art treasures—and gold teeth and watches from concentration camp victims—which were carried into Spain. In 1944 a devastating fire burned much of Canfranc to the ground and the station was closed once again. In 1946 it was reopened, and it remained operational until 1970, when a derailment on the French side destroyed one of its bridges.

By this time the railway was so rarely used that the French did not bother to repair the bridge. Despite periodic calls to reopen the line, Canfranc has remained closed ever since, and the opening of the 11-mile (18-kilometer) Somport road tunnel in 2003 has made the railway something of an anachronism, except for the two daily passenger trains between Canfranc and Zaragoza. Today the station provides access to the Canfranc Underground Laboratory, built underneath the Somport tunnel with cofunding by the Spanish government and the University of Zaragoza to conduct experiments into dark matter. The station building itself remains closed, a crumbling and incongruous outpost of urban elegance surrounded by rusted railway lines and buses, still waiting for the rehabilitation that has often been discussed but is yet to implemented.

In the summer of 2013 the government of Aragon opened the station to guided visits in an attempt to highlight the building's cultural value and prevent it from further disintegration. As is often the case in the Pyrenees, Canfranc's past has become its central attraction. Each year, on July 18, thousands of Spaniards take part in a reconstruction of the opening of the railway, some of whom are dressed in historical costume to play the role of Alfonso XIII and other dignitaries. In October 2017 the regional government of Aragon announced plans to reopen both the hotel and the tunnel itself, with co-financing from the Spanish government and the European Union. For the time being however, the railway into France remains unused and the station continues to molder, as it has done for more than half a century, a poignant and somewhat forlorn monument to one of the great follies of Pyrenean history—and a concept of "progress" that tends to be regarded very differently in the early twenty-first century than it was at the beginning of the twentieth.[5]

The Future in the Past: The Pyrenees in the Twenty-First Century

> Separating the Iberian Peninsula from the rest of the European continent, the snowcapped Pyrenees have always been a special realm, a source of legend and superstition. To explore the Pyrenees fully—the flora and fauna, the local cuisine, the remote glacial lakes and streams, the Romanesque art in a thousand hermitages—could take a lifetime.
>
> —Fodor's Travel, The Pyrenees Travel Guide, Fodors.com

In 1974 the author Robert Laxalt visited the Pyrenees to write a piece for *National Geographic*.[1] Looking down from the French-Spanish frontier toward the Vallée d'Ossau in the company of a local Aragonese shepherd, Laxalt delicately described a classic Pyrenean panorama that so many nineteenth-century travelers had sought and celebrated, "sprinkled with the golden buttercups of June and gashed along its flank by a torrent of frothing water. Peaks jagged as primitive spearpoints surrounded us, and a profusion of waterfalls dropped in white plumes to the valley floor." Laxalt also described a landscape that had been transformed by "painted new chalets and resort hotels. These stood on the outskirts of medieval hamlets with gray stone houses, guarded by the turrets of fortified churches. Ski lifts soared to the high peaks. Gigantic water pipes, two abreast, plummeted down the hillsides to a hydroelectric station. Once-secluded meadows bloomed with the blue and yellow and red tents of campers." Laxalt's shepherd companion openly lamented these unwelcome intrusions of modernity and described them as a manifestation of the "progress" that had once forced his two sons to abandon the Pyrenees and go "to the big cities for money."

Laxalt's meditation on the "enduring Pyrenees" was a more measured reflection on the ongoing transformation of the Pyrenees and the decline of the traditional life of the mountains that he still saw through the eyes of his emigrant father. Despite his anxieties about the degradation of the landscape, he also recognized the benefits that "progress" had brought to the Pyrenees. In the village of Saint-Lary, a French historian told him how tourism had stemmed the flow of young people to the cities and given them new and better-paid jobs beyond farming and agriculture. Such considerations influenced Laxalt's optimistic conclusion that "progress may alter the face of the Pyrenees, but it will be a long time before it erases the essence of its peoples."

More than forty years after Laxalt made these observations, "progress" has continued its inexorable advance through the Pyrenees. Today Vielha, the sleepy capital of the once-isolated Val d'Aran, is dominated by featureless high-rise ski buildings. Catalan valleys such as the Vall Fosca and the Vall de Boí have also been expanded by ski chalets and holiday apartments, while parts of the French Pyrenees are dotted with charmless ski villages that look as if they were put up in a weekend. Chairlifts, snowmaking machines, fast-food restaurants, and anonymous hotels add to the sense of intrusion and violation. New roads have accelerated the integration of the Pyrenees into the Anthropocene, bringing traffic, noise, and pollution to valleys that once rang with the cries of birds. Between 1990 and 2000, total traffic back and forth across the Pyrenees rose by 80 percent, and some valleys experienced an increase of 130 percent in the numbers of trucks crossing the mountains. Every day some seventeen thousand heavy trucks cross the passes at Biriatou and Le Perthus alone.

Ecologists in the Spanish and French Pyrenees have attempted at various times to block the expansion of ski resorts, the increase in truck traffic, and the installation of electric pylons and gas pipelines. In France, during the 1990s, the drilling of the Somport road tunnel was fiercely opposed by the communist trade union the Confédération Générale du Travail and also by the more militant "eco-activists" of the Comité pour la Sauvegarde Active de la Vallée d'Aspe (Committee for the Active Safeguard of the Vallée d'Aspe, CSAVA), which warned of the environmental impact of increased truck traffic on the Vallée d'Aspe. Such opposition was not universal. Even though the CSAVA saw the tunnel as the manifestation of a "Europe of business, desperate for new profits," the "European highway" was supported by many locals on both sides of the mountains, who regarded it in much the same way as a previous generation had regarded Canfranc—as a source of income and an instrument of economic regeneration. In 1994, six thousand people marched in Pau in support of the tunnel, where one speaker told them, "To live on the land, to work on the land, it's not enough to write some poetry and put a feather in your hat. You need an infrastructure worthy of a new century."[2]

These conflicting interests have continued to accompany the march of progress through the Pyrenees. Many visitors may find it difficult to contemplate the legoland ski villages, such as Gourette, near Eaux-Bonnes, or the dismal sight of a deserted ski station in summer, without a sinking feeling. But as Laxalt once observed, whole communities now depend on the tourists who come to them. Outsiders may lament the decline of the "traditional" Pyrenees and the cruder encroachments of modernity, but this transformation has not been entirely negative. In 1809 Joseph Wilson and Robert Andrew described the spa village of Barèges as "perhaps one of the most desolate places in nature" in winter, where the majority of its inhabitants "dare not remain in their houses, but remove furniture and belongings to escape avalanches and rockfalls," leaving "only a few invalid soldiers to preserve the warm sulphurous springs, which have given such a merited notoriety to the place, from being overwhelmed."[3]

One of the main reasons for the persistence of these avalanches, according to the eighteenth-century French engineer Antoine-François

Lomets, was the deforestation of their surrounding oak forests by the local population. "Because these slopes, being the first to be freed of snow by the sun and by avalanches, provide the first spring pasture for their sheep, Lomets observed, "the day they take them there, they forget that at home in the winter they have shivered with the fear of being carried away by the avalanches which they have stubbornly provoked."[4] Today the slopes above Barèges are thickly forested as a result of conservation and replanting, and the village that so many visitors once described as a gloomy Pyrenean purgatory for wounded war veterans has become a pleasant and laid-back base for recreational tourism.

Other Pyrenean villages have carried out similar works. For centuries the village of Aas, overlooking the Vallée d'Ossau just above Eaux-Bonnes, suffered regular snowfalls from the treeless hillside. Some houses in the village still have the old "double porch" system, which allowed snow to pass directly through their houses through doors built on two sides. In 1989, however, the local authorities installed snow barriers above the village and began a reforestation program consolidated by regular controlled tree burning to stimulate regrowth, which has succeeded in eliminating avalanches completely.

Even from an environmental perspective, therefore, the impact of modernity on the Pyrenees cannot be reduced to a conflict between "tradition" and "progress." The reintroduction of bears is an attempt by the French government to restore parts of the Pyrenees to their premodern wild state, yet the "traditional" Pyrenean shepherds have often opposed these efforts. If "progress" has brought roads, pollution, and commercialism to the Pyrenees, it has also brought national parks and conservation areas, which have protected mountains and forests from further unwanted encroachments. Contrary to some assumptions, the environmental degradation of the Pyrenees is not due only to the actions of outsiders. As early as 1683 some French Pyrenean forests and woodlands had become so drastically denuded of their trees that the government ordered every household to plant a tree annually. By 1780 the slopes of the Trône

du Roi (King's Throne) peak in the Vallée d'Aspe had been virtu-
ally stripped of pine trees in order to provide masts for the French
navy. The Pyrenean pastoral economy also contributed to the destruction, as sheep and goats destroyed young trees and fed on
shrubs.

Nineteenth-century visitors to the Pyrenees with much less interest in conservation than our own era were often shocked at the
misuse of local resources by the local inhabitants. Richard Ford
noted that many Pyrenean woodlands had "suffered much from the
neglect, waste and improvidence of the natives, who destroy more
than they consume, and rarely replant."[5] In Andorra, James Erskine Murray lamented "the great havoc and haste which the
ignorant charbonniers and woodcutters make in cutting down
the wood" and the primitive tools which obliged them to cut trees
quite high from the ground, leaving "the best and soundest tree left
to decay."[6]

Perhaps the greatest threat to the ecology of the Pyrenees in the
early twenty-first century emanates from far beyond the mountains
themselves. In the last hundred years Pyrenean glaciers have declined by 85 percent, and the decline has accelerated during the last
few decades. In 1842 Thomas Clifton Paris attempted to climb up
through the Brèche de Rolande via Gavarnie through a "smooth
glaciar that slopes to the distant circus" on the French side. On
contemplating the "huge slope of smooth ice, which went down
and down, and grew steeper and steeper" about a quarter of a mile
long up toward the Brèche, Paris "could not summon sufficient
resolution to attempt the passage" without crampons, and turned
back.[7]

When I passed over the Brèche from the other side in the autumn
of 2015, that glacier was an insignificant patch of ice and snow
barely fifty yards long. In 2008 Spanish researchers reported a
drastic regression of Pyrenean glaciers since 1980 and predicted that
all twenty-one remaining Pyrenean glaciers would disappear by
2050. These climatic changes are likely to have a long-term impact
on the ecology of the Pyrenees. As the mountains become drier,

they are likely to become browner and less forested. The reduction in the level of snow may deprive some of the lowlands of water and may also undermine one of the cornerstones of the Pyrenean tourist economy. In 2010 the European Environment Agency predicted that more than half the ski stations in the Pyrenees "will face difficulties in attracting tourists and winter sports enthusiasts in the future"—a prospect that may well consign some of the ski villages and chalet towns to the same fate as some of their abandoned villages and former spa towns.[8]

I was often conscious of these possibilities as I walked in the Pyrenees, in record-breaking temperatures that seemed higher every year. In the 1970s film *Soylent Green*, Edward G. Robinson's world-weary pensioner Sol checks into a voluntary euthanasia clinic to escape from an overcrowded and nightmarish urbanized world in which nature has largely disappeared or been concreted over. Robinson is put to sleep, serenely watching the photographs of lakes, mountains, and forests from his youth that no longer exist. If I were ever to find myself in a similar situation, I would not need to watch films to be reminded of such things. Images of those Pyrenean walks are permanently embedded in my mind: the dripping beech forest at the top of the Aspe Valley after a summer storm; the steep scree-covered slope below the Col de Petrachema as the bronze wall of rock to our left emerged through the drifting mist; the blue-tinged clarity of a mountain stream as we descended through the Marcadau Valley on a misty late afternoon; the kettle of vultures that cawed at one another above my wife and me as we walked toward Eaux-Bonnes high above a sea of mountains, cliffs, and tumbling forests; the sight of an ibex on the ridge below the summit of Canigou; the breathtaking magnificence of the Gavarnie Cirque; the forest-covered mountains that stretched in every direction during a descent toward Aulus-les-Bains.

Again and again I have found myself in a landscape that was as grandiose, pristine, and emotionally overwhelming as so many travelers have described it. In the course of these walks I often found myself thinking more about the past of the Pyrenees than I did about their future. Today the Pyrenees is a landscape that trades on its past and its history, a landscape crisscrossed with commemorative walking routes and "routes of memory" that have been walked by refugees, pilgrims, travelers, scientists, and soldiers. These walking companions often accompanied me on my own explorations.

I have tried to show the different ways in which the Pyrenees have been imagined and reimagined, and which have, at various times, transformed this random conglomeration of rock, earth, and stone into a place of beauty, terror, and enchantment and a mirror of our best hopes and worst selves. Perhaps now, even in these difficult times, when scientists have suggested that a human settlement on Mars offers some kind of future home for humanity, the Pyrenees can remind us that there is no better planet than the one we have.

In a world where so much seems to be crumbling and falling apart, we might take comfort and consolation from the triumphant words of Jacint Verdaguer engraved on the monument at the summit of Canigou:

What one century builds up, the next brings low
But God's enduring monument stands strong
Nor raging winds, nor war, nor wrath of men
Will overturn the peaks of Canigó
The soaring Pyrenees will not be bent.

Notes

INTRODUCTION: FROM THE SACRED MOUNTAIN

1. Friedrich Nietzche, *The Gay Science*, ed. Bernard Williams (1882, repr., Cambridge University Press, 2001), 230.

2. Simon Schama, *Landscape and Memory* (Vintage, 1996).

3. Robert MacFarlane, *Mountains of the Mind: A History of a Fascination* (Granta, 2008).

4. William Hazlitt, "On the Fear of Death," in *William Hazlitt, Essayist and Critic: Selections from His Writings*, ed. Alexander Ireland (Frederick Warne, 1889).

5. M. Ramond, *Observations on the Glacieres, and the Glaciers*, in *A Tour in Switzerland*, vol. 2, by Helen Maria Williams, appendix (G.G. and J. Robinson, 1798), 348–49.

6. Matsuo Bashō, *The Narrow Road to the Deep North and Other Travel Sketches* (Penguin Books, 1966), 143.

7. Nietzsche, *Gay Science*, 230.

1. THE LAND

1. *The Geographical Journal*, col 3, no. 2, Fe., 1894, p. 52.

2. Quoted in *À la découverte des Pyrénées/El descubrimiento de los Pirineos* (Château Fort Musée Pyrénéen de Lourdes, 2011), 62–63 (my translation).

3. Robin Fedden, *The Enchanted Mountains* (John Murray, 2002), 32.

4. Harold Spender, *Through the High Pyrenees* (A.D. Innes, 1898), 240.

5. Jules Michelet, *The Mountain* (Thomas Nelson and Sons, 1886), 83.

6. Silius Italicus. *Punica*, vol. 1, Loeb Classical Library Edition (William Heinemann Ltd, 1927), 147.

7. Diodorus Siculus, *Bibliotheca historica*, in *The Library of Diodorus Siculus*, vol. 3, Loeb Classical Library edition (Loeb, 1939), 197.

8. Strabo, *The Geography of Strabo*, vol. 2, trans. H.C. Hamilton and W. Falconer (Henry G. Bohn, 1856).

9. Ahmed ibn Mohammed al-Makkari, *The History of the Mohammedan Dynasties in Spain*, vol. 1, trans. Pascual de Gayangos (Routledge, 2002), 21–22.

10. Stendhal, *Travels in the South of France*, trans. Elizabeth Abbott (One-World Classics, 2009), 102.

11. Emmanuel de Martonne, *Geographical Regions in France* (Heinemann, 1962), 184.

12. Britan Jackman, "The Pyrenees: Walking with Condors," *Daily Telegraph*, February 9, 2002

2. THE VANISHING BORDER

1. F.J. Routledge, *England and the Treaty of the Pyrenees* (University Press of Liverpool, 1953), 66.

2. For a more detailed description of Velázquez's unfortunate mission to the Isle of Pheasants and the many tasks it entailed, see Carl Justi, *Velázquez and His Times* (Parkstone Press International, 2006).

3. Elisée Reclus, *The Universal Geography*, vol. II. (J.S.Virtue & Co., Limited, 1876), 97.

4. Pliny, *Natural History, Preface and Books 1–7*, trans H. Rackham (Folio Society, 2012), 147–48.

5. Thomas Glick, *Islamic and Christian Spain in the Early Middle Ages* (Brill, 2005), 53.

6. For a comprehensive history of the Peace of the Pyrenees and the Pyrenean border in general, see Peter Sahlins, *Boundaries: The Making of France and Spain in the Pyrenees* (University of California Press, 1989).

3. "AFRICA BEGINS AT THE PYRENEES"

1. Stendhal, *Vie de Napoléon* (Arvensa Éditions, 2015), 93 (my translation).

2. Dominique-Georges-Frédéric de Fourt de Pradt, *Mémoires historiques sur la revolution d'Espagne* (Perronneau, 1816), 70 (my translation).

3. William Z. Ripley, *The Races of Europe: A Sociological Study* (D. Appleton, 1899), 272.

4. Robert Harrison, trans., *The Song of Roland* (Signet Classics, 2002).

5. Albert Jean Michel de Rocca, *In the Peninsula With a French Hussar* (Greenhill Books, Lionel Levanthal Limited, 1990), 21.

6. Quoted in Charles Esdaile, *Popular Resistance in the French Wars* (Palgrave Macmillan, 2005), 210.

7. Vita Sackville-West, *Pepita* (Virago, 1986), 3.

8. Quoted in Peter Sahlins, *Boundaries: The Making of France and Spain in the Pyrenees* (University of California Press, 1989), 282.

9. Louis-Gabriel Suchet, *Memoirs of the War in Spain, from 1808 to 1814*, vol. 1 (Henry Colburn, 1829), 46–47.

10. Richard Ford, *A Handbook for Travellers in Spain* (John Murray, 1888), 514.

11. Caleb Cushing, *Reminiscences of Spain, the Country, Its People, History, and Monuments* (Carter, Hendee, 1833), 4.

12. Adolphe Thiers, *The Pyrenees and the South of France During the Months of November and December 1822* (Treuttel and Würtz, Treuttel, Jun. and Richter, 1823), 114.

13. Ford, *Handbook for Travellers in Spain*, 1103.

14. Jules Michelet, *The Mountain* (Thomas Nelson and Sons, 1886), 74.

15. Juan Valera, "Sobre el concepto que hoy se forma de España," *Revista de España* 1, no. 1 (1868), from *Obras completas*, vol. 2 (Aguilar, 1958), 737–51 (my translation).

16. Daniel Alexander Gómez-Ibáñez, *The Western Pyrenees: Differential Evolution of the French and Spanish Borderland* (Clarendon Press, 1975), 47.

17. Victor Fairén Guillén, *Una encuesta sobre las regulaciones internactionales de pastos en los Pireneos* (Instituto de Estudios Políticos, 1952).

18. Emmanuel Le Roy Ladurie, *Montaillou* (Penguin Books, 1990), 107.

PART II: PYRENEAN CROSSINGS

1. Will Durant and Ariel Durant, *The Story of Civilization: Rousseau and Revolution: A History of Civilization in France, England, and Germany from 1756, and in the Remainder of Europe from 1715 to 1789* (Simon & Schuster, 1967), 293.

4. SCHOLARS, PILGRIMS, AND TROUBADOURS

1. Quoted in John Tolan, *Petrus Alphonsi and His Medieval Readers* (University of Florida, 1993), 172–73.

2. J. Nicholas Entrikin and Vincent Berdoulay, "The Pyrenees as Place: Lefebvre as Guide," *Progress in Human Geography* 29, no. 2 (2005): 129–47.

3. For accounts of Gerbert's life and his intellectual adventures in Iberia, see Nancy Marie Brown, *The Abacus and the Cross: The Story of the Pope Who Brought the Light of Science to the Dark Ages* (Basic Books, 2010). See also Marco Zuccato, "Gerbert of Aurillac and a Tenth-Century Jewish Channel for the Transmission of Arabic Science to the West," *Speculum* 80, no. 3 (July 2003): 742–63.

4. *William of Malmesbury's Chronicles of the Kings of England. From the Earliest Period to the Reign of King Stephen*, trans., J.A. Giles (Henry G. Bohn, 1847), 173.

5. Philip K. Hitti, *History of the Arabs from the Earliest Times to the Present* (Macmillan, 1951), 589.

6. John V. Tolan, xiii.

7. It is not known exactly which routes Peter took on his journeys to and from Spain, but the fact that he visited a number of Cluniac houses, received a donation from King Alfonso VII of Castile, and assembled his team of translators at Nájera in La Rioja suggests that he stuck very closely to the main pilgrimage route through the Pyrenees.

8. William Melczer, trans., *The Pilgrim's Guide to Santiago de Compostela* (Italica Press, 1993), 93.

9. For more detail on this poignant and fascinating journey, see R.W. Southern, *The Making of the Middle Ages* (Yale University Press, 1953), 20–25.

10. Quoted in Andreas Petzold, *Romanesque Art* (George Weidenfeld and Nicolson, 1995), 18.

11. See Jeffrey A. Bowman, "The Bishop Builds a Bridge: Sanctity and Power in the Medieval Pyrenees," *Catholic Historical Review* 88, no. 1 (2002): 1–16.

12. Quoted in Roger Boase, "Arab Influences on European Love-Poetry," in *The Legacy of Muslim Spain*, ed. Salma Jayyusi (Brill, 1992), 465–66.

13. Ibid, 466.

14. M. Defourneaux, *Les Français en Espagne aux xIe et xIIe siècles* (Presse universitaires, 1949), (my translation).

15. Henry Kamen, *Early Modern European Society* (Routledge, 2005), 186.

16. Peter Sahlins, *Boundaries: The Making of France and Spain in the Pyrenees* (University of California Press, 1989), 174.

5. THE ZONE OF WAR

1. John Malcolm, *Reminiscences of a Campaign in the Pyrenees and the South of France, in 1814* (Constable, 1828), 254.

2. Malcolm, *Reminiscences of a Campaign*, 260.

3. Malcolm, *Reminiscences of a Campaign*, 261.

4. Titus Livius (Livy), *The History of Rome*, trans. Rev. Canon Roberts (E.P. Dutton, 1912), bk. 21, chap. 30.

5. W.A. MacDevitt, trans., *De Bello Gallico & Other Commentaries of Caius Julius Caesar* (Cosimo, 2006), 238.

6. Jean Froissart, *Sir Jean Froissart's Chronicles of England, France, Spain, and the Adjoining Countries* (Longman, Hurst, Rees, and Orme, 1808), 273.

7. Lynne H. Nelson, trans., *The Chronicle of San Juan de la Peña: A Fourteenth-Century Official History of the Crown of Aragon* (University of Pennsylvania Press, 1991), 76.

8. For an account of this little-known episode, see Jesús Gascón Pérez, "La 'Jornada de los bearneses': epílogo de la resistencia aragonesa contra Felipe II," *Bulletin hispanique* 106, no. 2 (2004): 471–96.

9. W.F.P. Napier, *History of the War in the Peninsula and in the South of France: From the Year 1807 to the Year 1814* (D. & J. Sadlier, 1873), 617.

10. Ian Fletcher, ed., *Voices from the Peninsular War: Eyewitness Accounts by Soldiers of Wellington's Army, 1808–1814* (Frontline Books, 2016), 205.

11. Roger Parkinson, *The Peninsular War* (Wordsworth Editions, 2000), 185.

12. Charles Esdaile, *The Peninsular War* (Penguin Books, 2003), 462.

13. Esdaile, *Peninsular War*, 463.

14. John Lynn, *The Wars of Louis XIV, 1667–1714* (Longman, 1999), 159.

15. Louis-Gabriel Suchet, *Memoirs of the War in Spain, from 1808 to 1814*, vol. 1 (Henry Colburn, 1829), 56–57.

16. For descriptions of the resistance operations and the Nazi/Vichy response in and around Canigou, see Rosemary Bailey, *Love and War in the Pyrenees* (Phoenix, 2008).

17. Blaise de Monluc, *The Commentaries of Messire Blaise de Montluc Mareschal of France*, trans. A.W. Evans (F.G. Browne, 1913), 446.

18. Edward Bell Stephens, *The Basque Provinces: Their Political State, Scenery and Inhabitants, with Adventures Amongst the Carlists and Christinos* (Whittaker, 1837), v–vi.

19. C.F. Henningsen, *The Most Striking Events of a Twelvemonth's Campaign with Zumalacarregui, in Navarre and the Basque Provinces*, vol. 1 (John Murray, 1836), 136.

20. James Erskine Murray, *A Summer in the Pyrenees*, vol. 1 (John Macrone, 1836).

21. George Wheeler, *To Make the People Smile Again* (Zymurgy Publishing, 2003), 42.

22. Richard Baxell, *Unlikely Warriors: The British in the Spanish Civil War and the Struggle Against Fascism* (Aurum Press, 2012), loc. 1525.

23. Vincent Brome, *The International Brigades: Spain 1936–37* (Mayflower-Dell, 1967), 40.

24. Brome, *International Brigades*, 45.

25. Baxell, *Unlikely Warriors*, loc. 1536.

26. Baxell, *Unlikely Warriors*, loc. 1536.

27. Lee memorably recounts his Pyrenean adventures and his short-lived participation in the Spanish Civil War in Laurie Lee, *A Moment of War: A Memoir of the Spanish Civil War* (The New Press, 1994). Nevertheless, his account has been critiqued by former International Brigadiers, including Bill Alexander, who have accused him of embellishment and even falsification.

28. For a full account of Operation Reconquest, see Ferran Sanchez Agustí, *Espias, contrabando, maquis y evasion: La II Guerra Mundial en los Pireneos* (Editorial Milenio, 2003). More recently, Robert Gildea's *Fighters in the Shadows: A New History of the French Resistance* (Harvard University Press, 2015) contains abundant information on the participation of Spanish Republican exiles in the French Resistance in the South of France.

29. For an account of the post–World War II anti-Franco resistance in the Aragonese Pyrenees, see Mercedes Yusta, ed., *Historias de maquis en el Piréneo aragones* (Piraeum Editorial, 1999).

30. For a biography of Sabaté, see Antonio Téllez Solà, *Sabaté: Guerrilla Extraordinary* (Cienfuegos Press, 1974).

31. For a fuller account of the Kruegers' work in the Pyrenees, see Bailey, *Love and War*.

6. SAFE HAVENS

1. Max Aub, *Obras completas*, vol. 4B, stories 2 (Valencia, 2006) (my translation).

2. Quoted in Rosemary Bailey, *Love and War in the Pyrenees* (Phoenix, 2008), 26.

3. Ignacio de Asso, *Historia de economía política de Aragón* (Zaragoza, 1798), 300 (my translation).

4. Quoted in Matthew Carr, *Blood and Faith: The Purging of Muslim Spain* (Hurst, 2017), 308.

5. Adolphe Thiers, *The Pyrenees and the South of France During the Months of November and December 1822* (Treuttel and Würtz, Treuttel, Jun. and Richter, 1823), 82.

6. Sabine Baring-Gould, *A Book of the Pyrenees* (E.P. Dutton, 1907), 88.

7. Arthur Koestler, *Scum of the Earth* (Eland Publishing, 2006), 114.

8. Mary Lowenthal Festiner, *To Paint Her Life: Charlotte Salomon and the Nazi Era* (Harper Collins, 1994), 119–20.

9. Koestler, *Scum of the Earth*, 94.

10. Lion Feuchtwanger, *The Devil in France: My Encounter with Him in the Summer of 1940*, trans. Elisabeth Abbott (The Viking Press, 1941), 148.

11. Josep Calvet, *Las montañas de la libertad* (Alianza Editorial, 2008), 46.

12. For Fittko's account of Benjamin's Pyrenean crossing, see Lisa Fittko, *Escape Through the Pyrenees* (Northwestern University Press, 1991), 103–15.

13. Frederic V. Grunfeld, *Prophets Without Honour: A Background to Freud, Kafka, Einstein and Their World* (Holt, Rinehart and Winston, 1979), 248.

14. Fittko, 111.

15. Carmina Birman, *The Narrow Foothold* (Hearing Eye, 2006). It is worth noting that some of the details provided by Birman regarding both the journey and Benjamin's death do not correspond with previous accounts. She herself is not even mentioned in Fittko's account, which may well be due to the vagaries of memory. Another unlikely theory posits that Benjamin did not commit suicide but was killed on Stalin's orders. See "Did Stalin's Killers Liquidate Walter Benjamin?" *The Guardian*, July 8, 2001.

16. There are many books on World War II escape lines. For a more unusual perspective on the Pat O'Leary line, see Antonio Téllez Solà's biography of Francisco Ponzán Vidal, *The Anarchist Pimpernel: The Anarchists in the Spanish Civil War and the Allied Escape Routes of WWII* (Christie Books, 1997).

17. See Calvet, *Las Montañas*.

18. See Russell Braddon, *Nancy Wake: SOE's Greatest Heroine* (History Press, 2009).

19. Quoted in Edward Stourton, *Cruel Crossing: Escaping Hitler Across the Pyrenees* (Black Swan, 2013), 248.

PART III: THE MAGIC MOUNTAINS

1. *Heinrich Heine's Memoirs: From His Works, Letters, and Conversations*, vol. 2, ed. Gustav Karpeles (William Heineman, 1910), 118.

7. PIONEERS: THE "DISCOVERY" OF THE PYRENEES

1. L. Ramond, *Voyages au Mont Perdu: Et dans la partie adjacente des Hautes-Pyrénées* (Chez Berlin, 1801), 347 (my translation).

2. Henry Swinburne, *Supplement to Mr. Swinburne's Travels, Being a Journey from Bayonne to Marseille* (P. Elmsly, 1787), 28–29.

3. Swinburne, *Supplement to Mr. Swinburne's Travels*, 18.

4. *À la découverte des Pyrénées*, 165.

5. *À la découverte des Pyrénées*, 129.

6. Henri Béraldi, preface to *Cent ans aux Pyrénées*, 7 vols., edited from 1898 to 1904 (repr., Les amis du livre Pyrénéen, 1977) (my translation).

7. Louis Ramond de Carbonnières, *Travels in the Pyrenees: Containing a Description of the Principal Summits, Passes, and Vallies*, trans. F. Gold (Longman, Hurst, Rees, Orme, and Browne, 1813), 132–33.

8. Jules Michelet, *The Mountain* (Thomas Nelson and Sons, 1886), 79.

9. Michelet, *The Mountain*, 43.

10. Quoted in *À la decouverte*, 118 (my translation).

11. Ramond, *Travels in the Pyrenees*, 58.

12. For a biography of Russell, see Rosemary Bailey, *The Man Who Married a Mountain: A Journey Through the French Pyrenees* (Transworld Publishers, 2005).

13. Bailey, *Man Who Married a Mountain*, 348.

14. Bailey, *Man Who Married a Mountain*, 16.

15. Bailey, *Man Who Married a Mountain*, 337.

16. Baron Bertrand de Lassus, "Midnight and Dawn on the Summit of the Great Vignemale," *Alpine Journal* 102 (1997): 197–205.

17. Quoted in Kev Reynolds, *Mountains of the Pyrenees* (Cicerone Press, 1982), 27.

18. Reynolds, *Mountains of the Pyrenees*, 279.

19. Charles Packe, *A Guide to the Pyrenees: Especially Intended for the Use of Mountaineers* (Longmans, Green, 1867), 12.

20. Packe, *Guide to the Pyrenees*, 26.

21. Francis Galton, *Memories of My Life* (E.P. Dutton, 1909), 189.

22. For accounts of "heroic-age" pyreneists and their descendants, see Reynolds, *Mountains of the Pyrenees*.

23. Bailey, *Man Who Married a Mountain*, 188.

24. Douglas Busk, *The Delectable Mountains* (Hodder & Stoughton, 1946), 44.

25. See Jerome Lamy, "'The Pyrenees Are Not Hollow': The Mountain as a Boundary Object," *História, ciências, saúde—Manguinhos*, no. 3 (July–September 2009).

26. Norbert Casteret, *Ten Years Under the Earth* (1939; repr. Zephyrus Press, 1975), 91.

27. Casteret, *Ten Years Under the Earth*, 11.

28. Henry Blackburn, *The Pyrenees: A Description of Summer Life at French Watering Places* (Sampson Low, Marston, Searle, & Rivington, 1867), 179–80.

29. Victor Hugo, *Victor Hugo's Letters to His Wife and Others (The Alps and Pyrenees)*, trans. Nathan Haskell Dole (Estes and Lauriat, 1895), 297.

8. VISITORS

1. George Sand, *Story of My Life: The Autobiography of George Sand* (State University of New York Press, 1991), 855.

2. Henry Swinburne, *Travels Through Spain in the Years 1775 and 1776* (J. Davis; for P. Elmsly, 1787), 4.

3. Quoted in Jay Williams, ed., *Life in the Middle Ages* (Cambridge University Press, 1967), 256.

4. For a more extensive discussion of changing cultural attitudes to mountains, see Robert MacFarlane, *Mountains of the Mind: A History of a Fascination* (Granta, 2008); Rebecca Solnit, *Wanderlust: A History of Walking* (Penguin Books, 2001).

5. Titus Lucretius Carus, *De rerum natura*, trans. H.A.J. Munro (Deighton Bell and Co., 1864).

6. Petrarch, "The Ascent of Mount Ventoux," in *Selections from the Canzoniere and Other Works*, trans. Mark Musa (Oxford University Press, 1999).

7. Quoted in Douglas W. Freshfield, *The Life of Horace Benédict de Saussure* (Edward Arnold, 1920), 9.

8. Marjorie Hope Nicolson, *Mountain Gloom and Mountain Glory: The Development of the Aesthetics of the Infinite* (University of Washington Press, 1997), 277.

9. Edmund Burke, *A Philosophical Inquiry into the Origins of Our Ideas of the Sublime and the Beautiful* (Oxford Paperbacks, 2008).

10. Charles-François Brisseau de Mirbel, *Mountain Adventures in the Various Countries of the World: Selected from the Narratives of Celebrated Travellers* (Roberts, Brothers, 1869), 114.

11. Ann Radcliffe, *The Mysteries of Udolpho* (Oxford University Press, 1998), 42.

12. Louisa Stuart Costello, *Béarn and the Pyrenees: A Legendary Tour to the Country of Henri Quatre*, vol. II (Richard Bentley, 1844), 12–13.

13. Victor Hugo, *Victor Hugo's Letters to His Wife and Others (The Alps and Pyrenees)*, trans. Nathan Haskell Dole (Estes and Lauriat, 1895), 298.

14. Joseph Wilson and Robert Andrew Riddell, *A History of Mountains, Geographical and Mineralogical*, vol. 2, (Nicol, 1809), 81–83.

15. William Gilpin, *Three Essays: On Picturesque Beauty; On Picturesque Travel; and On Sketching Landscape: To Which Is Added a Poem, On Landscape Painting* (R. Blamire, 1794).

16. Henry David Inglis, *Switzerland, the South of France, and the Pyrenees* (Whittaker and Co., 1835), 80.

17. Edith Wharton, *A Motor-Flight Through France* (Charles Scribner's Sons, 1908), 104.

18. Rosemary Bailey, *The Man Who Married a Mountain: A Journey Through the French Pyrenees* (Transworld Publishers, 2005), 323.

19. Bailey, *Man Who Married a Mountain*, 111.

20. Charles Baudelaire, "Incompability," PoemHunter.com, 2004.

21. Charles Baudelaire, *Paris Spleen*, trans. Louise Varèse (1869; repr., New Directions, 1969), 28.

22. For full text, see Algernon Charles Swinburne, *Selected Poems* (Routledge, 2002), 246–49.

23. Algernon Charles Swinburne, "Victor Hugo: En Voyage," *North American Review* 151, no. 409 (December 1890): 650–61.

24. *Heinrich Heine's Memoirs: From His Works, Letters, and Conversations*, vol. 2, ed. Gustav Karpeles (William Heineman, 1910), 119.

25. For full text, see Heinrich Heine, *Atta Troll*, trans. Herman Scheffauer (Sidgwick & Jackson, 1913).

26. Belinda Jack, *George Sand: A Woman's Life Writ Large* (Vintage, 2001), 124. Sand's intoxication with the Pyrenean landscape was also influenced by her complex emotional relationships with her entourage. Her Pyrenean

journey coincided with a crisis in her marriage that would eventually lead to separation. In the Pyrenees she became aware for the first time of her bisexuality—a discovery that produced a love triangle involving her husband and a male and female companion.

27. Quoted in Patrick Waddington, *Turgenev and George Sand: An Improbable Entente* (Barnes & Noble Books, 1981), 25.

28. Hilaire Belloc, *The Pyrenees* (Methuen & Co., 1909), 314.

29. Dominique Jarrassé, *2,000 ans de thermalisme. Economie, patrimoine, rites et pratiques* (Pu Blaise Pascal, 1999), 168 (my translation).

30. For an interesting discussion of Schrader's views on the relationship between art and cartography, see Hélène Saule-Sorbé, "En torno a algunas 'orografías' realizadas por Franz Schrader en los Pirineos españoles," *Ería* 64–65, 2004: 207–20.

31. The establishment of the "Chemin Mackintosh" was largely due to the efforts of Robin Crichton, president of L'Association Charles Rennie Mackintosh in Roussillon and author of *On the Trail of Monsieur Mackintosh: The Travels and Paintings of Charles Rennie Mackintosh in the Pyrénées Orientales 1923–1927* (Robin Chrichton, 2014). For more details on Mackintosh's last years, see also John McKean, *Charles Rennie Mackintosh: Architect, Artist, Icon* (Lomond Books, 2000).

32. Anna Klumpke, *Rosa Bonheur: The Artist's (Auto) Biography* (University of Michigan Press, 2001), 139.

33. Stanley Meisler, *Shocking Paris: Soutine, Chagall and the Outsiders of Montparnasse* (St. Martin's Press, 2015), 39.

34. Graham Robb, *The Discovery of France* (Picador, 2007), 307–10.

35. Sarah Bernhardt, *My Double Life: The Memoirs of Sarah Bernhardt* (William Heinemann, 1907), 60.

36. Henry Blackburn, *The Pyrenees: A Description of Summer Life at French Watering Places* (Sampson Low, Marston, Searle, & Rivington, 1867), 97.

37. François René Chateaubriand, *Mémoirs D'Outre-Tombe*, trans. A.S. Kline, *Poetry in Translation*, 2005, book xxxi, chap 1: sec 1, https://www.poetryintranslation.com/PITBR/Chateaubriand/ChateaubriandMemoirs BookXXXI.php.

38. Steve Cracknell, *If You Only Walk Long Enough: Exploring the Pyrenees* (Steve Cracknell, 2016), 86.

39. Jarrassé, *2,000 ans de thermalisme*, 168.

40. Edwin Asa Dix, *A Midsummer Drive Through the Pyrenees* (G.P. Putnam's Sons, 1890), 269.

41. Taine did not like Eaux-Bonnes at all, and spent some four pages doing as much as he could to put off potential visitors, in Hippolyte Taine, *A Tour Through the Pyrenees* (Henry Holt and Company, 1875), 120–24.

42. Octave Mirbeau, *Twenty-One Days of a Neurasthenic*, trans. Justin Vicari (Dalkey Archive Press, 2014), 3.

43. Blackburn, *Pyrenees*, 84.

44. Leslie Stephen, *The Playground of Europe* (Archivum Press, 2007).

45. Thomas Clifton Paris, *Letters from the Pyrenees During Three Months' Pedestrian Wanderings Amidst the Wildest Scenes of the French and Spanish Mountains in the Summer of 1842* (John Murray, 1843), iv.

46. Inglis, *Switzerland*, 99.

47. Sand, *Story of My Life*, 856.

48. Bernhardt, *My Double Life*, 60.

49. E. John B. Allen, *The Culture and Sport of Skiing: From Antiquity to World War II* (University of Massachusetts Press, 2007), 111.

50. See Bill McGann and Carol McGann, *The Story of the Tour de France*, vol. 1 (Bill and Carol McGann, 2006). Also see Geoffrey Wheatcroft, *Le Tour* (Simon & Schuster, 2013).

51. Edith Wharton, *A Motor-Flight Through France*, 106.

52. Quoted in Michael Foot, "Trotsky's Diary—a Poignant Document," *International Socialist Review* 20, no. 4 (Fall 1959): 122.

53. To be fair to Rahn, he was not the only writer to describe the Cathars in these terms. The nineteenth-century French historian Napoléon Peyrat described the caves and tunnels around Montségur as "our wild Capitoline, our aerial tabernacle, our ark sheltering the remains of Aquitaine from a sea of blood." Quoted in Stephen O'Shea, *The Perfect Heresy: The Life and Death of the Cathars* (Profile Books, 2000), 251.

54. See, for example, Nigel Graddon, *Otto Rahn and the Quest for the Holy Grail: The Amazing Life of the Real "Indiana Jones"* (Adventures Unlimited Press, 2008).

55. For an account of Böhmers's career and a history of the Ahnenerbe, see Heather Pringle, *The Master Plan: Himmler's Scholars and the Holocaust* (Hachette Books, 2007).

56. Graham Keeley, "Revealed: Himmler's Secret Quest to locate the 'Aryan Holy Grail,'" *The Independent*, February 6, 2007.

9. LOST KINGDOMS

1. Jacint Verdaguer, *Mount Canigó: A Tale of Catalonia*, trans. Ronald Puppo (Barcino-Tamesis, 2015).

2. Norman Davies, *Vanished Kingdoms: The History of Half-Forgotten Europe* (Penguin, 2012).

3. James Erskine Murray, *A Summer in the Pyrenees*, vol. 2 (John Macrone, 1836), 102.

4. Francis Miltoun, *Castles and Chateaux of Old Navarre and the Basque Provinces*, (L.C. Page & Company, 1907), v.

5. Jonathan Sumption, *The Hundred Years War*, vol. 2 (Faber & Faber, 2011), 317. For an English-language biography of Phoebus with detailed analysis of his political relationships with France and his neighbors, see Richard Vernier, *Lord of the Pyrenees: Gaston Febus, Count of Foix (1331–1391)* (Cambridge University Press, 2007).

6. John Joliffe, ed. and trans., *Froissart's Chronicles* (Harvill Press, 1967), 283.

7. Quoted in Vernier, *Lord of the Pyrenees*, 167.

8. Louisa Stuart Costello, *Béarn and the Pyrenees*, vol. II, 178.

9. Lady G. Chatterton, *The Pyrenees: With Excursions into Spain*, vol. 1 (Saunders and Otley, 1843), 267.

10. Costello, *Béarn and the Pyrenees*, vol. II, 55–56. Costello claimed to have encountered one of these historical ghosts herself, in the form of "a grey transparent figure in armour, the head covered in a helmet," which she glimpsed during a walk near the castle.

11. Quoted in Graham Robb, *The Discovery of France* (Picador, 2007), 20–21.

12. Henry Swinburne, *Travels Through Spain*, 13.

13. Jules Michelet, *The Mountain* (Thomas Nelson and Sons, 1886), 75.

14. James Erskine Murray, *A Summer in the Pyrenees*, vol. 1 (John Macrone, 1836), 162.

15. Harold Spender, *Through the High Pyrenees* (A.D. Innes, 1898), 58.

16. Bayard Taylor, *By-Ways of Europe* (G.B. Putnam and Son, 1869), 267.

17. Lewis Gaston Leary, *Andorra, the Hidden Republic* (McBride, Nast & Company, 1912), 97.

18. V.C. Scott O'Connor, *Travels in the Pyrenees: Including Andorra and the Coast from Barcelona to Carcassone* (Forgotten Books, 2017), 278.

19. "An Unknown Republic," *Chambers's Edinburgh Journal* 10, No. 244 (September 2, 1848): 165–66.

20. Dix, *A Midsummer Drive*, 174

21. Walter Kirchner, "Mind, Mountain, and History," *Journal of the History of Ideas* 2, no. 4 (October 1950): 412–47.

22. Stephen O'Shea, *The Perfect Heresy: The Life and Death of the Cathars* (Profile Books, 2000), 251.

23. Quoted in Charles Alfred Downer, *Frédéric Mistral: Poet and Leader in Provence* (The Columbia University Press, 1901), 93.

24. D. Víctor Balaguer, *Los Pireneos; Trilogía en Verso Catalán con Traducción en Prosa Castellana* (Talleres de Henrich y Ca, 1892), 55–56 (my translation).

25. Robert Hughes, *Barcelona* (Harvill, 1992), 348.

26. Hughes, *Barcelona*, 348.

27. Elisabet Andreu, Francisco Lagardera Otero, and Glòria Rovira Bahillo, "El excursionismo Catalán y los deportes de montaña," *Apunts: educación física y deportes* 41 (1995): 80–86.

10. MOUNTAIN PEOPLE

1. Louis Ramond de Carbonnières, *Travels in the Pyrenees: Containing a Description of the Principal Summits, Passes, and Vallies*, trans. F. Gold (Longman, Hurst, Rees, Orme, and Browne, 1813), 63.

2. Strabo, *The Geography of Strabo*, vol. 2, trans. H.C. Hamilton and W. Falconer (Henry G. Bohn, 1856), 232.

3. William Melczer, trans., *The Pilgrim's Guide to Santiago de Compostela* (Italica Press, 1993), 92.

4. Melczer, *Pilgrim's Guide*, 94–95.

5. Henry David Inglis, *Switzerland, the South of France, and the Pyrenees* (Whittaker and Co., 1835), 86.

6. Comte de Saint-Saud. *Contribution à la carte des Pyrénées Espagnoles* (Édouard Privat, Libraire-Éditeur, 1892), 17.

7. David R. Blanks, "Transhumance in the Middle Ages: The Eastern Pyrenees," *Journal of Peasant Studies* 23, no. 1 (October 1995): 64–87.

8. For details of shepherds' lives in this period, see also Emmanuel Le Roy Ladurie, *Montaillou* (Penguin Books, 1990).

9. Stéphanie-Félicité de Genlis, *A Short Account of the Conduct of Madame de Genlis, Since the Revolution, to Which Is Subjoined a Letter to M. de Chartres, and the Shepherds of the Pyrennees, a Fragment* (R. Morison & Son, 1796).

10. Ramond, *Travels*, 64–65. Ramond's observations of the inhabitants of the Pyrenees were another indication of the changing attitudes toward mountains and their inhabitants in this period. For the alpinist Horace

Benédict de Saussure, "The human interest in the Alps is no less than the physical . . . if there is anywhere in Europe where one may hope to find men who have exchanged the savage for the civilised state without losing their natural simplicity, it is in the Alps that one may find them." Quoted in Douglas W. Freshfield, *The Life of Horace Benédict de Saussure,* 289. Ramond's belief that the shepherds of the Pyrenees embodied "a sentiment equivalent to the idea of liberty" was written very much in this spirit.

11. Quoted in Sabine Baring-Gould, *A Book of the Pyrenees* (E.P. Dutton, 1907), 30.

12. Edwin Asa Dix, *A Midsummer Drive Through the Pyrenees* (G.B. Putnam's Sons, 1890), 245.

13. Dix, *Midsummer Drive,* 246.

14. Jean Louis Matocq, *My Journey from the Pyrenees to California* (Page Publishing, 2015).

15. Erskine Murray, *A Summer in the Pyrenees,* vol. 1, 49–50

16. Le Roy Ladurie, *Montaillou,* 114.

17. For a general history of the Bardaxí family and history of the Aragonese borderlands in this period, see Severino Pallaruelo, *Bardaxí* (Severino Pallaruelo Campo, 2002).

18. Théophile Gautier, *A Romantic in Spain* (Signal Books, 2001), 15.

19. Henningsen, *The Most Striking Events,* 135

20. Ramond, *Travels,* 104.

21. Rosemary Bailey, *The Man Who Married a Mountain: A Journey Through the French Pyrenees* (Transworld Publishers, 2005), 339.

22. Peter Sahlins, *Boundaries: The Making of France and Spain in the Pyrenees* (University of California Press, 1989), 241.

11. WILD THINGS

1. Peter Sahlins, *Forest Rites: The War of the Demoiselles in Nineteenth-Century France* (Harvard University Press, 1994), 6.

2. Phoebus's manual/homage has gone through many variants and adaptions over the centuries. The quotes and illustrations cited here are from *Medieval Hunting Scenes ("The Hunting Book" by Gaston Phoebus),* text by Gabriel Bise, trans. J. Peter Tallon (Miller Graphics, 1978).

3. For a full description of these gruesome procedures, see Charles Richard Weld, *The Pyrenees: West and East* (Longman, Brown, Green, Longmans & Roberts, 1859), 220–30.

4. Erskine Murray, *A Summer in the Pyrenees*, vol. 1, 243.

5. Edward North Buxton, *Short Stalks or Hunting Camps North, South, East, and West* (G.P. Putnam's Sons, 1892), 254.

6. T.H. Hollingsworth, "A Basque Superstition," *Folklore* 2, no. 1 (1891): 132–33.

7. Henry Blackburn, *The Pyrenees: A Description of Summer Life at French Watering Places* (Sampson Low, Marston, Searle, & Rivington, 1867), 143–44.

8. For a short account of bear reintroduction, in English, see Mick Webb, *Bear Mountain: The Battle to Save the Pyrenean Brown Bear* (Guardian Books, 2012). Also see M. Lyons, "The Death of Canelle and the Re-invention of the Pyrenees," *French History and Civilisation: Papers from the George Rudé Seminar* 6 (2015): 279–91, www.h-france.net/rude/rudepapers.html.

9. Charles Fréger, *Wilder Mann: The Image of the Savage* (Dewi Lewis Publishing, 2012).

10. Rosemary Garland Thompson, ed., *Freakery: Cultural Spectacles of the Extraordinary Body* (New York University Press, 1996), 78.

11. Weld, *The Pyrenees*, 225.

12. Sabine Baring-Gould, *A Book of the Pyrenees* (E.P. Dutton, 1907), 217.

13. Sahlins, *Forest Rites*, 30.

14. There are a number of accounts of de Lancre's reign of terror in Labourd. See Julio Caro Baroja, *The World of the Witches* (Phoenix Press, 2001); P.G. Maxwell-Stuart, *Witch Hunters, Professional Prickers, Unwitchers & Witch Finders of the Renaissance* (Tempus, 2005).

15. Mark Kurlansky, *The Basque History of the World* (Vintage Books, 2000), 95.

16. Baroja, *World of the Witches*, 176.

17. Henry Charles Lea, *A History of the Inquisition in Spain*, vol. 3 (Bibliobazaar, 2009), 234.

18. Rodney Gallop, *A Book of the Basques* (University of Nevada Press, 1970), 58.

19. Elizabeth Gaskell, *An Accursed Race* (Floating Press, 2016).

20. Louis Ramond de Carbonnières, *Travels in the Pyrenees: Containing a Description of the Principal Summits, Passes, and Vallies*, trans. F. Gold (Longman, Hurst, Rees, Orme, and Browne, 1813), 228. Ramond's views on the "cretinism" of the Cagots were in keeping with the assumptions of his time, which often depicted the inhabitants of mountains in this way, regardless of

whether they were Cagots. The Montagnards of the Valais region of the Alps were commonly depicted as cretins, and the philosopher Rousseau was one of the few eighteenth-century intellectuals to challenge this stereotype, when he praised the inhabitants of the Valais in the notes for his projected *History of the Valais*.

21. Ramond, *Travels*, 251.

22. Weld, *The Pyrenees*, 99.

12. GHOST TOWNS

1. Ismael Vaccaro and Oriol Beltran, eds., *Social and Ecological History of the Pyrenees: State, Market, and Landscape* (Left Coast Press, 2010), 97.

2. Ignacio de Asso, *Historia de Economía Política de Aragón* (repr. 1798, Consejo Superior de Investigaciones Científicas, Estación de Estudios Pirenaicos, 1947), 302.

3. Lorenzo Mediano, *The Frost on His Shoulders*, trans. Lisa Dillman (Europa Editions, 2012), 29.

4. Robert Laxalt, *Sweet Promised Land* (University of Nevada Press, 2007), 104.

5. This situation may be about to change. In October 2017, the regional government of Aragon announced plans to reopen the station as a hotel. That same month the regional government of Bordeaux told the BBC that it would be seeking to raise the 200 million euros required to re-open the railway line on the French side. After more than fifty years, Canfranc may yet have a future after all. See "Is Europe's ghostliest railway station about to rise again?" BBC News Magazine, October 1, 2017, www.bbc.co.uk /news/magazine-41445860.

EPILOGUE: THE FUTURE IN THE PAST: THE PYRENEES IN THE TWENTY-FIRST CENTURY

1. Robert Laxalt, "Enduring Pyrenees," *National Geographic* 146, no. 6 (December 1974).

2. G. Hayes, *Environmental Protest and the State in France* (Palgrave Macmillan, 2002), 190.

3. Joseph Wilson and Robert Andrew Riddell, *A History of Mountains*, 95.

4. Antoine-François Lomet, *Mémoire sur les eaux minérales et les établisse-ments thermaux des Pyrénées* (1794). Quoted in Steve Cracknell, *If You Only Walk Long Enough: Exploring the Pyrenees* (Steve Cracknell, 2016), 114–15.

5. Richard Ford, *A Handbook for Travellers in Spain* (John Murray, 1888), 515.

6. James Erskine Murray, *A Summer in the Pyrenees*, vol. 1 (John Macrone, 1836), 155.

7. Thomas Clifton Paris, *Letters from the Pyrenees*, 182.

8. European Environment Agency, *Alps—the Impacts of Climate Change in Europe Today*, March 17, 2010.

Index

animals: bears, 249–53, 277, 292;
    conservation and reintroduction
    of, 253–56; depicted in fiction,
    245–46; extinctions of, 248–49;
    hunting of, 246–48; in witch-
    craft stories, 265
al-Arabi, Sulaiman Yaqzan ibn, 27
Arabic (language), 57, 58
Arabic numerals, 55–56
Aragon (Spain): abandoned villages
    in, 279–82; invasions of, 73, 74;
    Llamazares's novel about,
    270–71; merged with Castile,
    203; population of, 272–73;
    smuggling in, 238, 242–43;
    during Spanish Civil War,
    87–89; during World War II, 94
Aragon, Crown of, 29
Arendt, Hannah, 109
Aristotle, 257
art: cave art, 152–55; depicting
    animals, 246; Pyrenees depicted
    in, 172–76, 179–82
Asso, Ignacio de, 101–2
astrolabe, 55–56
Atkins, Ray, 180–82
Atta Troll (Heine), 169–70
Atto, 55
Aub, Max, 100, 108
Auerbach, Frank, 180, 181
Aulus-les-Bains (France), 187

Baigen, Michael, 196–97
Balaguer, Josémaria Escrivá de,
    105, 216
Baligant (mythical), 38, 39
Barat, Jean, 277

Barat, Joseph, 277
Barbastro (Spain), 64–66
Barcelona (Spain), 89
Bardaxí, Felipe de, 237
Bareges (France), 186, 291
Barétous Valley (France), 46–47
Baring-Gould, Sabine, 107, 171,
    260–61
Baroja, Julio Caro, 266
The Baron in the Trees (Calvino), 141
Barrau, Louis, 123
Barreau, 147
basajaun (wild man), 257–58
Basques (people), 48; *Codex
    Calixtinus* on, 225; de Lancre on,
    264; emigration of, 275–76;
    Hugo on, 204; nationalism
    among, 215
Baudelaire, Charles, 167
Bayonne, Treaty of (1866), 32
Béarn (France), 29, 47
bears, 249–50; reintroduction of,
    253–55, 262–63, 292; trained,
    250–53, 277
Begouen, Henri (count), 153
Behold a Pale Horse (film,
    Zinnemann), 94
Belloc, Hilaire, 35, 171
Beltrán, Antonio, 89
Bénazet, Jean, 106
Benet i Capara, Josep Maria, 88
Benjamin, Walter, 112–17
Bennett, James Gordon, Jr.,
    160–62
Béost-Bages, 135
Béraldi, Henri, 136–37, 173
Bernhardt, Sarah, 183, 190

About the Author

Matthew Carr is the author of several books of nonfiction, including *Blood and Faith: The Purging of Muslim Spain*, and a novel, *The Devils of Cardona*. He has written for a variety of publications, including the *New York Times*, *The Observer*, *The Guardian*, and others. He lives in the United Kingdom.

Publishing in the Public Interest

Thank you for reading this book published by The New Press. The New Press is a nonprofit, public interest publisher. New Press books and authors play a crucial role in sparking conversations about the key political and social issues of our day.

We hope you enjoyed this book and that you will stay in touch with The New Press. Here are a few ways to stay up to date with our books, events, and the issues we cover:

- Sign up at www.thenewpress.com/subscribe to receive updates on New Press authors and issues and to be notified about local events
- Like us on Facebook: www.facebook.com/newpressbooks
- Follow us on Twitter: www.twitter.com/thenewpress

Please consider buying New Press books for yourself; for friends and family; or to donate to schools, libraries, community centers, prison libraries, and other organizations involved with the issues our authors write about.

The New Press is a 501(c)(3) nonprofit organization. You can also support our work with a tax-deductible gift by visiting www.thenewpress.com/donate.